Standing On Hi

Compiled By

Martha Holland Dobson

And they overcame him by the blood of the Lamb
and by the word of their testimony . . .
—Revelation 12: 11

Spirit-Filled Life Bible in the New King James Version
was used for all Scripture unless otherwise indicated.

ISBN: 1-59684-022-6

printed by Derek Press, Cleveland, TN

Dedication

This book is dedicated to our Lord and Savior, Jesus Christ, whose grace and mercy is evident throughout all of the testimonies in this book. To Him be the honor, praise and glory for the victories in the lives of all of those who have shared His work in their lives.

Acknowledgments

I wish to thank the following people without whom Standing on His Promises would not have been possible:

My husband, Ben Dobson, who has faithfully supported and encouraged me despite the demands on my time required to complete this book.

My friend, Diane Cash, who has faithfully proofread each page of this book.

Pastor Kenneth M. Hudson who has worked with me and encouraged me so much.

Jane Hudson who has supported this project through the Ladies' Ministries.

Irma B. Williams who has listened and shared with me so many times.

Karen Spalding who painted the cover and helped in so many other ways.

The Thursday and Friday night prayer groups who have prayed with me so many times over each aspect of this project.

And all of those who have tirelessly shared their testimonies.

Foreword

"Living Epistles." Peter called us "Living Epistles." How can we who are flesh and blood be living letters?

God challenged Israel in Malachi 3 to "prove Him" or "try Him." He says, "See if I will not keep my Word. Do what I say and test me, and I'll show you." God has proven over and over again that He keeps His Word. In this book Martha Dobson has compiled testimonies of "Living Epistles" who have dared to "try Him." One hundred testimonies of God's testing. One hundred times God has proven true to His Word. As you read these testimonies, remember that these are just glimpses of volumes of testimonies that could be written from each of the one hundred "Living Epistles."

Each Epistle represents volumes of accounts where God stood the test and proved Himself. God writes the "Epistles through the lives of His children. As the world reads the Epistles, let the world realize that these are letters to the world from God. These epistles tell of the great love and faithfulness of God.

Herein, lies evidence that God is true one hundred times out of one hundred. To the reader it should prove that God will always stand the test. God will be true a billion times out of a billion. God is worthy of our trust for He has never faltered or failed. As you, the reader, turn these pages, remember that the words written come from flesh and blood that has proven and tested God and found Him to be one hundred percent dependable.

Finally, the goal of this book is to share the message and the evidence from the "Living Epistles." Everything God says is true for you just as it is to the Epistles that gave these testimonies. You can do more than read from the "Living Epistles." You, too, can become a "Living Epistle" by trusting God. Immediately, you'll discover that God will stand every test. Enjoy your journey as you see glimpses of one hundred lives, paragraphs from one hundred "Living Epistles."

We are grateful for every paragraph and every life. We are especially grateful to Martha for compiling this wonderful volume of evidence of the faithfulness of God. God bless you as you test Him and He writes His Epistle through you.

Kenneth Hudson, Senior Pastor, Landmark Church of God

Introduction

And they overcame him by the blood of the Lamb and by the word of their testimony, and they did not love their lives to the death.—Revelation 12: 11

What an awesome God we serve! He is...

El Shaddai, our almighty God

Jehovah-Jireh, our Provider

Jehovah-Rophe, our Healer

Jehovah-Nissi, our Victory

Jehovah-Shalom, our Peace

Jehovah-Perazim, our Breakthrough

Jehovah-Shammah, our Abiding Presence

Jehovah-Tsidkenu, our Righteousness

Jehovah-M'Kadesh, our Sanctifier

In over one hundred testimonies in this book, Standing on His Promises, God receives the glory as the great I Am. People have shared from their hearts their stories of how God has ministered in their lives and given them the victory over sickness, sin, financial woes, confusion, misunderstandings, danger, addictions and so much more.

For over three years, I have been merely the typist. I have been so privileged to have the opportunity to listen as members of the Landmark Church of God and people with whom they are acquainted have opened their hearts and shared what God has done for them and through them. Seven pastors and evangelists, three pastor's wives, the taxi driver for a missionary and many lay people have lifted God's name on high in these testimonies.

The vision for this book came through a dream which God gave me three times. In the dream He told me to write a book and call it Standing on His Promises. He directed me to put in the book the testimonies of the people of the church and people they know. He reminded me of the scripture in Revelation 12: 11:

> And they overcame him by the blood of the Lamb and by the word of their testimony, and they did not love their lives to the death.

When God gave me this dream/vision, I felt overwhelmed and so inadequate for such a project. I went to my pastor, Bishop Kenneth M. Hudson and shared the dreams. I asked him to pray for confirmation from God. He did pray and at God's leading shared the project with the church body. I told God that I would do my best with His help to be obedient to what I believe He called me to do.

As I continue to study the Bible, I see time and time again that God loves to use people who seem the least prepared and least able. He often does not use the qualified; rather He qualifies those whom He calls in order to confound the wise. Indeed, He has given me the courage to ask people for their testimonies, the wisdom to write and edit the testimonies and the tenacity to see the project to completion.

When I began this project, I thought that the book would have sections devoted to specific types of testimonies: healing, deliverance, salvation, finances, etc. As I continued to work, however, God directed me to put the testimonies in alphabetical order. Each testimony was to begin with a scripture pertinent to the testimony. The book was to be a ministry tool not to be sold for profit. I have followed God's leading in each of these areas. God also specifically designed the cover as He led Karen Spalding to share her painting, *A Sermon in Shoes*. Within the text is an explanation of this painting.

It is my prayer that....

People who do not know the Lord Jesus Christ as their personal Lord and Savior will read these testimonies and yield their lives to Him;

People who are sick will find the faith to reach out for their healings;

People who are discouraged will be encouraged;

People who have sin in their lives will find the courage to seek forgiveness from the Lord;

People who are living with addictions in their lives will find the courage to reach out for deliverance;

People who are experiencing difficulties in relationships will find the courage to mend the fences;

People who are walking through the "valley of the shadow of death" will find hope;

People who are walking in financially troubled waters will be encouraged;

And that everyone who reads these testimonies

Will be encouraged to seek a closer walk with the Lord;

Will rejoice over what our God has done; and

Will give Him all the glory, honor and praise!

Finally, I thank God for allowing me the privilege to write this book and all of you who have shared these testimonies. May the lives of all of you who read this book be blessed exceedingly, abundantly beyond all you could ask or think.

Contents

Sermon in Shoes

Do you know, O Christian, you're a sermon in shoes?
Do you know, O Christian, you're a sermon in shoes?
Jesus counts upon you to spread the Gospel News;
So walk it, and talk it, a sermon in shoes.
So live it, and give it, a sermon in shoes.
So teach it, and preach it, a sermon in shoes.
So know it, and show it, a sermon in shoes.

Sermon in Shoes by Ruth Harms Calkin.

A Sermon in Shoes

One day shortly after Martha had asked me to paint a cover for this book, I was praying about how I could possibly illustrate, Standing on His Promises. God showed me that I had already done the painting during a 1994 art class at Mitchell College. I titled the painting *A Sermon in Shoes* after a conversation with my husband, Bob. He said that he would like to have an interview with the shoes in the painting because they looked so eager to tell a story about the person who had walked in them.

I also remembered a song I used to sing with children when I worked with Child Evangelism called, *Sermon in Shoes* by Ruth Harms Calkin. Some of the words say:

> Do you know, O Christian? You're a sermon in shoes.
> Do you know, O Christian? You're a sermon in shoes.
> So walk it and talk it, a sermon in shoes.
> So know it and show it, a sermon in shoes.

Yes, indeed, Jesus counts on us to spread the Gospel news, to know the Gospel and to live it out in our lives; thus we are Christians in shoes. The SHOES, the first symbol in this painting, typify our Christian journey of faith. At first our steps are just baby steps. Later, as we learn to stand, they become sure and unfaltering as we lean on and depend upon the heavenly Father to firmly and patiently hold our hands.

Webster's New World Dictionary defines "stand" in part as "to submit to, to abide by, to hold on to, to deem important, to insist on or to be satisfied or convinced of." The word "standing" connotes one taking a position which is immovable, at rest, not likely to fade away, settled or permanent. It would make sense, then, that *Standing on His Promises* would include testimonies by people who had fixed their hearts on the promises of God. As the Psalmist in 56:7 (TLB) says:

> My heart is fixed, oh God. My heart is fixed:
> I will sing and give praise.

As God impressed me with this Scripture, He also brought to my remembrance Psalm 112: 6 (TLB):

> Such a man will not be overthrown by evil circumstances. God's constant care of him will make a deep impression on all who see it....for he is settled in his mind that God will take care of him.

As I recalled these Scriptures and the Holy Spirit nudged me about Bob's comment about interviewing the shoes, I realized that the image I sought for this cover had already been done.

The Bible, the second symbol in this painting, is a book of promises on which God's people can, indeed, fix their hearts. According to Webster, a promise is a declaration which gives to the person to whom it was made a right to expect or claim the performance or forbearance of a specified act. It is also that which causes or gives ground for HOPE, expectation or assurance especially of success or distinction.

In the Old Testament in Genesis 13: 15-17, God promised Abraham that his descendants would be multiplied, should possess the land of their enemies and would become the source of blessing to all nations. That promise was fulfilled in the New Testament in Christ, the promised Messiah, through whom we become the children of Abraham and receive the promise that we will be "blessed and be a blessing to the world."

We are blessed as we receive God's precious promises described by Peter in II Peter 1:3,4 (KJV). He tells us that, "all things pertaining to life and godliness are given to the believer through His divine power...." As believers, we are able to partake in His divine nature "through the knowledge of Him who has called us to glory and virtue." We never need doubt any of God's promises because His Word is totally trustworthy and backed up by His unchanging attributes. As I Thessalonians 5:24 says; "Faithful is He that calleth you, who also will do it," because as Titus 1:2 says, "He cannot lie."

As believers, we also have the hope of an inheritance in heaven described in I Peter 1:3:

> God the Father, through Jesus Christ, according to His abundant mercy hath begotten us again unto a lively HOPE by the resurrection of Jesus Christ from the dead to an inheritance incorruptible and undefiled, that fadeth not away, reserved in heaven for us who believe....

As we stand on God's promises, our shoes carry us on our journey down many different paths, unique to each of us; however, all of us battle the principalities in High Places warring for the souls of men. As we put on our armor—the shield of faith, the breastplate of righteousness, the sword of the Spirit (the Word), the helmet of salvation, truth around our loins (Ephesians 6: 14-17) and the strength of praise—we do so knowing that this battle is beyond our strength or skill to win. Our feet are shod with the Gospel of the Preparation of Peace as we choose the path to overcoming Victory. We are ordinary human beings whose steps are led by an extraordinary God as we clothe ourselves with God's armor and with the mighty weapons of prayer, the power of the blood of Jesus Christ and the anointing of the Holy Spirit. As II Corinthians 10:3-5 tells us, with these weapons, we are able to break through every stronghold, capture rebels and bring them back to God. In this battle, we hear the captain's cry: "Wherever the sole of your feet shall tread, there that land I have given you" (Joshua 1:3).

Someday, I imagine that we will "remove the shoes from our feet" as we come face to face with our holy and awesome God. We will see Him as never before. His presence will engulf us with warmth and eternal love as we sing praises and enjoy the company of angels around the throne. We will step from this life into Heaven, ushered into His presence with great joy!!! For now, however, we continue to be A Sermon in Shoes: walking, talking, and living vessels of the light of the world whose name is Jesus.

In this painting, the third symbol is the VESSEL which reminds us that though our bodies are temporal, they are given to us to be like a "container" for the dwelling of the precious Holy Spirit. Webster's says that scripturally, a vessel represents one into whom something is poured or stored for use. Vessels are depicted throughout the Bible. Some are vessels of brass, iron, silver and gold. Some are borrowed, and some are old. Some are empty, and some are full. Some carry wine, others water and oil. Some brought pleasure. Some brought honor while others brought dishonor.

This precious treasure—this light and power that now shines within us—is held in a perishable container, our weak bodies. This treasure shines out into the darkness of this world, and everyone can see that this power within must be from God and not our own.

We become earthen vessels who desire to be used for the Master's highest honor and glory. As He uses us, we learn that "the steps of a righteous man or woman are ordered of the Lord."

As we travel on our journey of faith we are often pressed on every side by trouble, yet not crushed or broken. Sometimes we are perplexed and ask, "Why do things happen as they do?" Still, we do not give up! Sometimes we get knocked down, but we get back up and keep on going! Instead of being preoccupied with the troubles all around us, we look forward to the joys in heaven, as yet unseen, and savor the joy of His presence every day of our lives here on earth.

As He calls us to walk in the paths of righteousness for His name's sake, we stand on the promise from the Word of God that,"The just shall live by faith" (Romans 1:17b). Those who live by faith standing on His promises do, indeed, have testimonies to share. For Paul said that we are "living letters of Christ"—not a letter written with pen and ink but written by the Spirit of the living God, not one carved on stone but in human hearts. Standing on His Promises, we continue to be *A Sermon in Shoes.*

Ann Baynard

Create in me a clean heart, O God, and renew a steadfast spirit within me. Do not cast me away from Your presence and do not take Your Holy Spirit from me.
—Psalm 51: 10-11

At the age of nine, I walked down the aisle all alone—no Mama or Daddy dragging me—just myself to accept Jesus into my heart. I didn't serve Him as I should, but I always knew His hands were upon me. I always felt that closeness and tugging at my heart when I did something wrong.

I grew up in an alcoholic, abusive home. I was never taken to church. No one got up on Sunday morning and went, but praise the Lord for Christian grandparents. My two grandmothers and grandpa took me to church and taught me the things of the Lord. I have three uncles who also were very inspiring to me. I would stay in one of their homes almost every weekend and would go to church with them. God brought me through a very difficult childhood.

I married at a very young age. My husband and I didn't always live and do right, but we did raise our two boys in Sunday School and church. God brought us through many trying and frustrating times raising our children. My husband and I both rededicated our lives to God when our children were very young. We both received the Baptism in the Holy Ghost, and our lives have not been the same since.

One of my favorite scriptures is Philippians 4:7:

> And the peace of God, which surpasses all understanding, will guard your hearts and minds through Christ Jesus.

There's a peace that only comes from knowing Jesus as one's personal Savior. Being filled with the spirit of God gives me power to witness to others, to pray for others and to better understand His Word.

I feel His love, His protection and His presence at all times. My daily prayer is Psalm 51: 10-11:

> Create in me a clean heart, O God, and renew a steadfast spirit within me. Do not cast me away from Your presence and do not take Your Holy Spirit from me.

There's power in just speaking the name of Jesus. Once my husband was choking on a hot dog. I knew he was choking to death. I laid my hand on his back and said, "Jesus." The hot dog came out. Another time we were driving on an interstate sandwiched between a van and a truck when a truck pulling a camper began passing us on the right side. I realized that the camper was coming closer and closer to my side of the car. It was weaving back and forth just ready to sideswipe us. I laid my hand on the window and said, "In Jesus name." The camper straightened up and went on. Oh, the name of Jesus.

Recently, on a vacation trip with my family, I was riding in a van with eight people. We were all talking, laughing and enjoying our day when all of a sudden my little one-year old grand niece began choking on food. Her mother began to panic. The child was fastened in her car seat, and no one could get to her and get her out quickly. I laid my hand on her and said, "Oh, Jesus." The food came out.

I love my Lord; and I thank Him for His mercy, His grace and His peace.

Bill Baynard

You are my hiding place and my shield; I hope in Your Word.—Psalm 119: 114

Unlike my wife, I was raised in a Christian home. I was brought up to go to Sunday School and to church. I guess I did it because my parents insisted. At the age of about seven, I walked down the aisle; and, in about the only way I knew how, I accepted Jesus into my heart. I don't think I really knew the true meaning of what I had done, but I just did what I had been told was the thing to do. Later in my life, I came to understand the truth of Psalm 119: 114:

> You are my hiding place and my shield; I hope in Your Word.

Through high school and into college, I went along leading a life like most of my friends were living. Nothing exciting happened for many years. I met Ann and fell in love with her, and we were married at an early age. We brought our two sons up in the church as I had been taught to do. I went along for many years living for the devil and doing nothing for Christ, my Lord. We went to a dead Presbyterian Church and left the Sunday services feeling nothing.

Sometime later, we had a Spirit-filled minister preach a revival in our church. For the first time, I felt a hunger in my soul. We had friends who had received the Baptism. I didn't know exactly what it was; but I knew they had something that I did not have, and I wanted it. Ann and I both received the Baptism at the same time with evidence of speaking in tongues. Boy did I ever learn what true joy was!

Several years went by, and I began to fall out of fellowship. I knew I wasn't living the life that God wanted me to live. I think Ann had prayed for God to get my attention and did He ever! Soon I was down with diverticulitis. I was rushed to Presbyterian Hospital in Charlotte with a ruptured colon. The doctor told me that I must have emergency surgery at once. He asked how to contact my wife, and I told him I would call her the next morning. He said, "Mr. Baynard, you need to let us contact her now." I refused, and he told me that he did not think I would come out of the operating room alive. Even though I knew I hadn't been living right, somehow I knew God's hand was upon me. Well, I did come out very much alive, though very sick.

My first night at the hospital, I woke up around three o'clock in the morning. I noticed a beautiful lady all dressed in white who I thought was a nurse. She was sitting in the window sill beside my bed. She wiped my brow with a cool towel ever so often. She was most beautiful and never spoke a word. Later in the morning, I asked the supervisor who this lady was that sat with me all night. She told me that no such person was in the room with me and that she had checked on me during the night and early morning hours. No one else had came into the room. I knew then that I had seen my angel. I had been taught that we all have an angel. I know it is true because I met mine. Thank you Jesus.

I am what I am today because of my very loving, caring and Christian wife and the love of God. I just can't praise God enough for His mercy and goodness to me. I am so undeserving, yet He loves me anyway and keeps His hand on me now and forever. Now more than ever, "I am persuaded that neither death nor life, nor angels nor principalities nor powers, nor things present nor things to come, nor height nor depth, nor any other created thing, shall be able to separate us from the love of God which is in Christ Jesus our Lord" (Romans 8: 38-39).

Reverend Benjamin N. Black

And as ye would that men should do to you, do ye also to them likewise.—Luke 6:31

Thoughts on Being Alone: A Testimony to the Truth

Lonesome has been described as, "Sad at feeling alone." Through the years, I have grown accustomed to the expressions of those who have from time to time felt they had reason to vent their feelings of frustration of hours, days or even months of living in the dark zone of being alone.

The pastor of our local church asked that I go to a nearby city to visit someone who was gravely ill. Surgery had been performed, and things were just not right.

The person was in a talking mood. As we approached the subject of faith, he pointed his finger at an old worn Bible lying close by. "That is my grandmother's Bible that I have over there. I like to read it because it has notes written in the margins by her very own hand." He paused and then told of a special note he had read while he lay there in his bed.

"If young people could only know what lonesome is or how it feels to be alone."

He then said, "I read this too late to do anything about it, for my grandmother is gone! I hope to live to share this with others along life's way."

This caught me by surprise. My mind, in a heart beat, went to days gone by. How many times could I have offered cheer, quieted the longing of a soul or reached out and touched another with just a, "Hello," or, "I just came by to say I was thinking of you today." This man was not alone in his discovery; for we all can learn from the past, or we can suppress reality and believe there is no emerging of consequence or the raising of conscious awareness.

The truth is I have been there! I have done that! The scary thing about all of this is expressed by an old cliché: "What goes around comes around," or as Grandmother's Bible does declare in Luke 6: 31, "And as ye would that men should do to you, do ye also to them likewise."

My thoughts went wild in that hour, and I began to think, "Will I be found someday, someplace, writing in the margin of my life, I am getting what I deserve, living in that dark zone of being all alone?"

Reverend Franklin D. Black

For I know that my Redeemer lives, and He shall stand at last on the earth: And after my skin is destroyed, this I know, that in my flesh I shall see God whom I shall see for myself and not another. —Job 19: 25-27

How Real is God?

I have had people ask me, "Who is God? Where is God when I need Him? If You're God why don't You just kill the Devil and get rid of all the sin in the world?" When I thought about the question, How real is God?, God told me to use my experiences to express this. How real is God?

In Job 2:9, we find a woman who wasn't as lovable as one would like her to be. She asked her husband,

> Do you still hold fast to your integrity? Curse God, and die.

In this verse, Job's wife displays her lack of spiritual insight and sympathy for her husband's condition. Job's response shows that unlike his wife, he knows that God is very real. He says in Job 19: 25-27:

> For I know that my redeemer liveth, and that He shall stand at the latter day upon the earth: And though after my skin worms destroy this body, yet in my flesh shall I see God: Whom I shall see for myself, and mine eyes shall behold, and not another; though my reins be consumed within me.

Question: How Real is God?

I graduated from the Williston-Elke High School in 1938. Our town had 1500 residents and was located in the center of a farming community. When I graduated from high school, I went looking for a job. I spent most of the summer searching for a job. None were available. My alternative, I thought, was to join one of the armed services; however, when I visited the court house in our county seat of Barnacle, South Carolina, I learned about the Civilian Conservation Corps (CCC) which had no time limit for enlistment. I enlisted and went to work for wages of $30.00 per month. The Army was over us.

I was put aboard a train with other men heading north. Where to? None of us knew. Late that afternoon I arrived in Winnsboro, South Carolina having completed my first train ride. We were put aboard a truck and headed to the CCC camp. We were given clothes, shoes and a bed in the barracks.

As a youngster, especially in the evening hours at the going down of the sun, the Holy Spirit had often spoken to me—the inner me—about my life. The Holy Spirit let me know that there was more of Him that I needed than I had. Without a doubt, God had reasons for bringing me to Winnsboro, South Carolina. He, God, had a young lady named Louise Hudson to become my future wife. She was nineteen years old. On May 12, 1939, in the Fairfield County Courthouse before the county clerk, we made our vows, and he pronounced us man and wife. Like my family, Louise's family was very poor.

Her mother was a very devout Pentecostal believer. She had great influence over me. I had been raised Baptist and Methodist. She kept telling me that without holiness I would never see God. She told me every Sunday that the Bible had Holy on the front. I don't know why I despised the word "holiness." She would tell me that without holiness no man shall see the Lord. She may not have had a lot of money, but she was rich in the things of God.

In my first few months I earned thirty dollars per month. Then I became Mess Sergeant at forty-five dollars per month. Louise and I began attending the Winnsboro Church of God. Reverend W. R. Craven was the Pastor. He was a great man of God. I remember riding to town with him. He would continue to praise God. I admired him. One particular evening during the worship, the Holy Spirit spoke to my heart. It was an awesome call. It was not an audible call like that of my son who received an audible call to go into the ministry. My call was on the inside of me. I listened to the Spirit as He spoke to me, but Satan also spoke to me. A great battle began inside of me. Satan's imps pressured me one way and the Holy Spirit another way.

When Adam and Eve sinned, all kinds of evil forces were unlocked on this earth. Satan is an opponent of God and man. The battle inside of me was heated. My outward reaction was to clutch the pew in front of me tightly. My knuckles turned white. I was proud that I had graduated from high school. When I sat down I always had my ring so people could see it. The battle inside of me was not a battle between God and Satan because God could immediately conquer Satan. The battle was whether or not I, Frank Black, would make that decision to heed the call of God or heed Satan's lies.

A brother of the church came to help me make the right decision. I was not too nice to him. He turned his slumping back to me and walked away. I was moved. I made up my mind and took Louise by the hand. Both of us moved into the aisle. We turned loose our hands. She went toward the ladies' praying area, and I went toward the men's area.

On my way down to the altar something very awesome happened to me. I felt so clean inside. Not only did I feel clean, I felt good! I began to shake by the power of God. Falling on my knees, I fell back on the floor. I was not hurt. I just kept trying to get up. One of the church brethren yelled in my ear, "Stay down, Brother Black." I obeyed, but the power on me caused me to roll from one side to the other. On this night I had worn my only suit, a blue serge one. I'd said before that one thing I'd never do would be roll. But I rolled from one side to the other. I mopped up the dust on the unpainted floor. I was a sight, but I had become a new creature in Christ Jesus. Thank you blessed Lord. How real is God? I believe that things that have happened in my life may be a blessing to you.

Question: How Real is God?

In Camden, South Carolina, my second pastorate, a young boy about twelve years of age poured kerosene on what he thought were dead coals, but they were hot living coals. There was an explosion and fire. The boy and his mother were burned seriously. Both were placed in the Kershaw County Hospital—the mother in the ladies' ward and the boy in the men's ward.

A tent of sheets was built over the boy who had burns over the entire body. On my hospital visits, I prayed for him plus others in the ward. On this particular day as I entered the hospital, the terrible odor of decaying burned flesh filled my nostrils. The boy was in the deepest of pain—his groans expressing the great pain. I pulled back a sheet and saw agony in the face of the boy. I spoke to him briefly and began offering a prayer to God. He was unable to sleep because of the pain. As I continued to pray, the boy suddenly stopped groaning and fell into a deep sleep.

I visited all the men in the ward and the ladies in their ward offering prayer. I was walking down the hall to exit the hospital. Suddenly, I heard a familiar voice crying out, "Preacher, Preacher come back and pray for me some more."

A few short hours later this boy received the greatest miracle healing any born-again person could ever hope for—death. Jesus stated to Thomas in John 14: 6,

> I am the way, the truth and the life: No man cometh unto the Father, but by me.

Question: How Real is God?

Matthew 6: 33 says,

> But seek ye first the kingdom of God, and his righteousness; and all these things shall be added unto you.

My greatest hurt came when I received a telegram stating that Louise and our baby were not expected to live. For five days and five nights, I traveled by train from Long Beach, California, to Birmingham, Alabama before I got word again about my family. A telegram awaited me at the train station. The telegram said that that my wife and baby girl were well. In me now was great rejoicing.

This experience affected my health for the rest of my life. How real is God? He's real! He took care of my wife and baby girl and saved their lives. Proverbs 3: 5-6 says,

> Trust in the Lord with all of thine heart; and lean not unto thine own understanding. In all thy ways acknowledge Him, and He will direct thy path.

Question: How Real is God?

I'll never forget an experience that happened as a child. I don't recall what I had done wrong, but Dad got the message.
When he got home, I was instructed to go to the peach tree and to get a good switch. Getting the switch, I had thought of notching it, but I didn't. I gave Dad the switch. His reaction was that it was not good enough. He told me to go get a better one. He accepted this one. He then began to remove his shirt and undershirt. He then said, "You are getting too old for me to whip." He gave me the switch and said, "I'm taking your whipping and turned his back to me. "Son, lay it on me." Dad's back was very white. His skin looked very tender. I never struck Dad one blow, but this was a whipping I'd never forget.

Likewise Jesus Christ loved us, and He stood before men who laid stripes on His back for your healing and my healing and our deliverance. Do you believe that God allowed His son to suffer in that way? He did. Not only that, but He went on to give His life, to shed His blood as the redemptive power to remove your sins and mine and to make us new creatures in Christ Jesus.

I want to ask you, "How real is God to you? How real is He to you this morning? I tremble inside of me when I realize that any person who does not have Jesus Christ in his or her heart or life, if a change is not made, is headed for hell. That's hard to say folks. Again I ask, "How real is God to you? Is He real enough to make the decision that Sister Black and I made to make Him Lord and Savior of our lives and to serve Him? If you need to know Jesus Christ as your personal Savior, will you make that decision now? I pray that you will not put this decision off.

Reverend Franklin D. Black

Then Moses stretched out his hand over the sea; and the Lord caused the sea to go back by a strong east wind all that night, and made the sea into dry land, and the waters were divided.—Exodus 14:21

Miracles Over???

McColl, South Carolina, a small town near the North Carolina border, has a population of about 3,000. Its income comes from two small textile mills and a farming community. Tobacco and cotton are the main sources of revenue for the local farmers. Most of the homes were built by the two textile mills and in later years sold to the employees. They were small, wooden frame buildings. The downtown area had a post office, furniture store, a 5 & 10 cent store, a Belks department store, a small hotel, a small cafe, a hardware store, a grocery store, a bank and a police station. The town was built around two major railroads that crossed in about the center of town. Highway number 15 is the main inlet and outlet of this small community.

Personally, I had never visited this community or passed through it until I was appointed the pastor of the Church of God by my state overseer at the 1952 General Assembly in Memphis, Tennessee. However, I did feel I was in the perfect will of God. On or about the first of September 1952, my wife Louise; my son Franklin, Jr., age nine; my daughter, Sandra Louise, eight; and my youngest son, Raeford L., age six (almost seven) and I moved to McColl, S.C.

We found a nice brick church built on a very small piece of property parallel with the railroad tracks. In fact, it was very, very close; and when the freight trains, some of them the longest I've ever seen rumbled by, we would have to stop the services and wait until the caboose passed by. The parsonage, a five-room block building with its bathroom on the small back porch, was built next to the church, or should I say, in the front yard of the church. It, too, was very close to the tracks; so we had to endure and suffer the consequences the rumble and roaring provided.

The house would shake and pictures would fall off the walls. One day all of the kitchen cabinets, with all of their contents—dishes, seasonings, etc.—fell with the sound of breaking glass and a rumble almost as loud as that of the train. Being this close to the tracks also gave us much anxiety concerning our three small children.

As the pastor, I was expected to host all the evangelists and their families in the small quarters of the parsonage. The previous pastor had been voted out and had had to leave. Upon our arrival, we were told that if they liked you, they would give you the shirt off their backs; but that if they didn't like you, they would take yours.

God gave us favor the next four years. Many souls were saved, sanctified and baptized in the Holy Ghost. About seventy people united with the church. We also saw many miracles and healings; and many followed the Lord in water baptism. The mill companies showed favor toward the church because previous pastors had supported them in resisting efforts to unionize the mills. Membership of the church was eighty-two; however, on a special drive by a former pastor, Reverend C.W. Barnes, attendance soared to above 500.

The potential was there. In fact, the last year of my pastorate, we averaged 286 each Sunday in attendance. The first month of our pastorate God blessed with seventeen converts, five sanctified, five baptized in the Holy Ghost, and fourteen new members. Because of the church's size and needed facilities, it was evident that this body of believers needed a new church. The piece of property the church owned was far too small to add to. Also, there was a great need for a new parsonage. Having just come through a major building project, I was very weary.

Two years later, however, a beautiful piece of property was offered to the church. It was much larger than the combined property on which the present church and parsonage were located. Also included in the offer was a two-story, unsightly, unoccupied building that was once a part of a college. The old building had eight rooms, each heated by one fireplace. It took two extra large chimneys to provide eight fire places. A business meeting was held, and the church voted one hundred percent to purchase the property and to build a parsonage. The cost of the property and building was $3,000. Immediately, Satan raised his ugly head. A high official of one of the mills told one of the members that we paid far too much for the property. This set tongues a-wagging—tongues that gendered discord, backbitings, and disunity. They did not know that within that old building was about $5,000 worth of priceless, unobtainable building materials.

Some of the sills were forty-five feet long, seasoned pine that we call "light wood." Termites could not attack this lumber. If punctured out this lumber would drip pine resin. The same kind of timbers were in the four corners reaching from the sills to the second floor top place that had been hewn out by expert woodsmen all in one piece. Other sills were made of cyprus. There were also many handmade 2x4's, 2x6's, 4x8's and 4x 10's.

At the set time, the men gathered at the old building to begin razing it. We began with prayer, and something unusual happened as we stood there. A window pane in the upper story, with nobody near, popped out and shattered. Everybody just turned and looked at one another. Then one of the men, Brother Tom Spivey stated that he believed it was an omen. Three teenage boys had volunteered to help raze the building. The work of tearing down and salvaging material was almost done. Sister Black and I had been visiting patients in the hospital in Bennettsville, South Carolina. Upon returning to McColl, we stopped to see how the demolition of the chimneys was progressing. One chimney had already been felled, and the other was ready to go. Bricks were hacked out somewhat resembling a tree that was almost ready for felling. I suggested that a long piece of timber be used to push it over. Two teen volunteers, W.L. Ingles and Chester Todd were busy hacking away. Brother Spivey answered me and said that the boys knew what they were doing since they had already felled the other chimney.

While we were talking, Ingles began twisting out a brick inside the lower fireplace with a crow bar. Suddenly the chimney began to topple. We yelled a warning to the boys. Todd looked up and saw the direction the chimney was going and ran in the opposite direction. Ingles did not look up but began running directly in the path of the falling chimney. I breathed a quick prayer and shouted another warning as did Brother Spivey.

At the second warning, Ingles dived forward with hands overhead as though he were diving into a swimming pool. In the car Mrs. Black saw tragedy in the making and closed her eyes and turned her head. She did not want to see this fine young man crushed to death. When the chimney was a few feet above the lad's head, a tragedy seemed inevitable; but the chimney suddenly stopped in midair, held there by an invisible force contrary to the law of gravity.

Suddenly the chimney began to shake and separate as though in an earthquake. Bricks began flying and dust filled the air. Ingles lay over some sills face down with legs and feet apart and arms and hands outstretched overhead. As suddenly as gravity ceased its hold, it took over again raining down bricks and chunks of bricks and cement. The sound was a big rumble and the crack of breaking timbers.

Brother Spivey and I ran to the aid of Ingles. There he lay with bricks and chunks of brick and cement between the arms and legs and around the entire body. The chimney parts were within inches of the body, but not one brick touched him. The sills on which he lay across were in splinters. We had just witnessed a great miracle.

I was immediately reminded of God's command to Moses in Exodus 14:16 to lift up his rod and stretch his hand out over the sea and divide it. Accordingly in Exodus 14: 21, "Then Moses stretched out his hand over the sea; and the Lord caused the sea to go back by a strong east wind all that night, and made the sea into dry land, and the waters were divided." As Moses obeyed, the children of Israel passed into the midst of the sea on dry ground because God divided the Red Sea as promised. Just as God performed miracles for His people, we learned that miracles are not over today. God continues to perform miracles for His people.

Ruth Black

Train up a child in the way he should go, and when he is old he will not depart from it.—Proverbs 22: 6

I want to thank the Lord for my Christian inheritance and for my family. I was raised in a family who taught me how to love God and who trained me in the admonition of Jesus Christ. They carried me to church as a child. My dad put me on the stage at church and taught me how to sing in front of a crowd and how not to be afraid because God was there with me.

They read the Bible to me every night and every morning. They prayed with me before I went to school and before I went to bed. They taught me how to pray and how to live a life in front of others. We used to go around to churches and sing together.

Now that I am older, I still try to live by that same pattern and to walk in the footsteps they taught me to walk in. I have five brothers and two sisters, and they all live for the Lord. Three have gone out and started singing for the glory of God. It's amazing to see what God has done. My parents raised us up according to Proverbs 22: 6:

> Train up a child in the way he should go, and when he is old he will not depart from it.

All of us are close to each other and living for the Lord. There has never been rancor, bitterness or even a cross word between us other than in jest. There were ten children in my mom's family and ten children in my dad's family. There were never any conflicts in either family. My grandfather Swails was a Pentecostal Holiness preacher. He passed these values down to his children and grandchildren. My dad's brother who is next to him in age is a minister who plants churches. I believe that the lack of conflicts in my parents' families and among my siblings and me is an awesome testimony to the faithfulness of God to those who live for Him and obey His word.

My dad would not allow me to date until I was married unless we went to church. I could only date on weekends and had a 9:00 p.m. curfew unless church lasted longer. My dad was strict, but I appreciate his strictness now. Unlike many other couples in today's society, my husband, William, and I are still married.

I was saved in Sunday School class when I was eight years old. The teacher was teaching a lesson called, *Little Children, Come Unto Me*. There were pictures of children on the lap of Jesus who was saying, "I died for you. I went to the cross for you." The teacher said, "You are His beloved child. If you're not saved, you can be in Sunday School. Jesus loves you just like you are." He put a chair in front of the class and said, "Someone here needs Jesus. Come forward. I'll pray. I'll be like Jesus. I'll hold you and pray for you like Jesus would." These words drew me to salvation.

In the sanctuary that day, I sat beside Dad. Tears were rolling down my face. My parents thought someone had hurt me, but my teacher assured him that no one had hurt me. He asked me to thank the Lord for saving my soul. As I did, my parents put their arms around me and began crying. I've tried to live my life in a way that would be pleasing to the Lord.

Sometime after we married, William became an alcoholic. We were separated for two and one half years while he was in service in Germany. We had two children. I'd filed for divorce and had sent him divorce papers. Our kids and I were staying with my mom and dad. That summer my Uncle Harris came to me and said that he wanted to take Russ, our three year old, with him to church camp. I was reluctant, but he promised to look after him; so I relented.

That Wednesday night was family night, so my dad and I went to camp to visit Russ. When I got to camp, a friend of mine, Bill Johnson, was standing there with his foot on a tree. He pointed a finger at me and said, "I want to talk with you." He said, "God has a message for you. God doesn't want you to get a divorce. Things will work out." Later when I saw Uncle Harris, he also said, "I want to talk with you." We went into the kitchen. He said, "The Lord said to tell you that you don't need a divorce. Things will work out." Then he said, "I've been praying for you. You're not going to be the first in our family to get a divorce." Uncle Harris and Bill Johnson had not spoken with each other.

That night I couldn't sleep and went out to sit on the swing on the porch. My mom came out, and I told her what they had said. The next morning at 9: 00 a.m., I called my attorney and said, "Joe, tear up the divorce papers." He said, "I've already done that. I had a dream last night that you were going to call me, so I got the papers out. I've already torn them up." I asked him what I owed him. He said, "Consider it paid in full." The next morning I had a collect call from William in Germany apologizing for all he'd done. I promised him I'd meet him at the airport when he returned home, and I did.

His alcohol problem ceased when he was saved at his sister's house in Dunn, North Carolina. He'd been drinking. Suddenly he said, "I want you all to pray for me." His sister said, "I will, even though at first we didn't think much about it. Then he asked the second time, "I want you all to pray for me." We knew he was serious, and we prayed. His sister led him to the Lord. God not only saved him, but He also delivered him from alcohol.

As we were driving home, he lit up a cigarette. The cigarette tasted awful, and he said, "Something is wrong with this cigarette." I said, "No, you've gotten saved. Nothing is wrong with the cigarette. It's you. God cleaned you up." He tried a second cigarette, and the same thing happened. He put that cigarette down, too.

God's hand was in all of it. If God can put my family back together, He can put anyone's back together. William was not raised in church, yet God brought him into the fold. Recently, William said, "You've taught me a lot—how to love God and how to wait on Him."

As Proverbs 22:6 says,

> Train up a child in the way he should go, and when he is old he will not depart from it.

My parents trained up their children in the way they should go. None of us have departed from our training. In this day and time, it is an amazing testimony to God's faithfulness and to the truth of His Word to find a family without conflicts between any of the siblings. As my family and friends stood on God's Word and prayed for our marriage, God also honored His Word as He repaired the breach in our marriage. If you do not have a personal relationship with Jesus Christ today and if you have not committed your life to Him, please do not wait. Time is too short for you to pass up this precious gift of salvation.

Elaine Brown

Who Himself bore our sins in His own body on the tree, that we, having died to sins, might live for righteousness, by whose stripes you were healed.—I Peter 2: 24

I have often stood on I Peter 2: 24 for healing. There was a time in my life a number of years ago when I continued to have a rash on my arms and face and in the bends of my legs. The rash itched constantly, and sores from the rash often broke open. One Sunday Reverend Exertion visited our church. When he returned home, he wrote me a letter. He asked if I believed in healing. He had anointed a prayer cloth for me according to Acts 19: 11. He told me to wear it and to believe for my healing. I did what he said, and the rash went away. God had healed me.

Another time I stood on this same Scripture for healing of depression. There was a period of time in my life of about a year when I experienced much anxiety, loneliness and despair. I had many ups and downs. I tried doctors, psychologists and medicine. I was even in the hospital once for thirty days. One of the medicines I took made me gain twenty pounds. Some days I felt as if I just couldn't get out of bed. I often had no energy. This wasn't like me. I was used to going all the time. The Devil tried to play tricks with my mind. I had lost my joy even though I knew better. I understood the Devil's tricks, yet it was hard. I prayed and prayed and prayed.

I believe that the depression was caused by overwork. I just couldn't say, "No," to people. I'd worry if I felt that I was not being everything to everybody, One day, however, I came to myself and said, "I'm not doing this anymore. I'm going to give this problem to the Lord." I began praising the Lord and came up out of a hole of dark depression.

The depression has never returned. Oh, sure, I have ups and downs like everybody does; but I have found a Man who will lift me up when I praise Him. His name is Jesus. There is truly no one in my life who is more precious to me than Jesus. Many times I have literally felt the loving arms of Jesus holding me and carrying me through life.

One day my husband Dennis and I were traveling in the mountains. I was sharing with him from a book on joy by Chuck Swindoll. I told Dennis that I felt strongly that I should go to the altar that Sunday and ask for prayer for my joy to return. I did, and God gave my joy back to me. It was wonderful!

I have stood on His Word in I Peter 2: 24:

> Who Himself bore our sins in His own body on the tree, that we, having died to sins, might live for righteousness, by whose stripes you were healed.

He not only answered my prayers for healing from a horrible rash and from depression but He also filled me afresh with His joy!

I have learned that as long as I keep my focus on Him and not on the problem, things always get better. If, on the other hand, I continue to focus on things that get me down, I will go further down. When I begin to feel down, I refocus and get my mind off the problem and onto Jesus. I get back up and think of all the good things Jesus has done for me. Indeed, there is no one more precious than Jesus.

Elsie Efird Brown

Trust in the Lord with all your heart, and lean not on your own understanding. In all your ways acknowledge Him, and He shall direct your paths.—Proverbs 3: 5-6

God has done so many miraculous things in my life that I hardly can mention just one. I don't see life as separate spectacular events, not connected to another, but as a sequence of events one leading to another.

I was born to a wonderful German father and a little Scotch Irish mother. They knew what it meant to "Love thy neighbor as thyself" (Romans 13: 9b), and they knew how to forgive trespasses done against them. They lived it everyday.

I was the youngest of six children. My parents worked for a prominent physician during the Great Depression. A house was furnished along with a small salary. My mother was thirty-five, and my dad was forty-two when I was born. I was born at home before the doctor came, just my mom and I. I weighed about five pounds and was a very sick child. The doctors gave my parents no hope of my living very long and ever being healthy enough to live a normal lifestyle. My parents had had their cup of sorrow in the loss of a baby girl. Even though they had two more children after that, they never recovered from the grief of that child of eight months old. She was sick only a few days.

Part of my dad's job was to oversee a large apple orchard and be responsible for the mixing of pesticides for the trees to be sprayed. With no laws governing the mixing and disposal of these poisons, my dad was subjected to the deadly effects, and his health went downhill as a result. My mother suffered from asthma, and her health was poor also.

When I was learning to walk, I fell and broke my right arm, both bones in two. My arm was dangling. They had to put me to sleep and operate. With a big cast on that tiny arm, I was pushing my little chair around and ran into a hot stove and burned the whole top of my hand severely. Back to the hospital again, and this, of course, was another setback to my already weak condition. I was surrounded by tender loving care and many prayers and a lot of faith.

Because of my childhood, I was not ever able to climb trees and run and jump and get loud like other children. My life was a continuous day by day of playing house and playing school. I had a pretend friend that I talked to all the time. At school he was helping me teach, and at home he was my ever present companion! I never once gave a thought as to what I would be when I grew up because at times it was questionable as to whether I would grow up or not.

This proves that when God has His hand on a situation, He will prove all the doctors and everyone else wrong. God had His hand on me! I always had a desire to learn more about Him. I grew up knowing how to pray. I laid my hands on my cats and prayed for healing. I loved going to church and singing the old hymns. I learned to read as a small child using the old hymnal of the Methodist Church. I remember sitting by the wood cook stove and singing my heart out. I would come across a word I didn't know and run to Mother. She would tell me the word, and off I would go again to my singing and worship. God was hearing my prayers and songs of praise and worship, and He was with me all the way. Nothing will ever take the place of the old hymns of the church in my heart. My dad and brother were musically talented, and I was surrounded with music.

My health improved greatly when I became a teenager. When I turned sixteen years old, the pastor and Sunday School Superintendent came to me and assigned me as the teacher of a class. Neither of them asked me if I had a relationship with Jesus Christ. They knew my parents, and they had confidence in me. I knew I wasn't saved, and I knew I loved the Lord. I took the class and enjoyed teaching it very much.

I met John W. Brown when I was seventeen years old. I fell in love with him. All I really wanted was to become Mrs. Brown and have a big house full of children. I wanted Mr. Brown to be like my pretend friend of my younger years. We married and had four wonderful, healthy children. When my firstborn was an infant, we were at church on a Sunday morning. When the altar call was given, I didn't have to be coached to go and kneel down and repent of my sins and give my heart to the One who had loved and kept me all the way. What a joy to know my sins were under His blood at last, and everything was all right between me and God.

My children were everything to me. My life was wrapped up in being the best wife and the best mother that I could possibly be. One evening after supper, I gathered the children around for Bible study and prayer. This was a common meeting and something I looked forward to and knew was right. While I was teaching my children, the Holy Ghost spoke to my heart. It was so real I will never forget it. He said, "Will you teach My children?" I said, "Why yes, Lord, I will gladly teach your children!" In my human mind I thought that He meant the four little ones at my knees. As time went on and I continued to teach Sunday School, Ladies' Ministries groups and Bible School and then to direct Bible School, I still knew I had God's calling but I still thought He meant doing just what I was doing.

One day the burden came on my heart and then on my husband's heart for me to return to school, get my certification and go and teach children who had not been touched in a church situation. I was so scared, and I didn't really have the desire to go back to school. God would not let me alone; neither did He let my husband alone. Finally, I said, "Yes." I took two classes at the community college just to see if I could do it! My husband and children were very supportive, and all went well. I graduated with honors and then went on to the university where I graduated with honors again. Then I went on to get a graduate degree with a commendation from the Board. Never did I come near to tragedy. If I did, I was not aware of it. My children and I studied together and worked together, and it was fun. I continued to teach at church and go on with my duties. God was with me all the way.

I have had the opportunity to teach other people's children in some capacity for forty-six years now. I have taught in public school for twenty-five years. I have had the golden opportunity to witness for Christ to educated people and the downcast. All need the Savior. There have been times when meeting with someone, I prayed and asked God how to conduct the meeting. He has opened doors, and He has closed doors for witness. Some find that hard to believe, but when the Holy Ghost says, "Be quiet," then if we disobey and witness anyway, it is like casting our pearls before swine; and they will turn again and find you. If God says, "Yes, this is my little lost sheep. Tell them about me," then the door is wide open and what a thrill to walk in!

I must tell you about just one opportunity I had. There was a little child in my class who had no hope. I have seen many, but I'll tell you about just this one. I met with his mother. I learned that she and her boyfriend were living in sin, and the lifestyle was devastating to this child. He was not able to learn even though he had the ability.

God gave me His word for his mother. I spoke what God had said to speak. She listened and didn't say a word back to me. Later, our class went on a trip, and it was after school hours when we returned. The parents were there to pick up their children. This parent was in the crowd. She came over and told me she had to talk to me right then. I told her the doors of the school were locked. She said, "But I have to talk to you today." I unlocked the doors, and we went into my classroom. She sat down beside me like a little girl, very close. She looked up at me and said, "I couldn't get away from what you told me the other day. I went to church and went to the altar and gave my heart to Jesus. I told my boyfriend that no longer would I live in sin. I took a stand. I now have peace in my heart, and I wanted you to know it!"

What joy! Yes, the laws say no Bible and no prayer in public schools, but my God is so real that He can't be locked out, and He can't be outlawed! We don't have to wear a sign on our backs or carry a megaphone to shout it out. We just have to know Who we know and what we know and obey and leave the rest to Him! He has it all in control! To God be the glory!

One thing I have learned is to never lean upon our understanding but to trust in the One who has all the understanding as it says in Proverbs 3: 5-6. God knew all the time what He wanted this little girl to do, and He healed me and gave me the strength and the ability. He has proven the devil to be a liar over and over again! I look forward to seeing my Jesus face to face and telling Him how much I appreciate Him leading me one step at a time down life's pathway.

Esther Brown

But He was wounded for our transgressions, He was bruised for our iniquities; the chastisement for our peace was upon Him, and by His stripes we are healed.
—Isaiah 53:5

On December 3, 1994, I woke up with swelling and pain in my left leg and ankle. Within a short time, they started turning black and blue. Because I could not walk, my sister and my son took me to the doctor. The doctor took one look and rushed me by ambulance to the hospital where I remained for twenty-one days completely on the flat of my back.

The doctors working with me told me that I had blood clots throughout my entire foot and leg. They said that my leg was dying and that they would have to remove it to save my life. They brought papers for me to sign for the removal of my leg. I refused to sign them believing that if I prayed, God would heal me. A few hours later, they told me that my leg was dead (My mother and niece had died from blood clots).

One of my sisters got ahold of my church for prayer. Through God's mercy and grace, my leg gradually came back to life during the next year. The large blood vein had been completely destroyed, but small ones were developed to take its place.

I had been told that I would not be able to climb stairs, and that eventually, I would not be able to walk. I would end up in a wheelchair. Isaiah 53:5 says that we are healed by His stripes. Because people joined me in prayer, I was healed. Today, I am able to climb stairs and to walk. I have no need of a wheelchair. I give the Lord all of the praise!

Calvin Burrell

Honor thy father and thy mother that thy days may be long upon the land that the Lord thy God is giving you.
—Exodus 20:12

I've had a lot of close scrapes that were not serious. The closest I have ever come to getting killed was during World War II just before the Japanese surrendered. I was selected to go to a supply depot in the Philippine Islands near Tacloban instead of the front line. When I got there, there was a lot of war damage. I could have been sent to the front lines, but God in His mercy looked after me. I was nineteen years old. I was on the water, mostly the Pacific, for sixty-three days. I was in the army as a volunteer from 1944-1946. I was discharged from the enlisted army in Medlar. I came home while most of my friends in the service are dead. My survival during this time was just due to the mercies of God.

I remember that even at three and four years of age, I believed that Jesus was the Christ. Often times as a child, when my parents took me to church, they would bring me home asleep. I learned at a young age to honor my parents as I did throughout my life.

I've had several different jobs in my lifetime. I was living in Hiddenite and working in mechanics in 1947 when I needed to put a clutch in a 1937 Chevrolet. I had hitchhiked to Statesville to East Front Street to get a clutch from a junk yard. After I bought the used clutch plate, I hitched back. It was 1947. I was in my daddy's yard putting in the clutch. There was nobody there but me and God. I said, "God if You'll help me to be a good mechanic, I won't rip people off like people have done to me."

I improved in my ability to work on cars and specialized in automatic transmissions. In October 1955, I went to the General Motors training center where I specialized in mechanics. I worked on automatic transmissions for forty years and two months. I have honored my promise to God not to rip people off, and He has taken care of me.

My wife was sick for seventeen years. It took all the money I could scrape together to take care of her. I was robbed twice.The robbers put a knife all the way through my arm one time and busted my head another time all for $5.00. But through God's grace, I was still able to work. This shows what a person can stand if he doesn't give up. God's extended my life, I'm sure, because at my age so many of my friends are dead.

In 1961, my brother David and I bought an airplane. We spent twenty-one months rebuilding the airplane. It was in A-l shape. On May 28, 1961, we were going to fly over the raceway about eight miles from the Mooresville airport when the oil line came loose. We landed in a wheat field and rolled over. The right landing wheel broke as we eased on back. We tore the airplane up. We had flown about 2,000 hours. I feel like the good Lord took care of us that day. It wasn't our time to go. The Federal Aviation Authority commended us for choosing the site we chose and sticking to our decision. He told us that had we made a different decision, David and I could have been killed.

Exodus 20:12 says, "Honor they father and thy mother that thy days may be long upon the land that the Lord thy God is giving you." Throughout my life, I have honored my parents. I believe that God has rewarded this by protecting me and providing for me.

David Burrell

I can do all things through Christ who strengthens me. —Philippians 4: 13

I'd never been sick to amount to anything in my life; but in 1993, when I was sixty-three years old, I got sick. I knew that I could do all things through Christ. I knew that Christ gives me my strength; however, I experienced the truth of this scripture firsthand when I became sick.

I didn't know what was wrong. I lost from 215 to 150 pounds. It didn't matter what I ate. I wasn't trying to lose weight, yet I continued to become weaker and weaker. I became so weak that I could not walk from the bedroom to the living room without sitting down to rest.

I went to one doctor who examined me and said that although he could find nothing wrong, he suspected diabetes. He told me that if I would get my sugar under control, I'd be o.k. He told me to keep my sugar to 150 or less. When I went back to the doctor, my sugar was fine, yet I was still getting weaker.

I went to another doctor who said that I was a diabetic but with other problems as well. He did an electrocardiogram (EKG) test and a treadmill test. He said that I had had a silent heart attack. He thought that I had congestive heart failure (CHF). He gave me four types of medicine to take and said that I'd never walk more than a half mile a day. He said that I would be 100 percent disabled. I said,"God made the human body. He's got an antidote for anything. It's up to me to find it." I developed neuropathy so badly that I could hardly walk. I felt like I was walking on needles. The medicine didn't help.

I started reading everything I could find on natural healing and nutrition. With God's help, I found information about a mineral I could take to cure CHF. I listened to a tape of another doctor whose patients had been cured of CHF by taking one milligram of Pycnogenol per pound of body weight per day. Another doctor recommended vitamins C and E. I took 2000 milligrams of vitamin C per day, 800 units of vitamin E each day and 240 milligrams of COQ 10. I stopped taking the medicine the doctor had given me.

I had been attending the Friday night prayer meeting at our church. One Friday night, I asked everyone there to anoint me with oil and to pray for me. As soon as they prayed, I felt God's power hit me from the top of my head down through my toes. The neuropathy has never returned.

Eighteen months after the doctor had said I would never walk more than a half mile at any one time. I returned to the doctor who checked me out in the hospital. He thought the medicine he'd given me was working. I told him that I had gone off the medicine. He had a fit and asked, "Don't you know you could have convulsions from stopping this medicine suddenly?" Two months later, this doctor did another EKG, a sonogram and blood work. After he read the test results, he came back shaking his head. He said, “I’ve been practicing medicine a long time. I’ve never seen anyone’s heart heal itself.” I said, “What’d I’ll tell you! Read the Book!”

I was back to walking two miles per day. Since October 1994, I haven’t been back to the heart doctor. Indeed, “I can do all things through Christ who strengthens me” (Phillipians 4:13). I believe that there’s nothing impossible with God. If we’ll seek Him first, He’ll guide us to where we need to be. God healed me for a purpose. He gave me a testimony to share so that I could minister to others. I’ve shared this testimony with many people. God says that if I seek Him, He’s able to do “exceedingly, abundantly above all that (I can) ask or think....” (Ephesians 3: 20).

Standing on the Promises

Standing on the Promises of Christ my King,
Thru eternal ages let His praises ring;
Glory in the highest, I will shout and sing.

Chorus
Standing on the Promises of God,
Standing, standing,
Standing on the Promises of God, my Savior
Standing, standing,
I'm Standing on the Promises of God.

Standing on the Promises that cannot fail,
When the howling storms of doubt and fear assail;
By the living Word of God I shall prevail.

Chorus

Standing on the Promises I now can see,
Perfect, present cleansing in the blood for me;
Standing in the liberty where Christ makes free.

Chorus

Standing on the Promises of Christ the Lord,
Bound to Him eternally by love's strong cord;
Overcoming daily with the Spirit's sword.

Chorus

Standing on the Promises I cannot fall,
Listening ev'ry moment to the Spirit's call;
Resting in my Savior as my all in all.

Chorus

Dennis Byrd

For all the promises of God in Him are Yes, and in Him Amen, to the glory of God through us.—II Corinthians 1: 20

As Dennis Byrd grew up, he learned to depend on God by watching his parents live their faith believing that, indeed, God's promises are true. He saw a vivid example of his father's faith as a child one night at church.

"I was at the altar praying," he said. "I knew that my shoes had holes in them, but it didn't bother me because of the mom and dad that I had. They had been teaching me what was important. My pastor noticed that my shoes had holes in them and returned my Dad's tithe to him. He told my Dad to take the tithe money and use it to buy me some shoes. My Dad refused saying, 'It's not my money. It's God's money.' The next week, God provided a pair of shoes for me."

Dennis continued, "The thing of it is, Dad knew I needed shoes, but he depended upon God. All those years growing up, God never failed us. I've always had all I needed. My parents put their faith in God.

I learned how important living for Him is. Just watching them live their lives as they did taught me much. Watching people live their faith is more important than just hearing them tell what they believe. Children see the truth then, and it becomes real to them. Today I've got more than I need. There's an old song by R. Kelso Carter, *Standing on the Promises* that says,

> Standing on the Promises that cannot fail,
> When the howling storms of doubt and fear assail;
> By the living Word of God I shall prevail
> Standing on the Promises of God,
> Standing, standing, Standing on the Promises of God, my Savior
> Standing, standing, I'm Standing on the Promises of God.

"I'm grateful today for parents who understood that 'all the promises of God in (Jesus) are Yes.' I'm grateful that they lived their faith in front of me, 'Standing on the Promises that cannot fail,' and teaching me the necessity of depending upon and living for God."

Dee Calhoun

Cast your burden on the Lord, and He shall sustain you; He shall never permit the righteous to be moved.—Psalm 55: 22

People talk a lot about the miracles of Christ; however, we have all been doubtful from time to time. People just don't truly understand what miracles are until they experience one of their own. I would like to take time to share my miracles from Christ with you. Let me start by saying that once a person has had a miracle from the Lord, he or she will only want to know the good Lord more and more. Deuteronomy 29: 3 speaks of God's miracles.

> ...the great trials which your eyes have seen, the signs, and those great wonders.

On April 19, 2002, I was in a very serious auto accident. I was pinned in my vehicle for one and one half hours before I was found. I had fallen off to sleep and hit a tree head on. It was very early morning, and I remember that I went into a curve. I saw bridge reflectors ahead...., and that's all I remember until I woke up. I actually crossed the bridge without hitting it! Who drove me across the bridge? I believe that the good Lord helped to guide my car, for had I hit the bridge head on, I would have been killed instantly!

My car was light green, so it was very hard to see; and I was about fifty feet off the highway, I do not know who found me and called 911, but to that person I say, "Many thanks. May the Lord bless you whomever you are!"

When I woke up, it was still dark, and I remember not being able to move and trying to wave my arm out my window and trying to yell for help. At that very moment, a warm feeling came over me. I remember saying, "Lord, I'm not afraid to die. I know I'll come to heaven." I remember asking the Lord to please help me. I was so afraid to leave my children. Psalm 23: 1 says, "The Lord is my Shepherd; I shall not want." I thought about this verse, and I said to myself that I knew the Lord wouldn't let me die.

It seemed as if a lifetime had passed before I heard a voice call down to me and ask if anyone was in the car, if I was o.k. and if I could move. I replied that I was not o.k. and that I could not move. That person then came down beside the car. I remember asking him not to leave me. I had my arm out the window. I could feel a hand holding my hand; but when I turned to look, I don't remember a face being there. I remember hearing the voice telling me to hang in there, that help was on the way. I still get chills when I talk about it!

I believe the Lord sent me a guardian angel to be with me. I remember someone holding my hand, and then I remember a paramedic in front of me. I had someone tell me that I did have a first responder holding my hand the whole time I was being cut out of that mangled mess! I'm sure that is true, but no one will ever get me to believe that I didn't have a guardian angel holding my hand for one and one half hours before help arrived. I believe that an angel was there with me just as in Matthew 1: 20 an angel appeared unto Joseph telling him not to fear:

> But while he thought about these things, behold, an angel of the Lord appeared to him in a dream, saying, "Joseph, son of David, do not be afraid to take to you Mary your wife, for that which is conceived in her is of the Holy Spirit.

I was pinned in the car for one and a fourth hours while I was being cut out. I had the whole front end of the car on my legs! I was air lifted to Carolina Medical Center in Charlotte, North Carolina where I spent almost two months. I was in the trauma unit for over a week. I had four to six broken ribs and damage to my liver, gallbladder and right lung. It's a miracle that I'm still alive! Praise the Lord.

I also had my right leg broken in four places. After only three weeks in the hospital, I was told that I might have to have my foot taken off and never be able to walk again. I have a dead bone in my foot. I had no circulation in my foot at all. I was told that with physical therapy I might be able to walk on that foot by January 2003, almost a year later. In May 2002, I started to get feeling back into my foot. I came home the end of May. I had some physical therapy at home, but I couldn't walk on that leg and foot. By August 2002, I was walking and driving a car again. Praise the Lord! That's another miracle!

I now have a metal rod in my knee and eight pins inside my foot. I walk with very little limp, and I still have had no physical therapy. Why have I had no physical therapy? Because my husband of nine years cancelled my medical insurance after my accident. He also moved my personal things and my children out of my home the second week I was in the hospital in order to move his girlfriend into our home.

In August 2002, my children and I moved into public housing with nothing at all. I mean nothing! My husband didn't give us anything! Boy, oh, boy the Lord loves me! Within one week people were bringing us everything! Thanks to all the family, friends and churches that helped get us all these things we needed.

Then miracle number five happened. We have everything we need now. Thank you Lord! As if we haven't been through enough, however, the car that the court made my husband give the children and me has a lot of problems, but you know what? The Lord is keeping that car safe for us because we don't have the money to fix it.

Miracle number six happened next. See what I mean about you can't have just one miracle! I'm not finished yet....At Christmas 2002, I didn't have much money for the children for Christmas, so I had someone give my name to the toy drive sponsored by the South Yadkin Baptist Association. I went to the toy drive to buy toys at reduced prices. When I got ready to pay, I was told that the toys for my children were free. Praise the Lord. My children had the best Christmas ever! Thank you Lord!

Miracle number seven hasn't happened yet. Even though I don't have any more miracles of my own to share with you, I know that the Lord is not finished giving us miracles and blessing us! We still have a road ahead until we get completely back on our feet and put all the pieces back together, but the Lord will see us through. Indeed, as Psalm 55: 22 tells us to do, I have found that whenever I have cast my burden on the Lord, He has sustained me.

I would like to give a special thanks to all the doctors and nurses at Carolina Medical Center in Charlotte, North Carolina, to all of the first responders and firemen who helped with my rescue, and to paramedics Teddy Phillips and Lisa Bean who with the Lord's help worked quickly to save my life! Thanks for all the prayers and support from all the churches that helped to aid in my quick recovery. Please continue to pray for my children and me. May the Lord bless each one of you and keep you safe.

Scriptures That Helped Me the Most in the Hospital

Psalm 9: 9-10, 13	Deuteronomy 33: 27	Proverbs 17: 8
Psalm 18: 2	II Thessalonians 3: 3	John 6: 37
Psalm 27: 5	Philippians 1: 6	Romans 8: 38-39
Psalm 40: 1	Ephesians 1: 13	Matthew 21: 2
Psalm 46: 1	Psalm 55: 22	Psalm 142: 5-7

Earl Cater

Before I formed you in the womb, I knew you. Before you were born, I set you apart. I appointed you as a prophet to the nations. —Jeremiah 1: 5

My entry into this world was a minor footnote to Mamie Eisenhower's birthday. When I was young, my mom would remind me each November 14th that it was Mamie Eisenhower's birthday. She said it long enough and loud enough that I still think of Mamie on my birthday.

I was the fourth child born in the first five years of my parents' marriage. I have an older sister, a brother born two years before me, a brother born one year before me who died shortly after birth, a sister born five years after me, and a sister who is really my cousin. She was born ten years after me and adopted when she was four.

We lived in a small two-bedroom house, and my grandmother shared the second bedroom with my brother and sister. I slept in the baby bed in my parents' room until my grandmother passed away. Until I was four, hardly a day passed without my name being used in an argument. My mother named me Earl to spite my grandmother, and my grandmother never let my mom forget it. More often than not, I was referred to as "that child," and "that phrase" always defined me in relationship to the family. I was an unwanted pregnancy and an unwanted child. At best, I was an inconvenient disruption to the household.

As a young child, I was active, inquisitive and bright. I explored everything, tried everything, imitated everything and questioned everything. I was very verbal. As an adult with children of my own, I now know from experience that children like me cause extra work, an extra challenge and added frustration to the parental day. This fact of my identity worked to make my own circumstance more painful. There were plenty of bumps along my life path but one mountain-sized event. In fact, my life pivoted on this event for a very long time. This moment did more to shape and define me as a person than any other factor.

It started shortly after supper on my fourth birthday. We had just eaten the cake and ice cream, and I was playing with my new tow truck when I began to feel sick. I was laughed at for having eaten too much, but my stomachache did not go away. After I developed a fever, the doctor was consulted; and I was taken to the hospital for what turned into a ten day siege and fourteen days of abandonment. I had been struck with acute appendicitis and had had that little worm removed. The ether used to anesthetize me gave me pneumonia, and I spent ten days in an oxygen tent.

Any small child would be traumatized by these things. During my fourteen days of hospitalization, I saw my mom once while I was in the oxygen tent and once after the tent was removed. I was virtually alone and abandoned to strange monsters who wore funny clothes and tormented their victims with machines and needles. Afterward, I was saddled with the burden which the whole episode placed on my family. I was told that it was my fault that it happened.

Eight months later my grandmother passed away, and I was moved into grandma's bed with my brother; but I slept very little after I returned from the hospital. I had terrible nightmares from the trauma. Each night a large humming machine guided by people in green and white clothing came after me. Each night I awoke in a cold sweat and fought going back to sleep because I knew they would kill me. My life was in danger.

I went to my mom for comfort. I went only once. She was sitting in a red vinyl rocker just inside our living room. I crawled up on her lap and curled into a trembling fetal ball. I was immediately pushed off her lap and ridiculed. In a loud sarcastic voice, she announced to the people visiting our home that evening, "See my tiny little baby," and then ordered me back to bed with the threat of a spanking.

The next morning my older brother was sitting on her lap. She was reading to him, and so I tried to crawl up on her lap alongside of him. I was physically pushed off of her lap again and told that she was not going to have an oversized baby on her lap. I never went back to my mom again for anything!

The next fall, still four years of age, I was pushed into kindergarten. My mom's diatribe still echoes in my mind: "I will not have THAT CHILD in THIS HOUSE with a BABY to care for!"

My younger sister was due in a few months, so I started school without knowing my numbers, letters, colors or how to tie my shoes. I was not even fully potty trained. No one bothered teaching me any of those things until one of my teachers took issue with my level of achievement. By third grade my premature start in school caught up with me, and I spent a second year in the third grade trying to catch up. A new friend in the fourth grade taught me how to properly tie my shoes. The same friend taught me how to tell time in the fifth grade.

One day when I was eight, my brother and I were dreaming about what we would do when we grew up. He said he wanted to be an engineer and build things. I said I wanted to be an artist or an architect and design things. My mom praised my brother and said he could be anything he wanted to be. She then looked at me and said, "You are so stupid that you will be lucky if you make it through high school." It was my misfortune that I believed her.

This past year my brother and I were looking at some family pictures together when I noticed a couple of things that were very revealing and which stirred deep emotions within me. The fact is that my face was absent from most of those pictures. In the pictures where I was present, I was either at a distance from the others, in a corner or partially cut off because the photograph had been centered on my sister and brother. The pictures never revealed a smile.

In the midst of those pictures there was a group photo taken at a family reunion shortly before my fourth birthday. Out of the twenty-eight people in that photograph, I was the one sitting alone in the corner facing the rest of the people. Then I remembered. Each time a picture was taken, my mother would twist my ear and tell me that if I messed up the picture she would use a switch on my bare bottom.

I was severely punished often, slapped around the house on occasion and constantly threatened. Daily I was reminded of my lack of value and told I was stupid. At the end of each grading period, I was threatened with deprivation if I did not bring my grades up. Then my mom would tell me that I was an embarrassment to her personally. I was often reminded not to bother returning home at night if I did anything at school to embarrass the family or discredit the family name.

I am not telling this story because of my hurt or to gain your sympathy. I am telling this story because I want you to know that Jesus is victorious over the worst hardships that a person could possibly face. The people charged with responsibility for my life treated me as though I had no value and told me I had no value. As a result, I lived under the power of their words and actions. I was deeply hurt and very bitter until the day Jesus changed my life.

Oh, I still struggle to understand why I was unwanted and the target of my mom's bitterness and rage. I do not have an answer. I can only guess that my inconvenient arrival coupled with the loss of a baby one year earlier were in some way contributing factors.

Since my mom held grudges from her childhood, it is possible that I reminded her of the persons in her past who hurt her and that she struck out at the thing which troubled her not realizing that she really was striking out at me.

One bright spot in my childhood which worked to shape my life in a more positive direction took place on April 17, 1960. I had to wait another thirteen years to begin understanding the meaning of this event. Then I had to wait another twenty-eight years before I could fully appreciate its significance, but its unfolding was life changing and well worth the wait. It is good that we are not always allowed to see the end from the beginning.

April 17, 1960, was Easter Sunday. It was one of the two days each year when my parents would dress up. They would dress us up, and we would all go to church. Normally, we children were dropped off at Sunday School while our parents would have coffee and donuts at a local cafe, but on this Easter Sunday I had a Divine appointment.

On this day I audibly heard the voice of God. The church we attended was a strong, fundamentalist, King James only, Bible-thumping Baptist church with deeply rooted traditions. It still is. Praise be to God that His set will and counsel does not always respect the traditions and values of man. It was in this stodgy environment that God chose to speak to me in a voice strong and clear. In fact, I turned to my brother and asked him, "Whad'u say?" He punched me and answered, "Shut up stupid. We're in church!"

That morning at nine years of age, I heard the Lord God of all creation audibly say, "Before you were born, I knew you; and I have called you to stand in the pulpit and preach." He gave me something I could hold onto and something which by the sheer power of the words has worked to save my life. There was no one with whom I could share my revelation. I did not at that time understand it, and so I tried to become more involved in the church's program. My parents did everything possible to discourage my increased participation. By the time I was thirteen, I had totally withdrawn from all church activity and was pursuing a worldly course.

Thirteen years after I heard the voice of God, at age twenty-two, I was invited to a neighborhood Bible study. I went because a couple of friends of mine from high school and their new spouses were going to be in attendance. At that home Bible study the hostess gave an invitation to salvation. With every eye closed and every head bowed, she invited anyone who did not know Jesus as Lord and Savior to look up at her.

I was embarrassed and could not even raise my head. I knew in that moment that I did not personally know Jesus and that He had not transformed my life. In Baptist Sunday School I had heard all of the right stuff. I believed the Bible was true, and I believed that Jesus was Savior. I just did not own any of that knowledge. He was not my Savior, and I was suddenly aware of that fact.

I went home and asked Him to forgive me of my sin and to enter into my life. The moment I completed that prayer, I was filled with the presence of the Holy Spirit, and I again heard the voice of God. He said, "Before you were born, I knew you; and I have called you to stand in the pulpit and preach." At twenty-two years of age, I was beginning to understand what had taken place Easter of 1960. I surrendered myself to answer the call of Jesus upon my life. The date of my decision was April 17, 1973. It was thirteen years to the exact day from the first moment that at age nine I had heard the call of God on my life. God does have a wonderful sense of humor.

My parents despised my decision. I was harangued and harassed for being baptized and for choosing the pathway of obedience to my calling. My mom has since stopped speaking to me because I displease her with who I am and what I have become. In one of my last conversations with her, she punctuated her displeasure with me by telling me that with all of my education I could make real money if I would get a real job.

Before she severed her ties with me, God brought to light a wonderful secret that had been hidden since my mom's birth in 1923. It is so wonderful that it is truly the greatest revelation of God's abiding presence that any one person could ever hope for. In 1988, my mom had some heart problems, and the doctor wanted to proceed with a heart catheterization. The preliminary tests and x-rays indicated a congenital defect, and the entire family was called to be present because of the risk involved. They really did not expect her to survive.

We were told that other heart surgeons would be observing the procedure because she had a very rare heart condition. The doctor then drew a picture of mom's heart to show us its unique shape and function. The doctor drew an odd shaped single chamber heart and explained that since he had never seen one functioning in an adult and had never worked on one, he did not know what to expect. It is a condition which normally causes death within a few days of birth. As a pastor, I have conducted funerals for infants born with this condition. It is a very unfortunate birth defect—a defect from which people do not graduate to adulthood!

Why is this so important? The answer reaches back to my mom's birth. My mom was a twin weighing only two pounds at birth. She was born at home without modern medical care. The doctor came around several days later to check out the babies. Her twin died during that precious first week of life. My mom was so small that they kept her in a shoe box at first. It is incredible to believe that she lived at all, but the fact is that she did live and become an adult who carried and delivered five babies of her own into this world. Medically speaking, she should have died with her twin those first few days of life. She certainly should not have been able to work, marry and bring any babies into this world. She is a medical miracle!

Now if you understand basic genetics, you have already grasped the significance of my mom's life. I would not be here if my mom had not lived! My dad certainly would not have married my mom if she had died in accordance with her medical condition. This means I would have never been born! My presence in this world is totally dependent on the fact that my dad, and only my dad, married my mom, and only my mom. My existence is owed to their loving sexual activity which eventually produced me. Any other combination would not have produced me! It took a divine act of God's will to keep my mother alive and a world war to bring my parents together so that I could happen. This sounds arrogant. It is simply true.

I am the only believer within my immediate family who has answered my great grandfather's plea for the salvation of his lineage. When the Lord spoke to me at nine years of age and again at twenty-two, He quoted a piece of scripture. When I heard it, I did not know that it was a Bible verse. The passage from Jeremiah l: 5 is the call of Jeremiah the prophet:

> Before I formed you in the womb, I knew you. Before you were born, I set you apart. I appointed you as a prophet to the nations.

When the Lord of all creation said to me, "Before you were born, I knew you; and I have called you to stand in the pulpit and preach," He acknowledged His sovereign decision to call my life into being for His purpose. This means that He needed my mother and my father to accomplish this task. He meant for me to be from the very beginning, and He does not make mistakes. Preserving my mother's life was part of His plan to fulfill His purpose in me.

Perhaps you have a parent you despise. It could be that you have good reason. I certainly spent some time hating my mom and wishing my dad had married someone else. Humanly speaking, I also had good reason for my hatred; but I must tell you something, and you must hear it. You would not exist if both of your parents were not your parents. Someone else might be in this world as a child of your mom or your dad, but you would not be here. You cannot hate your father or your mother. To hate and despise them is to hate and despise yourself, for your presence on earth cannot be separated from their presence any more than life itself can be separated from the God who gave it.

Oh, yes, humans charged with my care treated me like trash. I have been rejected and despitefully used. I have been physically and emotionally abused. I have been deprived of things considered basic to life, but the people who did these things were only tools in the hand of the enemy of God. The truth is that from the very beginning of my life, and before, the one who has always hated the work of God has tried to undo the blessing which God has planned.

If you do not believe this, first consider how I alone among my siblings was despitefully treated. You must also consider how, as a pastor, I have had numerous coup attempts on my ministry and on my life. These attempts on the future of my ministry include:

1) One who decided I should be fired because I did not have enough education to be her pastor. I was a part-time pastor in a small rural church, and at the time that she raised her army against me, I was two weeks short of the same degree she held, a B.A.

2) One who decided that because I was licensed to ministry and not ordained for ministry, I was unfit to be his pastor. At the time that he raised his army against me, I was in the process of evaluation for ordination. When I was hired by his church, I had been hired with the understanding that I was proving my calling in preparation for ordination.

3) One who decided I had not given enough praise and credit to her for the work that she had done in the church. She took offense at my insensitivity and raised her army of supporters against me. The truth is that I had sent her a personal thank you and had publicly made mention of her contribution in church. I erred in not groveling deep enough for her taste.

4) One who decided he did not like the changes that took place in church under my leadership. He raised his army against me because the growth of the church had made him personally uncomfortable by the presence of too many strangers.

5) One who did not like the fact that I would not release the name of a person who in confidence had confessed to writing a nasty anonymous letter. She raised her army against me because I was protecting someone who had offended her. The truth is that it is my solemn duty to protect the pastoral confidence of all confessions, even when I do not agree with the actions and behavior of the person making that confession.

With these are cases of slander and gossip too numerous to count. The person who cursed me publicly in church because I took a stand against the manipulative politics he and his wife were using on the church is an example. The church board which agreed as a group to pretend poverty in order to force me to the lowest wage possible knowing that I would honor my sense of calling to the church anyway and knowing that I could not provide for my family on that wage is another example. Their calculated act enabled them to save face. You see, they figured they could force me into leaving through economic necessity if they decided they did not like me.

The benefit they would gain was the protection of their reputation by not firing another pastor.

Four of the above incidents made it necessary for me to move my family to a new ministry location. One of these incidents cost me a house which I built with my own hands and $25,000 in personal investment. As a result of this one incident, I will probably never own another home of my own. I have lost my financial advantage; and on a pastor's salary, it is unlikely at this point in my life that I will ever regain it apart from a miracle.

If you are still not convinced that the enemy of God would like to stop God's plan for my life and the blessing which God has for me personally, then take a look at this list:

1) In 1951, at six months of age, I contracted polio. The vaccine against polio was available in my hometown the very weekend I became sick, and I was the first to receive it. I suffered only minor nerve damage.

2) In 1952, at two years of age, severe ear infections damaged my inner ears.

3) In 1953, at two and one half years of age, I took some very strong medicine belonging to my grandmother, and I was rushed to the hospital to have my stomach pumped before I could be poisoned by it.

4) In 1954, at four years of age, my appendix was removed, and I nearly died from the pneumonia caused by ether.

5) In 1954, at four and three fourths years of age and on the first day of kindergarten, I fell seven feet and landed on concrete but only broke my left arm.

6) In 1956, at five years of age, severe ear infections scarred my inner ears.

7) In 1958, at seven years of age, I tripped on a wire and fell against the sharp edge of a tile block splitting the back of my right hand open. I bled heavily and had to be rushed to the hospital. I slightly damaged the nerves to my fingers.

8) In 1960, at nine years of age, I fell fifteen feet from a tree and landed on my back causing vertebrae to splinter and send bone particles through my muscle tissue. I walked away from the accident and am still walking.

9) In 1962, at twelve years of age, I was hit in the forehead with a baseball bat swung at full force. It threw me backward six feet through heavy shrubs but only split my right eyebrow.

10) In 1976, at twenty-five years of age, I had my tonsils removed and nearly bled to death. I was reinflated with four large bore IV needles one in each extremity.

11) In 1983, at thirty-two years of age, the Toyota I was driving was rear-ended by a Chevy El Camino. I was standing still in traffic, and the El Camino was traveling forty-five miles per hour. I suffered only bruises because I was warned of the oncoming car by the Lord and took some evasive action.

I have been harassed, mistreated, abused, accused, cheated and slandered throughout my life, so why am I not filled with rage and hate? Why have I not committed suicide? Why have I not murdered someone in rage? Why have I not become a child abuser, rapist or criminal? Why am I not in some pitiful jail? Why am I still a pastor?

In part the answer is caught up in that single sentence spoken to me when I was nine and again when I was twenty-two. The fact is that God has planned nothing but good for me. People who were not guided by the principles of scripture and surrendered to the power of God have done to me whatever seemed best to them. They were guided by the enemy of the things of God. They were the instrument of that enemy's plan to rob me of the blessing God planned for me before I was born.

My mom is living proof of God's eternal favor. My life is a testimony to the greater power of God to deliver, heal and preserve. As Paul declared in Ephesians 6:12:

> I struggle not against flesh and blood, but against rulers, against the powers, against the world forces of wickedness in the heavenly places.

Because of the pain of the things done to me, I have at times forgotten this simple truth, but in grace the Lord Jesus has always brought me back to understand that He has planned nothing but good for me. It is the forces of darkness that have tried to hurt me. People are just one set of weapons used by the enemy of God.

The second part of my answer is found in the words of Jesus. In more ways than I can easily recite, Jesus has spoken to the hurt which I have received and told me exactly what I can do with it. For the sake of space, I will mention only two passages where Jesus instructs me in this matter. Matthew 6: 14, 15 says:

> For if you forgive others for their transgressions, your heavenly Father will also forgive you. But if you do not forgive others, then your Father will not forgive your transgressions.

Matthew 7:2 says:

> For in the way you judge, you will be judged; and by your standard of measure, it will be measured to you.

I have chosen to be a child of God and not a child of this world. Since I have chosen the narrow gate and the straight way of being a follower of Jesus, I must forgive others the hurt which they have inflicted on me. The forgiveness which I claim from God through Jesus is in jeopardy if I do not freely lay my hurt down at the feet of Jesus and grant others the same forgiveness that He has granted to me.

When I cross into eternity, I do not want to hear my Heavenly Father say, "Receive from me the measure which you have measured out to others. In the same way you have refused to forgive others the wrongs you have suffered, I refuse to forgive you." Ouch! In better words, I will not choose to bear punishment before God for the offenses which others have inflicted upon me. If I hold onto those offenses, I chain myself to the person who has offended me through my refusal to grant forgiveness, I injure my relationship with God. I also continue the cycle of violence and inflict spiritual injury on those persons who have caused me offense and, thereby, bring condemnation upon myself.

Through foolish pride, I would only hurt myself by attempting to carry a burden which God has laid upon Jesus. This is a burden too great for any human to bear. In protest, you scream, "But it's not fair! They did______, and _______, and ________, and even _______!" (Please feel free to fill in your own blanks.) Why should I be punished when they wronged me. I have a right to be angry. God won't punish me because of something THAT person did." You are right. God won't punish you because of something that person did, but He will punish you for your refusal to grant that person the same grace and favor He granted you.

I also had my list of wrongs suffered, and I, too, could reel them off with a staccato voice. When push comes to shove and I feel hurt again, I still catch myself making a list of wrongs suffered. Forgiveness is not easy. Someone must bear the loss of the wrong suffered; and since it is God's prerogative to assign that burden to Jesus, why not let Jesus have it? Sometimes forgiveness is like eating a bad onion. The sour taste just keeps coming up. God does not ask us to pretend we are not hurt. He demands that we forgive that hurt.

Some people have trouble distinguishing between the lingering pain of the hurt suffered and forgiveness. Forgiveness is an act of willful obedience to God; hurt is a wound which must fester and heal. There are times when that means daily confessing our return to the pain of our hurt and laying it afresh onto the yoke of Jesus so that He can carry it for us. It is perfectly within His will for us to do this. All He asks is that we forgive the wrongs we have suffered. If that means granting forgiveness day by day until the fire burning in our heart is quenched, then we must continue to be faithful in granting that forgiveness.

The bottom line is this. God sent His one and only Son to die on the cross and pay the penalty of my sin. Jesus was innocent. I am not innocent. I am the one who deserved to die on the cross. The forgiveness He granted to me is beyond measure. My forgiveness of others, no matter how large the crime, is puny by comparison. The damage done to me by other humans is but a speck of dust in my eye when it is compared to the beam of the cross which I thrust into our Heavenly Father's eye with my own sinfulness. If you do not have a personal relationship with Jesus Christ, I invite you to turn to the last page of this book and ask Him to come into your heart today. I promise you that your life will never be the same again.

During Martha Dobson's trip to Israel from March 28 to April 9, 2001, she met Earl and Irma Cater. They were a part of her bus team. She felt so privileged to pray and to share with them during the trip. As Earl shared some of his testimony during the trip, she asked him if he would be kind enough to share it with the readers of this book. He was happy to oblige with the above testimony. It is a testimony filled with sadness and multiple challenges yet always with God's mercy, grace and divine providence. It's a heartwarming story of a man's ability to rise triumphantly above his circumstances through his dependence upon God's wisdom and hand. He and his wife pastor Methow Community Church in Methow, Washington.

George Conger

Is any among you sick? Let him call for the elders of the church, and let them pray over him, anointing him with oil in the name of the Lord.—James 5: 14

A Summer Accident and Healing

During the summer of 1982, I was out working in my garden on a warm Saturday afternoon. As I was tying up some tomato vines around a homemade chicken wire fence I had constructed, I poked a wire in my eye.

Having been a Christian most of my life, I thought I knew the Word; however, it was about this time that I had joined a Bible study and realized for the first time the true meaning of God's love, mercy and healing power for today.

After the accident I went into the house and told Nancy what had happened. We both knew I needed to go to the emergency room immediately; however, before we left, Nancy prayed and anointed me with oil I had received from the Oral Robert's ministry. This was in accordance with James 5: 14:

> Is any among you sick? Let him call for the elders of the church, and let them pray over him, anointing him with oil in the name of the Lord.

Upon arriving at the hospital, the doctor examined me and told me I had a "jagged" cut across the eyeball which was very serious. He gave me some medication, put a patch on my eye and told me to return in the morning. during that evening, I noticed I had no pain, only the discomfort of the patch.

The next morning when the same doctor took off the bandage and re-examined the eye, he exclaimed, "Holy Cow! It's gone! Yesterday there was a very deep cut across your eyeball, but now it is gone!" He was so astounded by all of this that he had another physician to come in and take a look. Needless to say, Nancy and I left the hospital rejoicing. Later that morning, I was able to stand before my church family and testify to what my Heavenly Father had done.

Since then, I have been delivered and healed from many things; and as I grow and learn more about what Jesus did for me, I can see that I am truly free and delivered from whatever Satan tries to put on me.

Cheryl Conroy

Trust in the Lord with all, and lean not on your own understanding; in all your ways acknowledge Him, and He shall direct your paths. —Proverbs 3: 5-6

Cheryl's heart's desire has been to see her children grow up in the fear and admonition of the Lord. Life was not easy for her as she was growing up; consequently, Cheryl has struggled to overcome the many obstacles in her life so that her children might have a more peaceful life undergirded with God's strength and power.

Several years ago, God began to impress her to pray for a teachable spirit. "I used to do things only in a logical way. I never used to listen. I used to tell Him what I wanted," she said. "When you're aggressive, it's hard to get in a humble spirit; but I've learned that even though I feel insignificant, God says that I am significant.

"There was a time that I was too busy to listen to God." God has answered Cheryl's prayer for a more teachable spirit giving her a close relationship with her children that affords her many opportunities to share her faith.

"I can see where the Lord has brought me from," she related. "My mother loved us," Cheryl shared, "but she didn't know how to be a good mother. She wasn't taught. She provided material things. She was too busy in the world." Because of the example her mother had set for her, Cheryl was determined to be the best mother she could be to surpass her mother and to teach her own children well.

When Cheryl was twelve years old, her father had a stroke and was placed in a Masonic home. Unable to deal with her husband's illness, Cheryl's mother divorced him. She moved her family to Florida when she remarried. Her second husband was an alcoholic fireman with quite a temper. Very insecure and naive, Cheryl's mother who was not an alcoholic, could not seem to see how many problems he had. Cheryl's father who had been such a good man died about two years after they moved to Florida.

Her step-father could be quite nice when he was not drinking, but under the influence of alcohol, his personality altered. "He lied to me," she said. "He didn't like me and criticized everything I did because his daughter had died of a brain tumor." She continued, "If I said anything, he'd take after me. He was physically and emotionally abusive. One time he pushed me from the kitchen to the dining room. I hit the chair so hard that I broke it. That was the start of my back problems today.

"Sometimes he'd get mad at Mother and go to the basement and turn the music up so loud that we couldn't sleep. One night I couldn't take any more and walked four miles with my suitcase to my Aunt Edna's house.

"My stepfather liked it cold, and my mother liked it hot. One night a couple of days later," Cheryl recalled, "while he was very drunk, he blew out the pilot light on the furnace so that she wouldn't have any heat. He neglected to turn off the gas causing a concentration of gas in the air." That night when her mother started relighting the pilot light, a fire erupted from the gas in the air. She was taken to the hospital with second degree burns.

Her mother decided to leave him and joined Cheryl at her aunt's house. Cheryl's mother divorced Cheryl's stepfather but moved to Virginia two years later and remarried him. Her children and family begged her not to remarry him. (Cheryl believed he was mentally ill.) They managed an apartment complex. Cheryl was nineteen years old and refused to live again with him; consequently, Cheryl paid room and board to live with her single Aunt Elizabeth. Two years later her mother died of cancer. She remembers that, "He was awful. I'd put up with him to see her. Later when he died, I was glad. I was rid of him.

"It was a gradual thing. God dealt with me to forgive him and her. I came to realize that she didn't do what she did to hurt me but out of her own insecurity. I knew to have peace I had to do it (forgive her). It's a commandment." I said, "Then Lord, you'll have to help me with this because I'm so resentful of what he did to our family." After my mother died, we went to pick up things my mother had designated for me and my sister; and he'd taken them all and sold them."

Eventually, Cheryl was able by the grace of God to forgive her mother and her stepfather. As she says, "My Sis and I say we know God had his hand on us. At sixteen years of age, my cousin Kurt came over to my house one day and led me to the Lord. My mother wouldn't take me to church; but when I'd stay with my Aunt Elizabeth, we went to church. I also had a little help from my cousin Kurt while he was in service. Maturing in my faith, the Lord continued to draw me to read the Word. It got me through; and when I was twenty-nine I rededicated my life to the Lord."

Proverbs 3:6 reads,

> Trust in the Lord with all your heart, and lean not on your own understanding; in all your ways acknowledge Him, and He shall direct your path.

This has become one of Cheryl's favorite scriptures. Each time the Holy Spirit directs her to this verse, she is reminded of how far God has brought her, of how good He has been to her; of all the obstacles He has helped her overcome; and of how much He has changed her as she has allowed Him to renew in her a teachable spirit. It is her prayer that her children and grandchildren will learn many of the lessons she has learned at a much younger age than she. Cheryl longs to leave her children and grandchildren a legacy of strong Christian values, of assurance of God's strength and power for every situation they might encounter and of God's faithfulness.

Harvey and Dee Cranfill

And my God shall supply all your need according to His riches in glory by Christ Jesus.—Phillipians 4: 19

They Walk Among Us

Many stories are told about the sighting of angels and their effect on our lives. Many are fabricated and expanded until their effect is either discounted or laughed at by non-believers. Some stories, however, are simple and so clear in their meaning that it is hard to discount them as fabrications or tales.

I have always believed that angels do exist and that they do cover the earth, to and fro. I believe that their purpose is not to be understood by man, but only by our Creator; and that they do His bidding. I also believe that the mind of man cannot comprehend their reasons or the facts that surround their deeds.

It is only through our faith and knowledge of the love of our Savior that we are permitted to make contact with these angelic beings. Some come to serve our immediate needs; some to sustain us in times of sorrow and some to view our actions and to sometimes help in guiding our deeds. Sometimes our faith is strong; sometimes it's weak and sometimes we're without faith. Despair is something that can sometimes consume us and make us lose our faith. It is in times like this that I believe that angels sometimes are chosen by God to give us a boost and renew our faith.

One such moment came in my life and showed me that God does extend a helping hand to us if our faith is strong enough. In 1988, for whatever reason, my wife and I had had several setbacks in our financial lives and had finally ended up in the county in North Carolina where I had been born.

Our finances were very low, and we were trying to make a go of a small cafe in a rural area. Our business was very marginal, and we were in great need of finances just to meet our obligations. A note was coming due which had to be paid, or we would lose our business. We had saved most of the payment, but it was due the first day of the month.

It was the last week of the month, and my pastor and his wife were having lunch in our cafe. My wife and the pastor's wife were in the kitchen serving lunch. Business had been slow, and we had put only thirty dollars in the register that morning. That was all the money that we had to start the day on.

Business was almost non-existent, and the pastor and I were sitting in a booth. We had all had prayer, and he and I were discussing problems that we were having in our church and ways to try to increase our membership.

The cafe was on a secondary highway (two lane), and you could see for a mile in each direction. No other buildings were near us at all. An open field behind the cafe and a home about half a mile away were the only things close to the cafe. Our two cars were parked in front of the cafe.

While the pastor and I were talking in the booth, the front glass door opened; and a man in old, but clean clothes came in. He had nothing with him. I looked out the window and saw no car, so I assumed he was on foot. He went to the counter, and my wife waited on him. He asked her for a glass of water. She served him the water, and he requested nothing else.

I looked at my pastor, and he looked at me. We both had the same thought—that the man had no money and was probably down on his luck and walking wherever he was going. I got up and walked over to the man and spoke to him. He was quiet and very orderly. I sat down beside him and asked if he had eaten. He informed me that he did not have any money but did not ask for anything. I called my wife over and told her to fix him a meal of whatever he wanted and told him it was on the house.

He thanked me, and I returned to my seat with my pastor. The man ate the meal and drank the drink that my wife served him. He thanked her and came over to me and thanked me. Then without further comment, he went out the front door. He was tall and thin and only had the clothes on his back as he left our cafe.

As he left, I got up to see which way he was going and if he had any transportation. I went to the door and looked out and did not see him. I went out the front door, and my pastor followed me out. We walked around the building, and he was nowhere to be seen. The road and the field were empty, and no one was in sight. Going back inside the building, we told our wives that we had seen nothing, and they both looked to see if they could see him. He was nowhere to be found.

In a few minutes the pastor and his wife started to leave, and he wanted some change for a paper outside. He gave me a dollar, and I opened the cash register to give him change. In the register where normally there would have been twenties if we had had any that day, there were two crisp new one hundred dollar bills. I showed these bills to my pastor, and we were all amazed and could not figure out how they got there. No one had been in the register but me on that day. We had had very few customers, and they had paid with small bills. The total of our receipts only totaled about thirty dollars which would have given us about sixty dollars in the drawer.

That afternoon, I took the two hundred dollars and put them with the rest of the money we had saved for our payment. It gave us enough to write a check and make our payment. No one ever saw the man again.

"I was thirsty, and you gave me drink. I was hungry, and you gave me food" (Matthew 25: 35). Suddenly, I knew without a doubt that I had been in the presence of an angel sent by God to help me in my time of need.

Some will say, it's only a quirk of faith—an accident to be explained away, and that I was mistaken in the facts; but for me, it was a sign that when we are faithful to our Savior's wishes, He will be faithful to our needs.

This is only one of many times that the grace of God has sustained us in our times of need. When our faith is strong, God is close. When it is weak, God can only let us make our lives whatever we choose. Sin is the separator, but faith is the glue that can repair and replace all that we have need of in this world. God is always there to pour out His love on us. It is up to us through faith to accept His gifts to us.

Lee Dages

But the Comforter, which is the Holy Ghost, whom the Father will send in My name, He shall teach you all things, and bring all things to your remembrance, whatsoever I had said unto you.
—John 14: 25 (KJV)

I choose to begin my testimony with John 14: 26 because this scripture has unlocked so many other scriptures for me. It's been a doorway or a key for me to the Living Word.

I'm the oldest of six children and was born in Newland, North Carolina in 1941. I was born again in 1951 and baptized in the Holy Spirit in 1971. After that I was baptized in water.

My mother was Baptist, and my dad was Catholic. There was no Catholic church in Avery County, just a chapel in the summertime. If my dad had wanted to, he could have taken us elsewhere to a Catholic church, but he didn't. He allowed us to go to the Baptist church. My parents took us to church or sent us. They didn't go with us. even though my parents didn't go to church with me, I was blessed by them; yet, I don't recommend that other parents not go to church with their children.

In 1951, when I was ten years old, I went to a Presbyterian revival. One night I was sitting on the back pew when I felt someone pushing me to go down front to accept Jesus Christ. I knew that it could not be a real person pushing me because there was no one behind me, but I didn't go down front. I finally followed the leading of the Holy Spirit and gave my heart to the Lord.

That night I told my mother about my experience, and she said that I should tell Daddy. I told her that I wasn't comfortable telling him because I didn't think he would approve. She told me that he would be happy; yet it was much later before I actually did tell him. Later my mother asked why I hadn't told my father about my conversion. She said that he was happy for me. I told her I had decided I could be a Christian and keep it to myself. It was not good for a ten year old boy to try to go it alone. We need as much help from others as we can get to grow in Christ.

When I graduated from high school, my family and I moved to Corpus Christi, Texas and built a Putt-Putt golf course. On July 5, 1959, after pulling out from an intersection, a car I hadn't seen hit me in the door on my side knocking me 150 feet sideways. As the car rolled over, my brother, sister and I were all thrown out.

My brother and sister received bruises and skin abrasions over most of their bodies. My sister had a partially severed finger and three broken ribs. My brother had a three quarter inch separation of the sacroiliac and a crushed pelvis. The impact of the accident crushed three of my vertebrae and cut my spinal cord in two which left me paralyzed from the waist down. The severity of my injuries from the accident impacted my whole family. To help me adjust to my paralysis, my family moved back to North Carolina.

In the beginning, I was in denial about being paralyzed. I KNEW that I was going to get better. My positive attitude did help in many ways, but the doctors couldn't help my paralysis. I heard the doctor tell my mother that I'd be in a wheelchair the rest of my life. For the first nine years after the accident, I refused to use a wheelchair. I used braces and crutches and went to Appalachian University. I graduated in 1965, with a degree in Industrial Arts. The next nine years of my life I used a wheelchair, braces and crutches. From 1977, until now, I have had the use of a wheelchair only.

Over the next thirteen years, I taught school for eight years in between operations. I began teaching school in 1965, and underwent a series of operations that kept me from finishing the school year. I had a bone disease called osteomyelitis caused by a staph infection which got in the bones I sit on and began eating them away. By 1975, the disease had gone underground and eaten away the top one and one half inches of my left femur.

In 1975, I had an operation on my left femur to take out the diseased bone. In one month in 1976, I had eight operations. I thought the doctors would keep on operating until there was nothing left to operate on. That was really discouraging. I thought I was going to die. In 1976, I read an article in *Prevention Magazine* about Hyperbaric Oxygen Tank treatment and went to Allentown, Pennsylvania, for the treatment which seemed to put the staph infection into remission.

During all of this time I experienced high fevers and excruciating pain. In the eighties, I began to have periorectal absesses and had several operations for them. In the nineties, I had five major operations for a hernia with methicillen resistant staph infection. (The staph infection couldn't be treated with methicillen antibiotics.) In January 2003, I had another operation. To date I have had sixty-three major operations. Obviously, the injuries from this accident are still impacting my life.

When I experienced the Baptism of the Holy Spirit in 1971, my spirit man came alive. I was saved, but now I had such joy and such a deeper experience with the Lord. With the Baptism of the Holy Spirit, I have been able to go through all kinds of things that have happened to me in a way that I could not have before.

A doctor from my hometown had told me about the Baptism of the Holy Spirit causing me to read The Cross and the Switchblade, a book by David Wilkerson, a third generation Assembly of God pastor. I'd had this book for three years. Pat Boone played the lead in the movie based on this book.

When I read this book, I realized that something had been left out of my Baptist upbringing. My upbringing had caused me to be skeptical of the Baptism of the Holy Spirit. This doctor and the book had told me that if I'd read certain scriptures, I would receive the Baptism of the Holy Spirit.

I read every scripture in the Bible on the topic. If it said, *Holy Ghost*, *Holy Spirit*, *Spirit of Christ* or just the word *spirit*, I looked it up. I found more scriptures to verify the Baptism of the Holy Spirit than people had given me. Indeed, I found the Baptism of the Holy Spirit to be truth.

According to Acts 1: 13-15, one hundred and twenty disciples altogether including Mary the mother of Jesus and the brothers of

Jesus were gathered in one accord in the Upper Room when Jesus filled them with the Baptism of the Holy Spirit on the day of Pentecost (Acts 2). I decided that if this gift was so important that Jesus gave it to His family members, it must be important for me.

I began to seek the Baptism of the Holy Spirit; and on November 14, 1971, I knew I had received the Baptism including my prayer language. The Baptism of the Holy Spirit is such an awesome gift and weapon of spiritual warfare. As 1 Corinthians 14: 2 says,

> For he who speaks in a tongue does not speak to men but to God, for no one understands him; however, in the spirit he speaks mysteries.

As 1 Corinthians 14: 14 says, when I pray in a tongue, my spirit prays. I don't understand what I am saying unless I pray for interpretation. Satan does not understand either. Only God understands. With the Baptism of the Holy Spirit, we are able to do battle in the heavenly places against the principalities.

At times in my life, I've run away from my spiritual life, but I've never lost the help of the Holy Spirit. I just wouldn't have made it through all that I've been through in my life without the Baptism of the Holy Spirit. I believe that the Baptism of the Holy Spirit is critical for our daily walk to help us better understand Him and His Word. In order to get along with people, we must stay in the Spirit and ask Him to change us so our neighbors will see Jesus in us.

John 16: 13 says,

> However, when He, the Spirit of Truth, has come He will guide you into all truth, for He will not speak on His own authority, but whatever He hears He will speak, and He will tell you things to come.

So many things happen as a result of the Baptism of the Holy Spirit. as Acts 1: 8 says,

> But you shall receive power when the Holy Spirit has come upon you, and you shall be witnesses to Me in Jerusalem and in all Judea and Samaria and to the end of the earth.

Over the years I've helped others to receive this gift. At first I was upset with myself that I wasn't winning enough souls to the Lord. Now, however, I understand that the more people I can help to receive the Baptism of the Holy Spirit, the more souls which can be won because with this gift people have greater power and boldness to witness. When the Lord uses me to win souls or to help others to receive the Baptism of the Holy Spirit, it is not me—only the Lord who receives the glory.

Not only has the Lord used me to win souls for His kingdom since I received the Baptism of the Holy Spirit, but He has also given me victory over alcohol and nicotine. Except for a relapse of two cigarettes, I have had no cigarettes since March 1993. I know that if you're struggling with an addiction, He will get you through the darkest night. In 1986, I tried several times to take my life. Only the power of the Holy Spirit protected me. Since I received the Baptism of the Holy Spirit, each time I've been tempted to take my life, the Holy Spirit within me saved my life. This spirit of suicide is something addicts often battle. If you're struggling, first accept Jesus as your Savior. Then seek the Baptism of the Holy Spirit. It's where your strength lies.

On July 24, 1992, my battle with alcohol addiction came to a head. I got up and looked over at less than one half of a four liter bottle of wine in my room. I rolled into my kitchen looking for an ashtray and couldn't find one. I went to the refrigerator to get something to eat and saw my ashtray and food that one wouldn't use to slop hogs with. I knew that I must have fixed that food. I asked the Lord, "What has happened to my crazy life?"

I told Him that I would no longer promise Him that I'd quit drinking and smoking. (I had been drinking off and on for a period of twenty-seven years.) I asked Him to help me even if I had to check in with alcoholic people. I had a very misinformed idea about people who are alcoholics. On that day I was willing to do anything to change.

One month and a half later, I got a ticket for DUI (driving under the influence) and went to jail for three days. I decided to stay there instead of trying to post bond. I learned more during those three days in jail than I ever wanted to learn about this side of life. I spent the last night of my confinement explaining the Baptism of the Holy Spirit to an inmate who began talking with me. He said he saw something different in me. Here I was a Christian in jail! I couldn't see how that was possible. He had killed someone. I have found that no matter how far a man runs, he can't outrun God. God has continued to put people in my path.

When I got out of jail, the judge sent me to a twelve-step program. I was going to wait eighteen weeks to decide if I was an alcoholic. One morning two weeks and one day into the program, I asked God if I were an alcoholic. He said, "Yes." I said, "Wait a minute, God. Are these people really just trying to talk me into saying that I'm an alcoholic?" He said, "No." I didn't hear an audible voice like Paul on the road to Damascus, but I knew that it was Him speaking just as I know the voice of any other family member. After all, He is my Father and my Brother. I have been sober from July 24, 1992, until now—eleven years.

I attend an anonymous twelve-step program. The program is unnamed because the leaders have found that it is best not to allow personalities and egos to flourish. I respect the anonymity. As a Christian recovering alcoholic, this delights me as it allows me to openly give credit to Jesus. The Lord has helped me to become sober and stay sober through this program just as He has helped two cousins and many friends to become sober at home or in church rather than in a twelve-step program. He alone gets all of the honor and the glory for accomplishing this in my life.

The Holy Spirit keeps drawing me back to Him. He delivered me. He is such a sweet person. Time after time, I used to write on a can of beer or a bottle of wine, "Lord, help me never to do this again." I knew the Lord as my Savior and as the Baptizer in the Holy Spirit, but I just couldn't fight my addictions. He let me reach what was the bottom for me. Then I went to jail.

The Lord showed me that He was in the twelve-step program. God has used me within a program which is dedicated to Him to lead people to the Lord. A lot has happened in my life. I have learned that no matter what may happen to you the Lord Jesus will send someone to help you with any problem you may have if you will just ask. He's done it for me, and He can do it for you. As John 14: 26 says,

But the Helper, the Holy Spirit, whom the Father will send in My name, He will teach you all things and bring to your remembrance all things that I said to you.

The Holy Spirit teaches me everyday how to be more like Jesus. I want to be a soul winner who just can't quit. I've come so close to dying so many times, yet He has protected me each time. I even found that I can pray for my own healing. Once I laid hands on myself and prayed. The decubitus ulcer was gone the next morning. I have had ulcers like this last for four years. That is the power of the Holy Spirit! Indeed, the Holy Spirit will teach us all things. He has taught me so much about praying for myself and others. I know that the Lord has protected me over and over again because He has a purpose for my life. Just as He has brought me out so many times, He'll bring you out of any valley if you will but ask Him.

Maria Devore

Here I am. Send me.—Isaiah 6: 8

From the time I was seven years old, I was so torn over whether to be a nurse or a missionary. Like Taylor Hudson, I held on to Isaiah's verse, "Here I am. Send me." As I grew older, I was surprised to learn that I could be both.

As I headed into my teenage years, my desire for missions in third-world countries grew stronger. I went on a missions trip to the Solomon Islands with an Australian mission team. I was empowered by the experience. I could live off the Word. The natives were friendly, and I didn't have a care in the world. That's definitely the life! I didn't even mind the heat, the noon showers, the mud, the bugs or the toads. Just the Lord and me—we would conquer the third-world. There was never a thought of America. Why they had everything. They certainly wouldn't need me. Surely a life of sacrifice was what was meant for me.

1 Bump in my plan. There was no job for me in New Zealand once I graduated from nursing school. The answer to my prayer—A children's hospital recruited me to Little Rock, Arkansas. I'd

found out that a missionary needs some experience to be useful in the field; so I packed and nine months later arrived in the United States of America.

Later I took part in a Mexican missions trip. I was pursuing a position in Romania in the orphanages when #2 Bump in my plan hit—Jeff Devore. Love can sidetrack you a little at times. Somewhere in our first year of marriage, I battled with failure. Surely, I was supposed to sacrifice myself in the wilds of Africa or somewhere very remote where I'd have to depend on the Lord, but not in America where I had every commodity and was self-sufficient. I really didn't even need God to provide my needs. Oh, how the prideful fall, and they do fall hard!

"Lord, here I am. Send me." Oh, the sacrifice to give up the control strings of my life—to daily strive to serve in a self-serving world. That is now my mission—to be a missionary in a very needy America.

Martha H. Dobson

And we know that the Son of God has come and has given us an understanding, that we may know Him who is true; and we are in Him who is true, in His Son Jesus Christ. This is the true God and eternal life. —I John 5: 20

To Thine Own Self Be True

Grandma, I remember sitting on your knee.
"To thine own self be true," you'd say to me.
Only one man ever perfected this quest.
He never faltered. His way was always true and best.

A man came to our door one day.
He'd come to talk business, not to play.
"Come join the Klan," he said to my Dad.
Even as a child, I wondered how so many could be so bad.

Grandma, I remember sitting on your knee.
"To thine own self be true," you'd say to me.
Only one man ever perfected this quest.
He never faltered. His way was always true and best.

Why, Mr. Charlie worked for us. He was so good.
How could anyone seek him out behind a hood.
So his skin was black, and ours was white.
Did that make his way wrong and ours right?

Grandma, I remember sitting on your knee.
"To thine own self be true," you'd say to me.
Only one man ever perfected this quest.
He never faltered. His way was always true and best.

Why should skin color make someone bad, I thought.
The idea that one's religion made him bad, I'd never bought.
It's not color or religion that matter. It's the heart.
From people with prejudices such as these I had to part.

Grandma, I remember sitting on your knee.
"To thine own self be true," you'd say to me.
Only one man ever perfected this quest.
He never faltered. His way was always true and best.

I went to school. They said I was fat.
I saw no difference between skinny and fat from where I sat.
Whether the heart was white, black, brown, yellow or red,
On these distinctions I would not be fed.

Grandma, I remember sitting on your knee.
"To thine own self be true," you'd say to me.
Only one man ever perfected this quest.
He never faltered. His way was always true and best.

On a farm I grew up. Little money we had;
But we had food, clothes, and a home—no need to be sad.
Yes, my clothes were homemade, not store bought
But for finer clothes any search would have come to nought.

Grandma, I remember sitting on your knee.
"To thine own self be true," you'd say to me.
Only one man ever perfected this quest.
He never faltered. His way was always true and best.

I was the girl who loved books and studied hard to learn.
From such paths I was told girls should turn.
The boys won't like you if you're too smart.
From books and good grades you really should part.

Grandma, I remember sitting on your knee.
"To thine own self be true," you'd say to me.
Only one man ever perfected this quest.
He never faltered. His way was always true and best.

I knew that into the ministry I should head.
"There's no way you can make a living," my Dad said.
"I'll send you to college only to be a teacher or nurse."
"O.K.," I said. "I'll study languages. Will that be worse?"

Grandma, I remember sitting on your knee.
"To thine own self be true," you'd say to me.
Only one man ever perfected this quest.
He never faltered. His way was always true and best.

My roots were Protestant, I knew,
Yet in so many directions, I blew.
I had to find my own faith to which I'd be true.
Each path I took had a different hue.

Grandma, I remember sitting on your knee.
"To thine own self be true," you'd say to me.
Only one man ever perfected this quest.
He never faltered. His way was always true and best.

I found the truth. My Lord, He's so real!
This joy I've found, It can heal!
I pray out loud. Some say it's bad.
I raise my hands in praise. Some say it's just a fad.

Grandma, I remember sitting on your knee.
"To thine own self be true," you'd say to me.
Only one man ever perfected this quest.
He never faltered. His way was always true and best.

I love the Word. With Him I love to be.
You're not coming to the party? We'll see.
You're not doing drugs or drinking?
No, my faith is tried and true. To the other I'm not sinking.

Grandma, I remember sitting on your knee.
"To thine own self be true," you'd say to me.
Only one man ever perfected this quest.
He never faltered. His way was always true and best.

You speak in tongues, you say.
"We know," I heard them say, "you're going the wrong way."
Your family and your friends know best, don't you think?
No, my heart knows best. I didn't even blink.

Grandma, I remember sitting on your knee.
"To thine own self be true," you'd say to me.
Only one man ever perfected this quest.
He never faltered. His way was always true and best.

You're going to the Arab Gulf, you say.
Don't you know women don't go alone so far away?
You should stay home and have kids. It's the better way.
But other cultures I need to understand. I must do it my way.

Grandma, I remember sitting on your knee.
"To thine own self be true," you'd say to me.
Only one man ever perfected this quest.
He never faltered. His way was always true and best.

My husband said he's headed out.
Marriage is too much responsibility, no doubt.
Now you're single and divorced. This church is old.
We couldn't have you here you'd break the mold.

Grandma, I remember sitting on your knee.
"To thine own self be true," you'd say to me.
Only one man ever perfected this quest.
He never faltered. His way was always true and best.

You want to make a difference, to do your best.
Don't you know without mediocrity, you'll have no rest.
Your search for excellence brings our weaknesses to light.
We'll fight everything you do to cause a blight.

Grandma, I remember sitting on your knee.
"To thine own self be true," you'd say to me.
Only one man ever perfected this quest.
He never faltered. His way was always true and best.

Now into ministry you say you're bound.
Can't you be satisfied? Don't you know that most women there
are not found?
Overseas to the mission field? Don't go.
You don't understand. It's not the mainstream but my Lord's heart-
beat which must be so.

Grandma, I remember sitting on your knee.
"To thine own self be true," you'd say to me.
Only one man ever perfected this quest.
He never faltered. His way was always true and best.

But those people are Arabs, and there's a Jew.
I understand those who will go are so few.
Their politics are different. They're not human.
Oh, but to God they're precious. They have a soul. Can't you see
it? I can.

Grandma, I remember sitting on your knee.
"To thine own self be true," you'd say to me.
Only one man ever perfected this quest.
He never faltered. His way was always true and best.

Those people speak English. Those speak French.
One's good. The other's bad.
But I looked instead and saw a human heart.
I felt so sad.

Grandma, I remember sitting on your knee.
"To thine own self be true," you'd say to me.
Only one man ever perfected this quest
He never faltered. His way was always true and best.

You can't have her in your home.
She's black, don't you see?
No, I see a human being like a butterfly,
Ready to be set free.

Grandma, I remember sitting on your knee.
"To thine own self be true," you'd say to me.
Only one man ever perfected this quest.
He never faltered. His way was always true and best.

You can't teach them English. Their skin is brown, and they're lower class.
But through the eyes of Christ, I see love and an an opportunity I can't pass.
They're never on time. They won't do it your way. Better keep them at bay.
I see beautiful brown hearts that'll enrich my day.

Grandma, I remember sitting on your knee.
"To thine own self be true," you'd say to me.
Only one man ever perfected this quest.
He never faltered. His way was always true and best.

Care about those children. How can you dare?
That a tear is wiped away and a life made better I care.
But they're dirty, and their parents uneducated, you say.
Oh, but dirt washes away as the soul beneath appears to bless my day.

Grandma, I remember sitting on your knee.
"To thine own self be true," you'd say to me.
Only one man ever perfected this quest.
He never faltered. His way was always true and best.

But your home, you see's, not in the best neighborhood.
For money, you see I'd never trade my soul even if I could.
It's Friday. We're having a party. Won't you come just for fun?
Friday's prayer group. I know it seems that from my peers I do run.

Grandma, I remember sitting on your knee.
"To thine own self be true," you'd say to me.
Only one man ever perfected this quest.
He never faltered. His way was always true and best.

What will the neighbors think? That's not how things are done.
Really? Who'll be counted for what's right. They're few. Most people run.
What would Jesus do, I wonder anew.
He'd stand with truth, I believe, with the few.

Grandma, I remember sitting on your knee.
"To thine own self be true," you'd say to me.
Only one man ever perfected this quest.
He never faltered. His way was always true and best.

Grandma, I remember sitting on your knee.
"To thine own self be true," you'd say to me.
Oh, I've tried so hard. It's come with pain, you know.
Yet, I'll continue to choose the narrow way even so.

Grandma, I remember sitting on your knee.
"To thine own self be true," you'd say to me.
It's cost me friends, you know.
Going against the status quo. It's not popular when the party line you don't tow.

Grandma, I remember sitting on your knee.
"To thine own self be true," you'd say to me.
The prejudice is rampant everywhere, it seems.
Bridging the differences is feared by many teams.

Grandma, I remember sitting on your knee.
"To thine own self be true," you'd say to me.
Sometimes I feel so weak and so alone.
Often taking a stand means no one has a hand for loan.

Grandma, I remember sitting on your knee.
"To thine own self be true," you'd say to me.
Pray for me, will you—one more time?
Don't stop believing in me. I have more mountains to climb.

Grandma, I remember sitting on your knee.
"To thine own self be true," you'd say to me.
I want to make a difference—open eyes through the innocence of a child to see.
To see a world not colored by prejudice but through hearts of love, let it be.

Grandma, I remember sitting on your knee.
"To thine own self be true," you'd say to me.
To thine own self be true. I've tried.
Sometimes I've laughed. Sometimes I've cried.

Grandma, I remember sitting on your knee.
"To thine own self be true," you'd say to me.
My Lord never faltered. He perfected His quest.
Many times I've faltered though I've given my best.

Grandma, I promise, I'll never rest. I'll strive to always be true to myself.
I'll use binocular vision to see past outer trappings to the heart at its best.
I'll help lift a tear to the Fountain of Living Water, not put it on a shelf.
I'll see people, not through faults, but as God's finished product—His best.

Grandma, I promise, I'll never rest. I'll always strive to always be true to myself, to stand.
I'll help replace a child's tears with hope.
What can I give but myself working only as clay molded by the Potter's hand.
Perhaps one smile, word, or extended hand will enable someone to cope.

Grandma, one more time will you hold me on your knee?
Grandma, one more time, will you hold my hand when the stand I take costs me dearly?
Yes, my dear. Come sit on my knee. Give me your hand.
Go, and to thine own self be true.

Martha and Ben Dobson

Behold, I will do a new thing; now it shall spring forth; shall ye not know it? I will even make a way in the wilderness and rivers in the desert. —Isaiah 43: 19

In October 1999, twenty years after I had spent three years teaching school in Saudi Arabia, my husband, Ben, and I were privileged to travel to the Arab Gulf as a missions prayer walking team to support long-term workers who lived there.

As Isaiah 43: 19 says, we believe that God is doing a new thing in the desert as He raises up prayer teams and professionals to go to countries closed to the Gospel where pastors and professionals cannot go. Many of these countries are in the 10/40 prayer window, a map which shows the nearly 1 billion Muslims in 3,800 unreached people groups who have yet to hear the wondrous message of the Gospel and who follow teachings contrary to the very foundation of the Gospel. Just as God is doing a new thing in the desert, He continues to do a new thing in the hearts of His people as they spend time in the Word and in prayer.Throughout the years, we have watched God continue to develop a new creation in our lives.

God stretched our faith as He burdened our hearts and opened doors for us to travel to the Arab Gulf region. Once God had confirmed in our hearts and in the heart of our pastor that this journey was His design, we watched in amazement as God dealt with the hearts of our employers to release us from our jobs for fifteen days and as He touched the hearts of people to support us financially. In five weeks we had the $5200 required by Firestone, the largest missionary organization in the world to Muslims, for our travel, lodging, food, training and general support. Our God is such an awesome God!

We had expected to have at least ten people on our prayerwalking team. God stretched our faith again when we learned that all were hindered from going by situations such as sickness and job concerns. We weren't trained as missionaries and had no degrees from Bible schools. We had been on only one missionary trip prior to this with four other couples to Germany. The staff of Frontiers spent one weekend training us prior to our arrival in the Gulf.

We wondered how God could use ordinary lay people like us. One night in my prayer closet, the Lord responded to all of my concerns about my worthiness and the messes I had made in my life when He said, "My child, no one is worthy but by the blood of Jesus, but you'll be obedient." We learned that He will use anyone who is willing to go to the,"nations, tribes and peoples," spoken of in Revelation 7: 9-10 because He does not necessarily call the qualified, but He always qualifies the called.

One night before our trip I was praying for the lost when God began to deal with me about my experience twenty years ago teaching French and English as a Second Language in Saudi Arabia. He told me that He had allowed this opportunity because He knew that one day I would intercede in prayer and witness to these people. "After all," He said, "you can't witness effectively and intercede for people you can't first love; and you had a good experience.

In my prayer closet in the last few years, God has been doing a new thing in my life, giving me tears for the lost. We saw the results of irrigation in the Gulf everywhere in gorgeous flowers and trees symbolic, I believe, of the new thing God is doing to bring spiritual streams out of the desert. It never ceases to amaze me that an omnipotent God chooses to partner Himself with people through prayer to accomplish His will. I believe that as we pray for these people, God will turn our tears to living water for this part of the world. Just as Christ wept for Jerusalem and weeps for the lost, He desires, I believe, for us to bring in the harvest in part through the prayers of tears.

For several years before we left, God had been doing another new thing in my life as President of Ladies' Ministries in our church. When I accepted this position, I asked God for only one thing—to help me to have such love for every lady that I would not see her faults and weaknesses. Rather, I would see her as His finished product. He has been faithful to help me learn to keep a guard over my lips (a daily process) and to maintain self-control even in difficult situations. Although I certainly have not mastered these qualities,

God has helped me to stop and think before I judge and criticize others from my own point of view. These are traits that would prove invaluable in cross-cultural interactions. I have found that when I take such weaknesses to my Lord and ask Him to help me crucify the flesh at the cross (Galatians 5: 24), He is faithful to honor my request.

The day before we were to depart for the Arab Gulf, our passports and visas had not arrived from the embassy in Washington, D.C. God stretched our faith developing in us patience and longsuffering as we continued to pray and war against the enemy, Satan was determined to keep us from going, but we knew that the source of our hope had already defeated him. We missed our first flight because we were retrieving our passports and visas as it left.

We experienced difficulties on most of our ten flights. When we arrived at the airport in Arizona, for example, for our return flight; we were told that we had no seats on the flight. When we missed our first flight, the airlines had cancelled our return tickets. Our flight from the Gulf to the United States had already been delayed by two hours. We were exhausted from our fourteen hour flight; yet, as we had done each time, we prayed and watched God, our Waymaker make a way. Fifteen minutes before take-off, the airline attendant found two seats together for us in the front of the airplane. Had those seats not been in the front of the plane, we would never have made our connection in Atlanta. Our God is, indeed, a Waymaker!

Before we left, people asked why we wanted to do this. We responded that we believe that the Lord's return is soon. We want the Muslim people to experience the greatest future, hope and miracle of all—salvation. We want them to know the joy we have that comes from a personal relationship with Jesus Christ. As God has continued to do a new work in our lives; we have also learned that although it is often difficult to be obedient to what God has called us to do; the consequences are worse for a lack of obedience.

Also, as Romans 1: 16 says, we are not ashamed of the Gospel. We have experienced its power. In 1994, after numerous orthopedic injuries (I had ankle and knee surgery.), my doctors told me that I would never work again full time, but God had other plans. I do teach full time without pain. I could not have done the prayerwalking that we did with these injuries. We serve a mighty God who is who He says He is in Exodus 15: 26, "the Lord who healeth thee." God has continued to stretch our faith to believe for healing as we have stood on Isaiah 53: 5 which tells us that by His stripes we are healed.

Many people asked us if we were not afraid to travel to the Middle East. Our answer was that our God was BIG enough to send us and to take care of us. In our lives God continued to do a new work in our hearts as we experienced the truth of Psalm 34:7 which tells us that the angel of the Lord encamps around about those who fear Him and delivereth them.

For example, several winters ago, Ben was thawing pipes in our water tank when the pressures unexpectedly rose. He heard a small, still voice tell him to go inside. Just as he obeyed, we heard an explosion like dynamite and looked out to see the well house explode and land across the fence. Had he not listened to the still, small voice, Ben would have been the one in pieces. Indeed, Jehovah, our Deliverer is alive and real today!

As a child, I was burned on a space heater and was afraid to light a match until I was in college. It took time to shake this fear. I learned that God had indeed taken away my fear when I boarded an airplane in Saudi Arabia which malfunctioned and was forced to land in a neighboring country because of government red tape. I remember not feeling afraid. II Timothy 1: 7 says that God has not given us a spirit of fear but of love and power and a sound mind. God did a new work in my life as He helped me to overcome my fears. I learned that as Daniel said in Daniel 3:7,

> Our God whom we serve is able to deliver us.

Through the years, God has been teaching us that as we give Him our cares and trust Him, we receive His peace in return. God has stretched our faith developing joy and peace in our hearts even in the most difficult of circumstances so that as Paul said in James 1: 2 we can count it all joy. Even when the flight had to emergency land or when our passports had not arrived causing us to miss our flight we were able to stand in faith with joy and peace because we knew that we could stand on His promises.

Before we left for the Arab Gulf, many asked us how much money we needed and how we planned to raise it. We said that we have learned that when we are in the center of His will, He always provides. Two years ago, we badly needed a vehicle. Everywhere we looked for a used Jeep like Ben wanted, we needed $8-$ 10,000 but had saved only $5,000. We agreed to borrow no money and to pray. The next day Ben saw just what he wanted at a car dealership where we had never done business. The price? $4,995. When I went to sign the papers the next day, the owner told me that he had gotten the jeep the day before and had planned to raise the price one to two thousand dollars but just felt for some reason that he should not. God has continued to do a new thing in our lives as He has taught us that He is more than able to meet our needs! We knew that if He was calling us to the Arab Gulf, He, Jehovah-Jireh would provide for us, and He did.

We have learned the power of prayer and that as Isaiah 55: 11 teaches, His promises do not return void. In fact, they accomplish what they are sent to do and even prosper in it. Once before I was to share a testimony at our church, I started to request a package at the post office when I lost my ability to speak and process language—a frightening experience for a language teacher. I could remember only part of my name and address and left in tears. I began to pray and rebuke Satan as best I could as I drove (I could do that.) to my mother's house to get her to take me to the doctor. Finding her not at home, I started to call a friend and the doctor but could not remember their names or telephone numbers.

About an hour and a half later, my speech returned in the doctor's office. Later, after many tests, the neurologist could find no problem. I stood on James 4:7 that because my life is surrendered to God; I can resist the enemy in the name of Jesus, and he must flee. I know that God was doing another new work in my life as He taught me that prayer changes things and the truth of Isaiah 54: 17—that no weapon formed against me shall prosper.

Once we arrived in the Arab world, we continued to see God's protective hand. He stretched our faith to believe that when we pray Psalm 2: 8; He will, indeed, give us the nations for our inheritance including the Muslim nations. As we walked, we prayed over homes, people, mosques, schools, the nation, the government, and the leaders that God would bring down the many spiritual strongholds. He always protected us.

One afternoon, we had gone out dune bashing with those we had gone to support. In the Gulf region people often drive their four-wheel drive vehicles as quickly as they can over sand dunes for fun. One night after the adults had all had a ride and were preparing a picnic, one man took the children for a ride. He was not driving fast when his vehicle lost its traction, went airborne and flipped over. We heard the windshield glass shatter and the children screaming. We ran to the vehicle and found that no one was hurt. The glass was encased in plastic and did not even fall into the vehicle.

We had our picnic and praised God singing, *The Name of the Lord is a Strong Tower*. When we returned home, we learned that God had burdened a man and his wife to pray for us at the same time as the accident was happening. What the enemy had meant for evil, God had turned to good. Oh, the power of prayer!

Traffic where we were was terrible. We had several near misses. One night as a member of our group was driving home from a prayer meeting, she hit a man who ran a red light. She called us from the police station and asked us to pray. The next day a witness appeared whom she had not seen at the scene of the accident. He affirmed that she had, indeed, had a green light. In court the next day, the man who ran the red light went to jail while she went free. Without the witness, she would also have gone to jail because the police would not have known whom to believe. She believes that the witness was an angel. Even in a country where the foreigner is always wrong, God's hand is not shortened (Isaiah 50: 2). Again, He stretched our faith to know through experience that according to Isaiah 59: 1:

> Behold the Lord's hand is not shortened that it cannot save; nor His ear heavy, that it cannot hear.

Ben and I both accepted Jesus Christ as our Lord and Savior when we were about thirteen years old. Later, as adults we both made a strong renewed commitment to serve Him. According to II Corinthians 5: 17:

> If anyone is in Christ, he is a new creation; old things have passed away; behold, all things have become new.

We understand that the development of this new creation is a continual process. God continues to develop a new creation in us as we submit our lives to Him by spending time in the Word and in prayer. As we are obedient to what He asks us to do, He continues to stretch us. As we allow Him to work, old things continue to pass away as we continue grow. Behold, He does do a new thing even in the wildernesses and deserts of our lives. Through the twists and turns in our lives He continues to develop the fruit of the Spirit, "love, joy, peace, longsuffering, kindness, goodness, faithfulness, gentleness, self-control" (Galatians 5: 22-23) into a new creation.

We are thankful for the opportunities and circumstances God has used in our lives to birth a deeper love for people especially the suffering and the lost. We are grateful that He has stretched our faith developing joy and peace in our hearts even in the most difficult of circumstances so that as Paul said in James 1: 2 we can count it all joy.

So many times in situations like our need for a vehicle, we have been able to rest in His peace without borrowing money or going in our own direction because of the new creation that He continues to develop in our hearts. When I was in and out of work with orthopedic injuries for two years, we saw His faithfulness as He taught us to stand in prayer and the Word in longsuffering and faithfulness.

Ben and I certainly have not mastered walking in the fruit of the Spirit. We know that we fall so short of what He would have us be. Sometimes it seems that we take one foot forward and two feet backwards. We are, however, most grateful for the day that Jesus Christ began a new creation in our lives. We are grateful for a Savior who does not give up on us as He, the Potter, works to mold us and make us into His image. We are thankful for the times and situations He has used to stretch us and for the opportunities He has given us to serve Him. What a privilege!

We are but weak and fragile earthen vessels (II Corinthians 3: 18) who can do nothing of their own power. As II Corinthians 4: 8 and 9 reads,

> We (may) be hard pressed on every side, yet not crushed; we (may) be perplexed, but not in despair; persecuted, but not forsaken, struck down, but not destroyed

because (we) "can do all things through Christ who strengthens (us)" (Philippians 4: 13).

If you do not have a personal relationship with Jesus Christ today, may we introduce you to Him. You will be a new creation. We can affirm that your life will never be the same again as old things pass away in your life and all things become new" (II Corinthians 5: 17).

Our journey with the Lord has been faith building, challenging, life-changing and exciting. We expect that you will also be amazed as you watch God birth a new thing in your life. May that new creation be exceedingly, abundantly beyond all you can ask or think. (Ephesians 3: 20)

Casey Durham

For God so loved the world that He gave His only begotten Son that whoever believes in Him should not perish but have everlasting life. —John 3: 16

I'm nineteen years old. I've been raised in the Church of God all of my life. My Dad is a retired minister of the Church of God.

Now to my spiritual life. Let me just start off by saying that I was saved at the age of six. I went down to the altar, and my Dad was by my side and helped me say the sinners' prayer. That was when I received Christ as my personal Savior. He has always been there for me in good times and in bad.

This past December, I was attending a small Church of God with my parents. There weren't many youth there, so God led me in a different direction to Landmark Church of God. I made a lot of Christian friends. God made my spiritual life stronger, and I became closer to Him. God has blessed me with the talent of singing. I started helping the church's choir, and I also started leading Praise and Worship in the youth services.

On March the l0th, I went to Winterfest with the Landmark Youth Group. God really strengthened me, and I drew closer to Him. I came very close to receiving the Baptism of the Holy Ghost. I have never experienced the feeling that I felt that weekend. On Pentecost Sunday, June 11, 2000, I received the Baptism of the Holy Spirit. I am drawing closer to God each day. I thank Him for sending me to Landmark and for letting me meet such great people.

Dot Edwards

God is our refuge and strength, a very present help in trouble. —Psalm 46:1

Many years ago when I was fourteen years of age, I went to a revival at Boulevard Methodist Church. At that time the church was on what used to be the Boulevard. People used to get up from their seats and go around asking different ones if they had ever been saved. I kind of dreaded to see them coming my way because I knew in my heart, even with all my Christian training, that I was lost.

On a particular night, we had a young preacher holding the revival. He kind of dressed like we all did with loud socks and Saddle Oxfords. He had a humor about him, and all of the teens were really interested in his sermon on Sampson and Delilah. He acted out how Delilah may have lured Sampson to get his attention and how she succeeded in doing so.

The Holy Spirit started to really get my attention. The preacher gave the altar call, and out I went from my pew. I believe God saved me the instant I moved into the aisle. I went down. After the prayer,

I moved back up the aisle and took hold of one of my friends. She was also saved that night. I've often wondered if that altar where I accepted Christ is still there.

When I was six or seven years old, my Dad used to take me to hear Preacher Mac Long in tent meetings here in Statesville. (His grandson, Ben Long, painted the fresco at the Civic Center.)

Christ has truly blessed me (with all of my faults), and He sent me a truly precious husband and children. We have had fifty-four plus years together; and, if I keep my right mind, I will never forget the night the Lord saved me. Through the years I've seen His hand so many times. He has, indeed, been my refuge, strength and help.

Debbie Evans

Trust in the Lord with all your heart, and lean not on your own understanding; in all your ways acknowledge Him, and He shall direct your paths.—Proverbs 3: 5-6

I grew up in the city. One summer night when I was fourteen years old, I was walking home from work. My job was at a fast food place, and it was about one mile away from home. I was still wearing my brown polyester pant suit and carrying a tote bag. It was somewhere around 9: 00 p.m., and it was just starting to get deeply dark.

Down the sidewalk, a man was approaching me from a distance. Being a city girl all of my life, I wasn't afraid of anyone; but this night my attitude was about to change forever. The man came near and asked me, "Do you want to smoke a joint?" I told him, "No." He then immediately grabbed me and started to carry me off. I told him, "I'll talk to you if you want," but he ignored me. I then hollered at the top of my voice, "God help me!"

All at once the man dropped me and took off in a high speed run! I was in a state of shock. This all happened in about a minute. I stood there gazing at this stranger running away. When I get to heaven, I will ask Jesus how He scared that evil man away. Did He put an angel in front of us with a gun or a sword? After all, Psalm 91 says,

> For He shall give His angels charge over you to keep you in all your ways.

I will never forget how the Lord spared me from great danger that night. I owe Jesus so much. I also thank God for a godly mother who daily lifts up her family in prayer. Fortunately, I learned the truth of Proverbs 3: 5-6 at an early age. When I screamed, "God help me," the night the man grabbed me, I did trust in the Lord with all of my heart. Indeed, He delivered me. Glory be to God forever!

Rick Farlee

The seventy-two returned with joy and said, "Lord even the demons submit to us in Your name."—Luke 10: 17 (*NIV*)

Smoking. Millions of people are addicted and want to quit. My wife, Sandy, was a smoker for over thirty years. Countless times she tried to stop, and a few times she succeeded briefly, only to pick the habit back up again. She was a "closet smoker." It was a burden of shame and guilt that she carried around. Every time she quit smoking, it became harder and harder to stop again. Prayer helped, but only seemed to ease the craving for a short time.

One night last February (2002), I was awakened about 3:00 a.m. with the impression that the Holy Spirit wanted me to lay hands on my wife and cast out that oppressive spirit. I was struck with the thought that demonic activity was an issue here. Obediently, as my wife slept restlessly, I placed my hand over her and said, "In the name of Jesus, spirit of Satan come out of her! I bind you and cast you into the pit of hell, never to return!"

My wife did not awaken, but immediately a deep growling groan came from way down inside of her like, "BRRAAHH....!" It was somewhat startling. Again, I said, "Evil Spirit in the name of Jesus, I cast you out of this house and into the pit of hell NEVER TO RETURN!" Next I prayed for angels to surround her and protect her. Instantly, my wife fell into a very deep, restful sleep. Her breathing was very deep and relaxed. I knew that she was at peace and could rest. For hours thereafter I praised God and thanked Jesus for using me that way.

The next day, unaware of any activity that occurred the previous night, I asked my wife how she was feeling. The response was, "Really good." When I told her what had happened, she was a little shaken to know of it. The good news is that my wife has not smoked, nor had the desire to do so since that day. Praise to Jesus for freeing her from that bondage! Shortly thereafter, we were both baptized in the Holy Spirit.

Sandy Farlee

Give and it will be given to you: A good measure, pressed down, shaken together, and running over will be poured into your lap. For with the same measure you use, it will be measured back to you.
—Luke 6: 38 (*NIV*)

Have you ever found yourself suddenly thinking about someone and felt compelled to call and check on them? Many years ago as a young mother of four, I became acquainted with another young mother of two children. Sadly, she had become a single parent; therefore, she often struggled to provide for her children. At this time, my own situation was grim, my husband having been layed-off from his job just a few weeks before Christmas.

Anyway, I obeyed that voice that kept speaking me; and I called my friend. I was so glad I did call her. You see, I was living in Ohio at that time, and December can be bitterly cold. Just that morning, it had begun to snow; and the snow was still coming down. The ground was covered already, but we knew we were going to get several inches of snow. Well, my friend was not able to get out to the grocery store before it started to snow, so she was just going to have to wait the storm out.

One of her children, her younger daughter, was handicapped; so she was not as easily mobile as I was even with my four children. After talking with her on the phone, I decided that I should take some groceries out to her. I had just one small problem though. I had no money for grocery shopping. As I explained, my husband was unemployed, and I was challenged to make meager ends meet.

Looking out my kitchen window watching the beautiful snow fall, however, I was inspired with a wonderful idea. I remember so well saying out loud, "Lord, I may not have money, but I have got food I'll share! I'll give her half of everything I have." The next few moments were the most thrilling and memorable of my life. As I opened cabinets, the closet, refrigerator and freezer, literally everything that I reached for doubled right before my very own eyes! It was a supernaturally joyous space of time that I shall never forget.

As I reached for a can of green beans, another seemed to appear right behind it and so on as I continued to reach for other food items. I remember specifically reaching for a bag of potatoes and having this cognizant thought, "I know I only have this one bag;" but again, as I reached and pulled the bag forward, there was another bag waiting to take its place."Wow!" I thought. The more I gathered the more I found. By the time I was finished, I had enough food and other supplies to fill my car. I was so excited and full of thanks.

Listen to the Holy Spirit when He speaks to you. You will be wonderfully blessed if you do. Luke 6: 38 (*NIV*) says,

> Give and it will be given to you: A good measure, pressed down, shaken together, and running over will be poured into your lap. For with the same measure you use, it will be measured to you.

Trudee Farley

Be still and know that I am God.
—Psalm 46: 10

When I am in a turmoil, "Be still and know that I am God," is usually the scripture that runs through my mind. For a couple of years, that Scripture became especially important to me. My son, Brian, who had been raised in the church and was such a good kid began to rebel. I lived in turmoil until I figured out that I had to let go of all of my anxieties and let God take control of my life.

When Brian was fifteen years old, he started turning his back on school, church and the world. He had been an excellent student. His test scores were off the chart. He was a great ball player whom the coaches loved, but he experienced some rough situations with those whom he thought were his friends. He also had mononucleosis which put him down and out for awhile. He quit hanging out with his "friends" and quit playing ball. Everything started to slide.

We moved from where he had grown up in Ohio to an area with a bigger school in West Virginia. We both knew people and had friends both places, and I needed to move for financial reasons. I didn't think it would be a traumatic move; however, moving from an eight room house to a four room apartment was difficult for both of us.

I thought Brian would spend time with the church friends he had known from summer camp. I didn't know that some of them were experimenting with drugs, especially marijuana. I think he spent more time drinking than he did doing drugs, but I know now that he did both.

My son began treating me with no respect. He wanted the car when he wanted it. He wanted to stay out late and didn't want to go to school. I had to lock the car with a car lock to protect my possessions. I locked my money in my room.

Brian left home twice. He took very little with him. I had many sleepless nights. I prayed and prayed. I prayed for wisdom and for strength to deal with my son and with whatever came my way.

One time when he moved out, I told him that I thought he should go to live with his Dad with whom he had had little contact since our divorce. I told him that I didn't want us to be enemies when he was grown. His Dad told him that he could come if he would cut his hair, wear no baggy pants and live by his rules. He wouldn't go and found some place else to live. Each time he left, however, he always came back. Brian told me later that he always knew that I was there for him because I would tell him, "I'll always love you. You are my son, but I don't always like what you do."

When he was with me, he went to school. That was my mandate. I gave him no choice. We had lots of battles. He was really defiant. I guaranteed Brian's principal that I would see that Brian arrived at school each day. I couldn't guarantee that he would stay once he got there.

At the end of his junior year in high school, the school counselor asked me to come to school to discuss Brian's grades. He'd barely made senior status. This was someone who had never had academic problems.

I always prayed, but I kept trying to fix everything myself. I would always think that there must be something else I could do. I felt so helpless. If someone had told me five years earlier that I would lose total control of one of my kids, I'd have said, "You're nuts." It was a pride thing. The stress of it all began taking its toll on me physically, and I felt totally lost.

The changes in my life didn't happen overnight. It was a gradual progression. I learned to be still and listen to God. The last time Brian moved out, I had no idea where he was. God gave me such a peace—that peace that passes all understanding. I was able to sleep at night leaving Brian in God's care. I was still concerned, but I could sleep and take care of myself.

During Brian's senior year, the situation got worse. He didn't graduate from school. He was shocked. This was the first big shock of his life. The second shock was when he began to think about what he would do after he graduated. He had no clue what he wanted to do with the rest of his life. He had thought about the Navy, but they wouldn't take him unless he had a high school diploma. He took the Navy's ASFAB test and scored lower than his brother had. He had always done better than his brother in school. Again, he was shocked and had to take a hard look at his life. He began to turn his life around.

He took a piano course as an elective. This teacher heard him sing and recruited him for the school choir. He loved it. That class kept him in school. During this time, he was asked to do a guitar solo. He was really nervous but did well. He made friends who liked him and appreciated his talent. By the time he graduated from high school, he had cut his hair and begun to wear better clothes. He also joined the Navy.

I believe that the Navy recruiters and the choral teacher had a lot to do with the turn around in Brian's life. I think God put them in his life to help him believe in himself again. I know that the changes in his life are a testimony to the power of prayer. I asked everyone I came in contact with to pray for Brian. I also know that when I learned to be still and listen to God, God began to really work in my life. The Word says, "Be still and know that I am God." When I released my son into God's hands—when I let go and let God, God restored my son to me.

Today, Brian is in the Navy. He is happy and married and successful. If you are experiencing storms in your relationship with your child, I encourage you to ask God to teach you to be still and listen to Him. Ask Him to help you to leave Your cares in His hands. None of us can do that without help, but with God all things are possible.

Note: Trudy Farley is a music teacher in Columbia, North Carolina whom Martha Dobson met while working with the North Carolina Teacher's Academy.

Jasper and Virginia Farmer

The effective, fervent prayer of the righteous man availeth much.—James 5: 16

At seventeen years of age, when a friend invited Virginia Farmer to a revival on Eighth Street, Virginia had no idea how much her life was about to change. She accepted someone's invitation to the altar where she could not stop jumping and shouting for joy as she was saved.

Soon, thereafter, she became hungry for the Baptism of the Holy Spirit. In her kitchen with her son Jasper crying while two friends prayed, God honored the desire of her heart by filling her to overflowing.

In the ensuing years, God developed her prayer life creating a giant prayer warrior who would touch many lives as she wept and groaned at the altar for the needs of her family and others. "I don't know what I'd have done if I hadn't prayed. I don't know what would have happened to my children," she said. God honored her prayers as each of her three children were saved.

She survived the first seventeen or eighteen years of a most difficult marriage because she had learned to pray. As she found herself married to an alcoholic, she also found that life was most difficult. She "just prayed and asked the Lord to help" her.

When her husband drank, like so many alcoholics, his personality would change. So many times God protected her as she and her children walked to her parents' home to avoid his outbursts. "Troy was tenderhearted and provided for me, but for some reason, he tried to pull me down 'cause I was living right, I guess," she remarked. She felt like a "peg legged man in a hole with a knot going in a circle." Many times she did not know what to do or which way to turn. Her life was rough; yet, God delivered her so many times because she continued to pray and to live a life completely surrendered to the Lord, Jesus Christ.

One Sunday morning, she got the children ready and left to go to church. Troy was returning with some groceries and told her that she could not go. When she told him that they were going to church, he threw the groceries on the street and broke the jug of milk. Even though milk spilled on her hose, she would not forsake her commitment to worship the Lord with her children.

Another Sunday, she asked the church to pray while the pastor anointed a prayer cloth for Troy. She pinned it to her husband's pillow believing for his deliverance from the bondages of alcohol and tobacco. Troy never knew that the prayer cloth was there, but one day he just stopped drinking. He never drank again. Later, he also quit smoking enabling his wife to stop coughing as she had done for so long from the second-hand smoke.

God had honored Virginia's prayers and delivered Troy from the bondages of alcohol and, yet he continued to refuse the gift of eternal life. Virginia, however, refused to give in and continued to pray for her husband's salvation. "Prayers are not always answered quickly," she commented. "He knew about God," she noted. "His father was a pastor and founded our church. In fact, he once told God that he would live for Him if He would save his son Everett's life."

When he was eight years old, Everett was hit by a bus as he rode his bicycle in front of it. He fractured his skull as he hit the parking light of the bus and was not expected to live. Jasper who was twelve at the time remembers witnessing the accident and seeing Everett's hair on the parking light. Troy was in the hospital himself at the time of the accident.

According to Virginia, it was a miracle that Everett lived; yet, when God saved Everett's life, Troy did not honor his promise to live for God. Virginia continued to pray, however, and lived to see her husband saved just before he died. God "just kept me by His hand. He kept me on my knees," she shared.

God honored Virginia's heart on two occasions when she was quite ill. Once she was diagnosed with pancreatic cancer. Her doctors felt that the cancer was so bad that surgery would not help. People prayed with Virginia. When she went back for more tests, the doctors were amazed that they could find no cancer. They refused to acknowledge God and said that they must have misread the X-rays. In fact, God had healed Virginia. The doctor's refusal to honor God's intervention, however, did not make her healing any less miraculous. Years later, when she needed gall bladder surgery, different doctors would find evidence to prove this.

Virginia was diagnosed with brain tumors. She was so sick that the doctors told her children that she was going to die. They said that they would do all they could to make her comfortable. Dr. Allen told her family that if she made it, it would be a miracle.

During this time, she also needed gallbladder surgery. The doctors said that she was too weak for the surgery but without it she would die. In fact, they believed that she would die either way.

Virginia was too sick to even recognize that she needed gallbladder surgery; consequently, her family opted for the surgery.

Afterwards, the doctor asked her daughter, Ruby, "Who did the surgery on your mother's pancreas?" Ruby replied that her mother had never had pancreatic surgery. "She must have had it," he said. "I saw the difference." Virginia's daughter, Ruby, told the doctor that God had done the surgery. The difference the doctor saw in her pancreas was proof of God's previous healing.

After the gallbladder surgery, Virginia, her family and her church family continued to pray for her to be healed of the brain tumors. The tumors disappeared. As Virginia said, "God didn't let me go then. I surprised those doctors with all the people praying. The Lord's been good to me, more than I deserve—more than all of us do."

As Virginia experienced so many twists and turns in life, her children continued to watch her pray and live her faith. They wanted to have similar deliverances in their lives. Jasper, for example, has seen God's hand so many times in his life.

One night, he was very depressed when he went to the Friday night prayer group. He was having problems with his eyes. After many tests in Winston-Salem, the doctor said that he had optic neuritis in both eyes for which no cure exists. The optic nerve was partially dead in his eyes.

Jasper began having great difficulty being productive at work. He became so depressed that he asked off from work as much as possible especially on weekends. He even talked with his supervisor about a leave of absence to get a hold of himself. At forty-eight years of age, he thought that he was going blind and that he would never be able to see his wife or boy again.

As he entered the church doors that Friday evening, he felt dark and gloomy. He was carrying such a heavy load as a small group of people began to pray. There may have been only a few people in that prayer meeting, but they knew how to touch God. Instantly, God healed his mind and the depression left. When he came into the prayer group, it was daylight outside. Inside he felt as if a storm were raging. He felt very dark and gloomy. When he left, the sky was dark outside, but inside the sun was shining for him. Jasper is now sixty-four years old. It has been sixteen years, and the problem of depression has not returned. Later, when he found himself concerned about his eyes, he asked his mother to pray. God gave her a word of knowledge for him that He would take care of him.

Another time, Jasper and his wife, Doris, needed a new well. They hired someone to drill the well expecting to not have to dig very far. The men told him that if they were able to get water easily, they would be gone when Jasper returned home from work. Shocked to find the men still there when he got home and to learn that the men had already dug 235 feet only to find a dry hole, Jasper went into the house and began to pray with Doris saying, "Lord, I know You can make water in that rock." The workers dug another thirty feet and found water. They thought they had fifteen to twenty gallons per minute; but when they checked again, they found that they had one hundred gallons of water per minute. God rewarded their prayers with wonderful water pressure and an abundance of water.

Throughout their lives through difficult times, Virginia and Jasper Farmer have proven that when we stand on the promises of God, the promises never return void (Isaiah 55: 11). God honored the fervent prayers of Virginia. In fact, God has continued to reward their willingness to stand with strength and peace.

Heather Gessler

The Lord will perfect that which concerneth me: thy mercy, O Lord, endureth forever; forsake not the works of thine own hands. —Psalm 138: 8

In February 2002, I felt that my world was turned upside down. With the dissolution of my marriage, I was struggling. Then, I was diagnosed with benign intracranial hypertension.

What is that you ask? Well, I wish I could explain that to you. I am not sure myself. All I know is what I could find in the Harvard School of Medicine Dictionary! It said that it is rare condition found mostly in young, overweight women. (I knew that I was a few pounds overweight, but....) It is swelling on the occipital nerve (the nerve connected to the eyeball).

This condition can be treated with medicine (for the rest of your life), or if that fails, a shunt. A shunt? Yes, a shunt. Sounds scary, doesn't it? It most certainly was! I just knew my life as I knew it was over. I was a volunteer fire fighter and an EMT in my home town. I had worked so hard to get all of those certifications. Now what? My goal was to become a full-time fire fighter. Well, not if I am on all that medication, and if I have a shunt in my head! I just felt that I was in a downward spiral—until God reopened my eyes.

I would like to say that my eyes were always upon the Lord, but they weren't. I became a bitter person. I was full of hurt, anger, resentment, embarrassment, you know all of those feelings that go along with divorce; so when a routine eye exam came back with complications, I was not very prayerful. As a matter of fact, I went the opposite direction. I refused to go to church with my family. All I wanted to do was sit in a dark room and throw myself a pity party.

My mother and stepfather were going to a wonderful, spirit-filled church; and every Friday night, they went to a prayer meeting. My mother began praying to God on my behalf. Mom stood strong on Psalms 138: 8:

> The Lord will perfect that which concerneth me: thy mercy, O Lord, endureth forever: forsake not the works for thine own hands. (KJV)

Mom went to this prayer meeting. Sitting in for me and being anointed with oil, she asked God to heal my body. Every Sunday she would invite me to church. One Sunday, I went. I had felt God dealing with my heart.

In the mean time, I had an appointment with a specialist. The Friday before my appointment, my mom was talking with another lady in the prayer group. Once Mom told her my doctor's name, Mom was filled with great joy. She just knew that God was going to heal me! As it turned out, the doctor and the lady in the prayer group were brother and sister! The members of the prayer group anointed my mother one more time. Once Mom stood up, she said that she knew, right then, that God had healed my eyes.

I went to church that Sunday, and I felt the conviction of the Holy Spirit. I knew that I was blaming God for my problems, and I knew that was wrong. I asked God to forgive me; yet, I was also praying that God would take care of my little brother. He was in a difficult time in his life as well. I never did come out and ask God to heal me although I am sure that is what He wanted. I was more concerned with God's forgiveness for me and God's mercy on my brother.

I went to the doctor on Monday. He ran a series of tests. I am not even sure of what all was done! I do know that I had a scan (like an X-ray) on my eyes done. This machine was one of only six such machines in the U.S., and it just so happened that there was one of those high-tech machines in Statesville, North Carolina!

The doctor would come into my room, look at my films and order another test. He came and went, came and went. Finally, he came into my room and pulled up a chair. He said, "Well, if you had something, it is there no longer! I have run every test that I have available. I just don't see anything!" My mother jumped out of her seat and shouted, "Praise God! Thank you, Jesus!" She just kept thanking Jesus. The doctor was quite disturbed with my mother's outbreak. He just tried to put some medical jargon off as to why my problem disappeared. (This had been diagnosed by two different doctors—an opthamologist and a neurologist.) If you remember, I said earlier that I would have this for life. This does not "go away." It is merely "controlled."

I was in complete shock! I didn't know what to say, but my mother did. Thank you, Jesus! Yes, thank you, Jesus! Isn't God good? God showed me that anything is possible. I mean, I knew that but didn't really comprehend that. I don't think people do until God intervenes. Sometimes God just gives us our morning wake-up call, and I think that was mine. God just allowed Himself to be supernaturally shown in my life. Just to say, "Heather, I love you, and I do care for you! Never forget that!" Never forget that. No matter how far we may stray from God, He will take us back, wash us, put us in new garments and make us whole again. Thank you Jesus! Thank you for loving me even when I couldn't love You. Thank you for dying for me, for I am so unworthy.

I praise God daily for what He did for me. I tell complete strangers about my miracle! If I don't know you, I soon will. I want to tell everyone what God did for me! I know this is not the only time God has intervened. I know this won't be the last. Thank you, Jesus.

Freida Gilberg

Call to Me, and I will answer you and show you great and mighty things, which you do not know.—Jeremiah 33: 3

I can never remember a time that I doubted my salvation. There were times in my life when my relationship with Jesus Christ was close and times when the relationship was not so close. I have always known that I was not worthy of this salvation, yet Jesus loved me enough anyway to die on the cross for my sins. As John 3: 16 says,

> For God so loved the world that He gave His only begotten Son that whoever believes in Him should not perish but have everlasting life.

I grew up in a good home and had a very happy home life. A turning point came in my life, however, when I was twenty-one and my father died. This was the first time that I had ever questioned my relationship with the Lord. No one gave me answers to my questions. The Lord took me on a nine-year journey searching for answers. This was a rebellious time in my life.

It was during this time that I met my husband in New York. I think that I knew that I shouldn't marry him, but I married him anyway. I was determined to stay married. I was convinced that the old adage saying that one should not divorce was true. I was thirty years old when I became pregnant. I told everyone that I was expecting. I would take my Bible and put it on my tummy as I prayed for my child. I prayed for a beautiful child, and God graciously granted my request.

During this time my husband moved to Florida because he was having an affair. His girlfriend became pregnant and lost her baby. My husband asked me to move to Florida saying that he wanted us to try to make the marriage work. My son, Steve, was born in Florida. During this time I really did call out to the Lord. I knew He was there. I just didn't know how to reach Him.

My mother came to Florida for a visit and encouraged me to find a church. One Sunday, I was on my way to a particular church when the Holy Spirit told me to go to a big church I'd heard about from a couple I knew who went there and raved about the church. Because their lifestyle didn't warrant such wonderful comments, in my opinion, I had not felt impressed to go prior to this time. Their life was one of wine, women and song. Fortunately, I followed the leading of the Holy Spirit and visited Coral Ridge Presbyterian Church. I came out a different person. I understood what Dr. D. James Kennedy was saying that day when he spoke about Jesus Christ. I had put my relationship with Jesus, prayer, going to church and time in the Bible aside; but on this day, the Holy Spirit was drawing me back to Jesus.

Things in my life became very difficult during this time. I worked in an insurance company and at a bar. Nobody ever told me that this was wrong, but in my heart I knew. I said, "Lord, I know I shouldn't be here. I guess You will just have to get me out. People would say to me, "You don't belong here." I'd find money people had left and give it back. One day my boss gave my job to his girlfriend. Jesus had answered my prayer and taken me out of the bar. God was teaching me to live the way He wanted me to live.

During this time my husband divorced me. He had tried to make the marriage work for about a year. Then he had more affairs. I also ended up in the hospital doubled over in pain from gallbladder problems. In surgery the doctor removed a pus bag the size of an orange from my intestine. When I came home from the hospital, people in my church were so good to me. They brought me food and ministered to me. My ex-husband had my son because I was too sick to care for him and threatened to keep him. The Holy Spirit impressed me to remain silent and pray for my son instead of fighting. God honored my prayers and brought my son back to me.

God put me in evangelism and discipleship programs at Coral Ridge, and my life really turned around. I truly learned the truths that transform. Those things have kept me clinging to the Holy Spirit since then. Through all the twists and turns in my life I never, ever doubted that God was. I may have had different understandings of who God was, but I never doubted that He was because I had been taught to believe as a youth. This truth was always taught in my home.

God has always been faithful. He has always placed me where He knew I would grow. Any good in my life is there only by God's grace. There's nothing good in me of myself. I've learned that being a Christian doesn't mean that life will be easy. God blesses and gives joy. He also allows turmoil in order to refine us, yet I know that His commandments are not burdensome. It is our faith that gives us the victory to overcome the world. As I John 5: l-5 says:

> Whoever believes that Jesus is the Christ is born of God, and everyone who loves Him who begot also loves him who is begotten of Him. By this we know that we love the children of God; when we love God and keep His commandments. For this is the love of God, that we keep His commandments. And His commandments are not burdensome. For whatever is born of God overcomes the world. And this is the victory that has overcome the world—our faith. Who is he who overcomes the world, but he who believes that Jesus is the Son of God.

Being a single parent was not easy; yet no matter how difficult it was, God had placed me inside that church at Coral Ridge. There I was secure, cared for and loved. By this time, I had lost both of my parents. God used these experiences, however, to teach me so that I could in turn help others going through divorce. He has brought me so far. I have learned to say with Maltbie D. Babcock:

> Be strong!
> We are not here to play, to dream, to drift;
> We have hard work to do, and loads to lift.
> Shun not the struggle; face it.
> It's God's gift.

Be strong!
Say not the days are evil—Who's to blame?
Or fold your hands, as in defeat—O shame!
Stand up, speak out, bravely,
In God's name.

There have been many twists and turns in my life. I've only shared the tip of the iceberg. As one dies to oneself there's so much, much more that God does in a person's life. The greatest lesson I've learned is to have faith to believe that God's promise is true. We learn this through obedience. I've learned that when I do a good work, it must not be "I" who receives the credit. It's to the glory of God. As God changes a life, a person finds that he no longer does the works for self but for His glory.

God's grace—God's riches at Christ's expense—is so awesome. Everyday He keeps me by His grace. I never cease to be amazed by the truth of John 3: 16 that, indeed, God loved the world so much that He sent His Son to die on the cross for my sins, that by believing on Him I should not perish but have eternal life. What a precious, priceless gift!

He's Been Faithful

Every word He's promised is true.
What I thought was impossible,
I see my God do.
He's been faithful, faithful to me.

Looking back, His love and mercy I see.
Though in my heart I have questioned,
Even failed to believe;
Yet He's been faithful to me

Every time I come back to Him,
He is waiting with open arms,
And I see once again(that)
He's been faithful to me.

Looking back, His love and mercy I see.
Though in my heart I have questioned,
Even failed to believe;
Yet He's been faithful to me

In my moments of fear,
Through every pain, every tear,
There's a God
Who's been faithful to me.

When all my strength was gone,
When my heart had no song,
Still in love,
He's proved faithful to me.

When I looked away,
The many times I could not pray,
Still my God...
He was faithful to me.

The days I spent so selfishly,
Reaching out for what pleased me,
Even then God was faithful to me.

—Carol Cymbala

Shara Gilreath

Through the Lord's mercies we are not consumed because His compassions fail not. They are new every morning; great is Your faithfulness.—Lamentations 3: 22-23

I grew up in a Christian home where I continually saw God's faithfulness at work. My mother was a preacher's kid. In fact, our family members have attended the Church of God now to the fourth generation in my life and the fifth generation in my daughter Cierra's life. The influence of Christianity was very strong in my family. I've heard my mother minister in almost every aspect of the church. She has spoken at meetings, preached, sung, worked as a youth director and directed a nursing home program among many other duties. I have truly been blessed to have such a heritage.

I was, however, a typical church kid. I'd live for the Lord for a while and then do my own thing for a while. I never had a very deep walk with the Lord growing up. I was accustomed to hearing the Word but was not accustomed to living as I should. When I graduated from high school, I went to Lee College. I spent the first year of college not really living as I should.

Then at the end of my freshman year, I found myself in a predicament. I felt as if my back was against the wall. I was at the end of my rope. I had no one to talk with. One night I was lying in bed when I felt fear and anxiety grip my heart. I couldn't seem to come up with any solutions to my dilemma.

Suddenly I began to recall years of Sunday School teaching and church teaching which said that when a person feels that there is no where left to turn, turn to Jesus. He's always there. I got up and went to the prayer room. My knees hit the floor, and I began sobbing and pleading with God to forgive me. I poured my heart out for about an hour saying, "God if you'll just take care of this situation, I'll live my life for you and serve you for the rest of my life." At first I felt no different when I left the prayer room; however, as I got closer to my room, I began to feel lighter. It was as if someone were dumping all of my worries off my shoulders.

That night as I fell asleep I felt completely at peace with no fear in my heart even though my situation had not been resolved. The next morning I got up determined to hold up my end of the bargain with the Lord. I began reading the Word morning, noon and night. Within a week my problem had taken care of itself. Everything just seemed to fall into place after that point. I received the Baptism of the Holy Spirit while kneeling alone on a bench in a church.

Since then, my walk with the Lord has been so beautiful. I call this my true salvation experience. Suddenly, God began to use me for the first time in my life. My voice changed, and the way I ministered to others changed. No longer was I just singing. Now I was worshipping as I sang under God's anointing. In fact, everything in my life changed.

One time I was ministering at a ladies' meeting in the Dakotas when the anointing became very powerful, and He began to use me in a way that I had never known before.The presence of the Lord filled that place in such a wonderful way. The Lord said to me, "You see what I'm doing now. There's so much more that I desire to do through you." I have learned that if I will remain faithful to Him in service, He will in His perfect timing and way bring His will to pass in my life and in the lives of my husband and children. I have, indeed, found that His mercies are new every morning. Great has been His faithfulness.

The song, *He's Been Faithful*, is my testimony. Indeed,

> In my moments of fear, through every pain (and) every tear
> There's a God who's been faithful to me.
> When all my strength was gone (and) when my heart had no song,
> Still in love He's proved faithful to me.
> When I looked away, (During) the many times I could not pray,
> Still my God...He was faithful to me. The days I spent so selfishly
> Reaching out for what pleased me, even then God was faithful to
> Me. Every word He's promised is true. What I thought was
> Impossible, I see my God do.

Every time I come back to Him, He is waiting with open arms, and I see once again(that) He's been faithful to me. Looking back, His love and mercy I see. Though in my heart I have questioned, even failed to believe; yet He's been faithful to me." Great is His faithfulness.

Tracy Gilreath

O Lord, You have searched me and known me. You know my sitting down and my rising up; You understand my thought afar off. You comprehend my path and my lying down, and are acquainted with all my ways. For there is not a word on my tongue, but behold, O Lord, You know it altogether. You have hedged me behind and before and laid Your hand upon me. —Psalm 139: 1-5

As I look back on my life, I know that from the age of five, God had His hand on my life. As Psalm 139: 5 says, He has "hedged me behind and before..." When I was five, my family and I had gone to a convenience store. Afterwards my brother and I began racing. My brother stopped running when he saw traffic. I kept running. My family yelled at me to stop, but I kept running. Little did I know that a UTS (United Telephone System) truck was coming. I was running full speed when I felt something hit me in the chest. My legs went flying outward as I went sliding toward the truck. The truck barely missed my feet. I fell backwards. I knew that an angel of God had protected me. Looking back, I realize that God had His hand on my life all along.

My dad was an alcoholic and was physically abusive. I lived in a difficult home situation. My parents were not saved. When I was eleven, we moved next door to my grandmother, my dad's mother, who was a Pentecostal Holiness evangelist. I often went to my grandmother's house. She had cancer and would ask me to read the Bible to me. One day as I was going out the door, she stopped me and said,"Tracy, God has His hand on your life. You're going to do something great for God." That thought never left me.

As a teen I knew the truth of Psalm 139:5, that His "hand (was) upon me," yet my family life continued to be difficult. I began drinking as a freshman in high school. Throughout my high school years there were lots of fights between my mom and my dad. My mom had gotten saved about the time we moved. My mom had gotten right with God, and my dad didn't like it. The more they fought, the more I drank. By the age of nineteen, I was a teenage alcoholic. A void grew and grew in my heart. I was trying to fill the void in my life caused by a poor relationship with my father.

As I continued to search for something to fill this void, I began to realize that alcohol and relationships were not doing it. My grandmother died, and my grandfather invited me to go to Shiloh Freewill Baptist Church with him. I had no background with church and didn't know what to do. But as Psalm 139 says, the Lord had searched me. He knew, "my sitting down and my rising up." He understood, "my thought afar off." He comprehended "my path and my lying down." He was "acquainted with all my ways."

The pastor preached on Judas Iscariot. I wondered why he kept talking about Judas's carrot. Suddenly, I knew that the void in my life would be filled if I would respond to the altar call. I went to the altar and poured out a lifetime of hurt. God filled me up.

I went on to college to pursue a pre-med degree at East Tennessee State University. When I was twenty-one, a friend of mine introduced me to the Baptism of the Holy Ghost. At first I thought he was crazy, but he showed me the truth in the Scripture. Every week I went back to church. I knew that there was more to this spiritual walk. I was hungry. As I studied the Word, I realized that he was telling me the truth. I went to my friend's room in the dorm and told him that I wanted the Baptism of the Holy Ghost. He prayed with me. I experienced such a powerful move of God that it was as if I convulsed in the spirit. I had never experienced God like that.

Six months later, God called me into the ministry. I started feeling a hunger to tell others about Jesus. I began to wonder about ministry. I told God that He was going to have to hit me over the head with a 2 X 4. If He was calling me into ministry, he would have to show me. At that time I was going to an Assembly of God church. I was in the altar praying for God to give me a confirmation of His calling on my life when I felt God's hand on my right shoulder. It felt as if He had His arm around me. I heard God speak audibly in my left ear. He said, "I've called you to preach." I turned around, and no one was there. I got up. I knew what God wanted me to do. Once again, He had laid His hand upon me.

That summer for the first time in my life, I went to youth camp as a counselor. While I was in the altar one night, I began travailing in the spirit. I experienced such spiritual pain that I felt as if someone were stabbing me in the stomach. While I was praying, I had a vision where I saw myself standing before thousands of teenagers preaching. I knew that I was called to youth ministry. I have been a youth pastor ever since.

After God called me into ministry, I felt Him directing me to Lee College to study the Bible in more depth. I graduated in 1992, from Lee College with a Bachelors of Arts degree in Biblical Studies. In 1997, I became ordained in the Church of God. Throughout my ministry God has, indeed, "hedged me behind and before" and kept His hand upon me (Psalm 139: 1-5).

Gilbert Hill

Wisdom and knowledge will be the stability of your times.—Isaiah 33: 6

Several years ago, Gilbert Hill experienced the miraculous, healing power of Jehovah Ropha, our Healer. This is his story. "I want to give a praise report for what the Lord has done for me," Gilbert said.

"On this Wednesday morning around 11: 00 a.m., I had been outside in the heat doing some things around the house when I sat down and began to feel weak. I went into the house and took a shower. After the shower, I began to lose the strength on my left side in my leg, arm and hand. This got my attention, yet I still got ready to come to Bible study. About ten minutes before time to go, I said to my wife, 'I am not able to go. I am not stable enough when I walk. You tell Irma the Pastor's wife at that time that I am not able to come.'"

"On Thursday morning, I called Brother Black, the Associate Pastor, and talked with him. He had prayer with me. Later, I also called Pastor Williams, and he had prayer with me. I had already called the doctor and gotten an appointment for that afternoon. The doctor checked me and my reflexes and said it was heat exhaustion. He said to drink plenty of liquids. After I came from the doctor, I called the Pastor's home and talked to Irma. I told her what the doctor had said. I also talked with Brother Black and told him and Sister Black that I was feeling better.

"The following Saturday, I still had a lot of weakness in my body on the left side. I told my wife that I could not practice the music on Sunday before Sunday School. I called Pastor and asked him to tell Eddie that I would not be there for practice, but that I would be at church. I wanted to be prayed for. Pastor said, 'Brother Gilbert, let's just pray right now and believe that God will touch you while we pray.'

"That evening I went to bed around 9:30 p.m. I got up Sunday morning at 6:00 a.m. I knew when I got out of bed and put my feet on the floor and walked down the hall that God had healed me. After prayer thanking God for my healing, I got ready and went to practice and gave a praise report to the church."

Each step of the way, God gave Gilbert the wisdom and knowledge promised in Isaiah 33:6 to know who to call for prayer and what to do. James 1:5-6 says:

> If any of you lacks wisdom, let him ask of God, who gives to all liberally and without reproach and it will be given to him. But let him ask in faith with no doubting....

When Gilbert asked God in faith believing for wisdom and faith, God rewarded him mightily. Now Gilbert encourages everyone to remember that, "The Lord gives wisdom and knowledge that we should use in all areas of life. The Lord is no respecter of persons. He will do for others what He has done for me!"

Pansy Holcomb

Now unto Him that is able to do exceedingly, abundantly above all that we ask or think, according to the power that worketh in us. —Ephesians 3: 20

When I was twelve, I accepted Jesus Christ as my Savior; and at fourteen, I dedicated my life to full-time Christian service. Believing that there was a great need for teachers and that the pay would be good, my parents would only send me to college to be a teacher. Now, I realize this choice to follow a secular career path kept me from my commitment to God for full-time Christian service.

That same year, I met the man I later married. For thirty-six years, I didn't realize that we were unequally yoked. Looking back, I remember that my parents were against this courtship and marriage. Young people, may I warn you to pay attention to the leading of your parents concerning your choice of a mate. I believe God has given parents an intuitive wisdom concerning your marriage partner.

When I married, I believe I stepped into God's permissive will for me—not His plan for me. In 1997, my unbelieving husband left me. I was devastated! I didn't know it then, but God was going to reveal Himself to me as my Husband according to Isaiah 54: 4b-6:

> For thou shalt forget the shame of thy youth and shalt not remember the reproach of thy widowhood any more. For thy Maker is thine husband; the Lord of hosts is His name....For the Lord hath called thee as a woman forsaken and grieved in spirit and a wife of youth when thou wast refused, saith thy God.

Truly, God, my Abba Father, and Jesus, my Chief Shepherd and Savior, have never left me nor forsaken me.

I had a wonderful husband who met my needs except for his repeated unfaithfulness. I also longed for him to share my spiritual hunger. Now, I know that since we were unequally yoked, we were unable to communicate and enjoy spiritual things together. After the children left, the empty nest syndrome set in; and having very little in common, he left me for another woman. After six months of seeking God to restore our marriage, I realized God had other plans.

It took a head-on collision which was my fault, a broken nose, a shoulder out of place, chest pains, and two numb knees to get my attention. I asked God, "Why am I the one having the wreck?" He answered me, "Until you get your eyes off the past and focus on Me, you are going to keep hitting things." This brought the reverential fear of the Lord upon me. Today, I take this very seriously. I still ask before leaving in the car, "Oh, Abba Father, am I focused on you today?"

Next, God led me to read James Dobson's book, Tough Love, which helped me to see that I had to let my husband go and follow I Corinthians 7:15,

> But if the unbelieving husband leaves you, let him depart. A brother or sister is not under bondage in such cases; but God hath called us to peace.

Now, three years later, I realize that it was God who delivered me from an unfaithful husband so that I could surrender my life to Him and His plans for me. I praise God that His hand was still upon me as I struggled through the wilderness. You know, God gave the children of Israel manna and water in the desert and led them with a cloud by day and a pillar of fire by night. Likewise, God blessed me with two dear children, two precious grandchildren and many memorable times. I have no doubt that even with our wrong choices, "all things work together for good to them that love God, to them who are called according to His purpose" (Romans 8:28).

God pointed out to me that from age fourteen to fifty-four—forty years, I'd walked in His permissive will, but now He would restore the opportunity to serve Him full-time. I believe God is giving me a chance to redeem the time of full-time service and commitment to Him that I vowed forty years ago. Isn't God awesome?

Now, I was ready to hear and obey God concerning the vision that He'd begun to birth in my heart even before the time I've spoken of above. Actually, in 1995 when my mother died, I began to get pieces of a vision which I tucked away in my heart—for I believed that I could not share this with my husband. I felt he would leave me if he knew that I wanted to pursue this vision.

At a Women's Aglow retreat during the praise and worship time, I remember seeing a picture of an open door in my mind's eye. God said, "I'm going to open a door that no man can close." A year later when Mother died, I again heard Him say, "You're going to use your mother's house to help hurting women." More recently, I've heard, "Remember the ladies you know who have had abortions? Now, you are going to save many babies alive." As I continue to surrender myself and all I have to the Lord, He is revealing more and more of His plan to me.

For the first two years after I retired from teaching, I became a jail minister. God used this time to let me see the great need for a Christian home for women and their children to keep them from their former environments and lifestyles. Then, I got my training to volunteer at the Pregnancy Resource Center. This led to the director of the center recommending Mother's House to a lady who came and successfully finished the 90-day program. Now, this delightful, young lady has a healthy baby girl, and God has helped her establish a home of her own. God is truly our El Shaddai, the All-Sufficient One, isn't He?

To begin with, three ladies and one lady's ten-year-old daughter stayed in my own home. Two of these came when a judge committed them into my care to keep them from going to prison. One mother had attempted suicide and needed to have a safe place for herself and her daughter. Another lady who stayed eleven months got a good job. Then her mother from California visited us and helped her get a car. The last time I talked to her she had an apartment and was seeking to get custody of her four-year-old daughter.

Then God worked through my pastor and his wife to get my church involved in the ministry. Just before Reverend Edward L. Williams and Irma B. Williams left Landmark Church of God in 1998, I told Pastor Williams about my vision for my mother's house. He replied, "Are you going to call the home My Mother's House?" Today, because of this, the ministry is called Mother's House. The next Sunday, Pastor Williams announced to the church that he was starting a Mother's House Fund to help establish and run the home.

Soon, a four-member board and a ten-member committee were formed to help me with the many decisions. By God's divine hand Mother's House was opened in September 1999. Today, Mother's House is a residential home for abused, addicted, battered and abandoned women and their children and/or families. The home is located in a country setting with a barn, garden, flowers, and a large yard. During the first ninety days the residents stay in the home. Their daily schedule consists of Bible studies, activities that teach independent life/communication skills, parent/child guidance, GED as needed, food preparation/preservation skills, and an Overcomers' Biblically-based 12-Step Program.

A second phase will let the ladies, children and/or families continue in a safe Christian environment as each one makes plans for the future. As some seek a job and others continue their education, again our focus is on God. His plans for each one are uppermost as we make the many decisions needed to establish their future. From September 1999 until May 2000, God has graced Mother's House with seven women and two children. Some exciting times have been when one of the ladies received Jesus into her heart and received the Baptism of the Holy Spirit. Others have gotten their license restored, a job and/or a car. Another has worked on her GED. Also, the children have been a joy and a blessing as they have brought new life and joy to the home. Only God knows what He has planned for Mother's House properties.

We've been given a two-bedroom,two-bathroom mobile home, three bunk beds, two baby beds, a toddler bed, and numerous clothes, appliances, furniture etc. Doesn't it sound like God has a lot planned for us? For example, just this week, God confirmed that He wants my home next door as a part of the ministry. God has provided someone to help with administration and day-to-day activities and a maintenance person.

God also opened a door for me to go into the poor areas of Appalachia to the Christian Appalachian Project in Kentucky to see what he has for us to do to help the homeless, poor, lost and hurting women and children there. In Isaiah 58:6-7, God says:

> Is this not the fast which I choose, to loosen the bonds of wickedness, to undo the bands of the yoke, and to let the oppressed go free, and break every yoke? Is it not to divide your bread with the hungry, and bring the homeless poor into the house; when you see the naked, to cover him?

In 2002, I collaborated with Teen Challenge for grant funding. In 2002-2003, we've ministered to two families of six. One has now successfully completed one year on their own. The other has finished the first phase of the program and are in preparation for going out on their own in the second phase of the program.

I am excited to see what God has planned as I continue to step into this "open door!" I want to thank everyone who has helped make this vision become a reality. Thank you for your prayers and support. Isn't it wonderful to know that we cannot even give a cup of cold water in the name of Jesus, but that He has promised to bless and reward it. (Matthew 10:42) Most of all, I want to thank my heavenly Father for redeeming my time and giving me another chance to serve Him with all my heart. I truly believe He is "...able to do exceeding, abundantly above all that we ask or think, according to the power that worketh in us. Unto Him be glory...by Christ Jesus throughout all ages, world without end. Amen" (Ephesians 3: 20-21).

Jane Brady Hudson

Is any sick among you? Let him call for the elders of the church, and let them pray over him, anointing him with oil in the name of the Lord: and the prayer of faith shall save the sick, and the Lord shall raise him up; and if he has committed sins, they shall be forgiven him. —James 5: 14

I would like to take this opportunity to share a special testimony. God has blessed my family and me many times and touched us both physically and spiritually. This particular healing, however, is one I would like to write about.

My father, Harry Brady, is seventy-five years old. Around Thanksgiving 2001, my Dad began getting very weak and tired. The doctor said my father's heart was out of rhythm. This was causing the weak condition. My dad went into the hospital in December for a procedure in which the doctor would try to shock his heart back into rhythm. Everything went very well for my father, and he was feeling much better. Unfortunately, in about two weeks his heart was off rhythm again. The doctor said he would try medicine this time. Although my dad was taking many new medications, he wasn't getting any better. He was so weak that he had difficulty getting his breath to talk or even get up out of the chair.

On Friday, March 15, 2002, my dad was hospitalized with congestive heart failure. He had gained over sixteen pounds of fluid. The doctor once again said that the problem was directly related to his heart's rhythm. As time passed, my dad became weaker and weaker. Many people were praying for my dad, but he just seemed to be getting worse.

In May 2002, we were in revival with Reverend Joel Talley. He had special prayer for the sick. I stood in for my dad. I distinctly remember the verse in James coming to my mind that night. Brother Talley asked one of the sisters in the altar to lay her hand on my chest and stomach. I truly felt God's touch during the prayer; however, my dad was only getting sicker. He came up for Joshua's high school graduation. He was so weak that my husband and brother-in-law almost had to carry him into the school. He was scheduled to return to the doctor on May 31, 2002. My mother just knew they would put dad in the hospital, and she told me to be expecting her call. Well sure enough, I was leaving work on May 31, and my cell phone rang. I just knew they needed me to come to the hospital.

I was wrong! Praise the Lord! It was good news. My sister was calling to tell me that dad's heart was back on rhythm! The reason he had been getting weak was due to all the other medications. The doctor quickly adjusted the doses, and dad was back to driving in about a week.

I realize my dad may get sick again, and his heart may even go back off rhythm; however, I know beyond a shadow of a doubt that God healed my dad the night I was prayed for in his behalf. God had to remind me not to get weary with my praying. He also had to remind me that sometimes things may look hopeless when He has already done the work.

I hope this testimony will bless you. I also hope that if you or a loved one needs prayer you will not hesitate to call for the elders of the church to anoint and pray over you or your loved one.

Bishop Kenneth McLellan Hudson

But my God shall supply all your needs according to His riches in glory by Christ Jesus.—Philippians 4: 19

God has been so good to me. There have been many instances where He has divinely intervened in my life. I have witnessed first-hand His miraculous power. I would like to share with you an incident that occurred early in my ministry. This is just one of many times that God has miraculously supplied my need.

When I was a young student attending East Coast Bible College, finances were very tight. My dad worked very hard to support our family and pay my way through school. There was very little money for extras. One weekend I came home from school to be with my family. One Sunday before church my dad gave me ten dollars and told me this would have to do for the next week. This would include buying my gas to return to school and any other expenses that I might incur. He was very emphatic that this would have to do.

I went to church and assembled in the choir as usual. During the offertory as my pastor was praying, the Lord spoke to me and told me to give ten dollars in the offering. The pastor had not expressed any special need. This was just a typical Sunday morning offering. I argued with God that the ten dollars was all I had. I needed gas to get back to school, and I knew the ten dollars would barely cover that expense much less any other incidentals. Without these ten dollars, I would probably not be able to return to school.

God continued to prompt me to give the money. The offering plate was getting closer, and I continued to struggle. Just as it came to me, I quickly pulled out the ten dollar bill and dropped it in the plate. I then began to worship God knowing that I had been obedient to His voice. The spirit of God moved during the offertory, and people began to worship. People began to fill the altar spontaneously, and I joined them as we were all blessed that morning. No one knew of my silent struggle over the ten dollars; however, God had assured me during the wonderful time of worship that He would supply all my needs.

As I left the church that morning, six different people came up to me and put money in my hand. Each of them expressed that God had led them to give the money to me that day. When I got home and counted the money, I had received six ten dollar bills. I had obeyed God by giving sacrificially. He abundantly supplied my needs. My ten dollar week became a sixty dollar week! That has been twenty-five years ago, and I can say unreservedly that He continues to supply my every need.

Eleanor Hughes

For I am the Lord who heals you.
—Exodus 15: 26

Eleanor Hughes has often seen the Lord's healing hand in her life and the lives of her children and grandchildren. She knows through experience that, indeed, the Lord Jesus Christ is Jehovah Ropha, the Healer. In 1958, her daughter Annette was born two months premature.

Prior to her birth, the doctor had told her husband that he feared for either her life or the life of the baby. He also said, "This is one I'll be glad to see get here." As Eleanor shared, "I had people praying for me. My sister was praying for me and felt led to get between the refrigerator and wall and pray for me. I had no fear. While I was in the hospital, Psalm 23: 4 kept going through my mind. Even under anesthesia, I kept standing on, "Yea though I walk through the valley of the shadow of death, I will fear no evil."

As Eleanor continued, "They were giving me blood to do a Caesarian operation, but before they got the blood in, the baby was born naturally. Both are alive today. God was with me then. People were praying. The next morning my husband came to see me. I said, "You know why the baby and I are both here and alive, don't you?" He said that the Lord had done it.

When her grandson, Dennie Marlow (Paulette's son) was two years old, he was taken to the hospital with Bright's disease, an acute kidney disease. The doctor said that if he could live beyond his twenty-fifth birthday, he would be all right. "One Sunday morning," Sister Hughes said, "Reverend B.N. Black, the pastor at Fifth Street Church of God, called me forth to let him anoint me with oil for Dennie. Dennie was healed and never went back to the hospital." Born on February 25, 1967, he is now in the year 2,000, thirty-three years old and continues to have no problems from Bright's disease.

Later, her granddaughter, Tammy (Judy's daughter). was born two months premature with an enlarged kidney. She was in and out of the hospital for about two years. She would often go into convulsions. As Eleanor says, "Reverend B.N. Black anointed me and prayed for her while she was in the hospital. She was healed and has had no more trouble with her kidneys or convulsions."

In all three instances Sister Hughes has seen that God is "the same yesterday, today, and forever." James 5: 14 says:

> Is anyone among you sick? Let him call for the elders of the church, and let them pray over him anointing him with oil in the name of the Lord. And the prayer of faith will save the sick, and the Lord will raise him up.

When Eleanor was anointed with oil by the pastor, God did raise up Dennie and Tammy and heal them.

As she stood on the promises of the Word, God took her fear. As Isaiah 55: 11 teaches, those promises did not return void, but accomplished what they were sent to do and even prospered in it. God honored the prayers of the righteous who were praying for her and healed her and her baby. For as James 5: 16 says, "The effective, fervent prayer of a righteous man avails much." Indeed, our God is the Lord God that healeth. What a loving, awesome God.

Ibrahim

Peace I leave with you; My peace I give to you; not as the world gives do I give to you. Let not your heart be troubled, neither let it be afraid.—John 14: 27

I was fourteen years old. I did not understand what was going on. I don't know what to do. It was a hard life. Everybody was busy about themselves. I was working driving a taxi on the Mount of Olives.

One day God sent a lady who wanted to go to Nazareth. I don't know how to come to Jerusalem from Nazareth. I go around the city seven times. She began laughing. I say, "Why are you laughing?" She told me that she had dreamed this.

In the beginning I give her my address. She preach and send Bibles. I was interested to read. It was important to go out from my problems. In the beginning I don't take an answer. The lady come every week. I feel rest and peace in my heart around her. She came for about six months. I was not serious with her.

She told me why I am here. She teach me how to live life and be a nice person. Then I was working eighteen to twenty hours per day. I had no place to go. I had no friends. Then she tell me to work eight hours. She said that my health was more important.

God opened my heart. Now I test it. It work. Now my family is everything. Now I don't play games. I say, "God you control me." Now I have my own cab. God just provided. Now I can't go back. I want to continue. I like the rest and peace I feel. I tested the food. Now I keep coming back. I know when people are true. I know you all are true.

Note: Martha Dobson met Ibrahim in 2001 when she was in Israel. He was her taxi driver. He is an Arab Christian believer in secret. He and his wife invited her, her friend Barbara and Kathleen Runyon to his home for lunch where he shared his testimony. This is his testimony.

Sandra Black Jackson

Through the Lord's mercies, we are not consumed because His compassions fail not. They are new every morning; great is your faithfulness....The Lord is good to those who wait for Him, to the soul who seeks Him.—Lamentations 3: 22,23,25

In June 1999, Sandra Black Jackson, who was living in California, made a testimonial tape as a special Father's Day gift for her father, Reverend Franklin D. Black, Sr. The following testimonial praises God for His miraculous intervention and work in her father's life and in her husband's life. She can, indeed, testify that God gives rest to those who labor and are heavy laden when they put their trust in Him and are not offended because of the Lord Jesus Christ.

"Dad, there are many, many times that you have been healed, and Mom. I don't know how many times they said you weren't going to make it. I told someone the other day that my Dad had nine lives. That's the way I feel because God has restored your life many, many times.

"I remember how hard you worked. I remember how hard you worked to build churches. The first church I remember was in Camden, South Carolina. I remember that you dug a big hole, and I fell in it. Then, I remember all the work you did in McCall when you built the house there. And Mom, I remember when the dishes all fell down when the trains came across the railroad track.

"I remember as a little girl when we would get scared when Dad would fall out because he'd fall out under the anointing of the Lord. We were scared, but God never wanted us to have that kind of fear.

"And Dad, I remember that every time you went somewhere, my middle name was Go. I even loved to go with you to church. Wherever you went in Bakersville, California, I just wanted to be with you. And when we went to the Old River Church of God, of which you were district pastor, I just loved going. I remember all of the preaching.

"It's been so hard for me, and I know it's been hard for Mom, too, since you retired. We were so used to your ministry and the things that you said and the way you pastored and loved your people. It was so hard to find a minister that does that and loves God like you do, Dad.

"I know that you sat at your desk many times wondering where the money was going to come from. God always answered you. God always kept you. He always kept the family. I'm so thankful for all your prayers. During the years that I raised my children, I know it was your prayers and Mom's prayers that brought me back to the Lord.

"I'm thankful for the church in Statesville. They love you, and they have shown it. A lot of people say they love you, and a lot of people do love and support you; but, you know in your heart that the people in Statesville really mean it. I'm thankful for that.

"I love you this Father's Day. There's no other Dad I would rather have had. God gave me a Dad and a Mom for whom I shall always be grateful. I'll never be able to convey how much I appreciate God's love for giving me you and Mom.

"I also appreciate so much what God did in my husband Dorman's life in 1999. On March 24, 1999, Dorman went into the hospital to have a valve replacement and open heart surgery with two by-passes. Recently, Dorman and I were sitting on our porch talking about this experience. I was expecting Dorman to be excited with me at what God had done, but I realized that he didn't remember much about what he'd gone through.

"When Dorman had surgery, everything went very well, and we'd gone home and gone to bed. During the night, I called the nurses three times. They told me that everything was just fine and that I should get some rest. When I went the next morning to the hospital, they met me and asked me if I knew he'd had a stroke and could not talk. His right side was paralyzed. This threw all of us into shock because we'd believed that everything was going to be fine.

"Dr. Desota, the heart specialist, came in and talked with us. He told us that a sliver of plaque that had gotten loose from the plaque around the heart had gone to his brain. He said that it'd be days, maybe weeks before we'd know all the damage. Two hours later, the neurologist gave us the worst scenario—that Dorman would never be the same. He'd had a stroke; he could not talk or feed himself; he could not eat; and he did not know what was going on. This went on for about three days.

"On the third day, the doctors moved him to step-up, step-down care. In the Intensive Care Unit as a patient improves, he is moved twice before he is well enough to be moved to his own room. Dorman doesn't remember being moved. The nurses started therapy and started feeding him. They put a thickener in his drink so he could swallow. It seemed that he wasn't getting better. On the fourth day, they had him sitting up. Dorman was laughing and seemed to be like himself. He still couldn't tell you who he was. He came and went at that time. It was so wonderful when he could finally say who I was; yet, the doctors still didn't see much improvement. The therapist said that he'd have to go through a hospital stay to get physical and speech therapy.

"On the fifth day, the hospital staff said that they were making plans for him to go to another place for this therapy. I said, 'No, I think he's going to go home.' My children kept saying, 'Mom, you've got to listen.' But I just knew—I remembered praying on our porch. God had told me that he'd come home a whole man. I had to lean on that because I was going to bring him home.

"On the sixth day, the therapists all came in and said, 'I don't see any reason for him to go to therapy. He's walking and going to the bathroom by himself; he's feeding himself; and he can do everything he'll have to do for himself at home.' Some things weren't right. For example, he had difficulty with days and months.

"Then the doctor came in and told me what a miracle this was. He and the neurologist had written on paper what a miracle this was. That day the heart specialist had come in Dorman's room every hour, seven or eight different times just to watch the improvement.

"The heart specialist had not been to church in years. The next Sunday, he went to church with his mom. He told me that he knew what God had done. He asked, 'If I ever need prayer, may I call on you and your family? I know this had to be God.' He said that the neurologist also knew that this had to be the work of the Lord. People just don't make that kind of recovery.

"As Dorman and I were on our porch talking about what God had done, I understood that he didn't realize half of what had gone on. He was upset because he forgets. He has come a long way. God is still healing him. I have no doubt that there's a full recovery ahead for Dorman. I know it's coming.

"I love the Lord. I wanted to give this testimony because I know the miracle is there, and God has been so good—not only the miracles that happened with you, Dad, but the miracle that has happened with Dorman. I know that in the last days, it will be such testimonies that will bring people to the Lord. These are miracles that need to be told."

God has provided miraculous healings in the lives of Sandy's father and husband and desires to do the same for his hurting children throughout the world. Sandy has seen His faithfulness as described in Lamentations 3: 23. Indeed,

Through the Lord's mercies, we are not consumed because His compassions fail not. Great is Your faithfulness....The Lord is good to those who wait for Him, to the soul who seeks Him.

Throughout her life, Sandy has been with her mother and father many times when the doctors said her father would not live. Instead, they saw God heal him. She saw how hard her father worked in ministry and building churches. No matter how weary her mother and father were, they always put their trust in God according to Matthew 11: 6. When they were weary, God always gave them rest as He promises in Matthew 11: 28. Likewise, when Dorman was in the hospital and Sandy was weary, God gave her rest because she put her faith in Him. He'll do the same for you who read this testimony.

Ralph Jarvis

Those who wait on the Lord shall renew their strength. They shall mount up with wings like eagles. They shall run and not be weary. They shall walk and not faint. —Isaiah 40: 31

When Sue and I first got married, I was Baptist, and she went to the Church of God. Back then, mixing religions was about like mixing races to many people. We were kids. We didn't see a problem with belonging to different denominations; however, we let other peoples' reactions drive us out of church instead of being strong enough to find a church we could both go to. We got out into the world.

The longer I was out in the world (thirty years), the worse things got. During that period of time, I got into the motorcycle scene, alcohol, drugs and partying. Sue and I partied together. The longer I was out in the world, the deeper I got, and the further I got from the Lord. I not only used drugs; I sold drugs. But today the old Ralph is dead and buried. I'm a new man born again in Jesus Christ.

When I was out in the world, through it all the Lord was with me and watching over me. I should have been dead because of many of the things I was into and the places I've been. I've had many, many motorcycle wrecks. I always came out with no more than a scratch. I'd drive 150 miles per hour as drunk as a skunk. We'd go to motorcycle rallies. Some of the people I hung around with were really rough. Most of them are dead now. I finally got out of the motorcycle scene and withdrew to a few friends I could party and do drugs with.

I didn't want any friends I couldn't do drugs with. I didn't want anyone around me who'd disagree with me or say anything about the drugs. Sue left me one time because of marijuana. I wouldn't tell her I'd quit smoking. She came back. That was God's grace. One reason that I think she put up with me was because of a Dear Abby article in the paper. A lady wrote in that she had a wonderful husband except that he smoked a little pot. Abby said that the woman should thank the Lord for what she had. She told her not to worry about a little pot. Sue said to herself that Ralph must be o.k. then.

I kept telling myself I was going to quit drugs and straighten up. This went on for about four years. I believe that this was God's hand telling me that the drugs were wrong. Instead of quitting drugs, however, I began to use harder drugs like cocaine. I really didn't care much about cocaine. My involvement was selling the drug. I did some stupid things when I was doing drugs. On vacation I'd take the marijuana with me on airplanes. I never got caught. At some point, however, I asked God to help me. Once you get God involved, you're in trouble. God nudges you. If you don't listen, He nudges harder. It's like He knocks you on the head and says, "Didn't you hear Me?" The next time He knocks you on the head with a sledgehammer. It took the sledgehammer for me.

I hadn't sold a lot of drugs up to that point. A guy at work asked me for a few ounces of cocaine. It turned out that he was working for the Federal Bureau of Investigation (FBI). They'd busted him. Then they busted me. When they came to my house, they had local, state and federal agents together. They charged me with five counts of trafficking and selling cocaine. When they came, I'd been doing some cocaine. They searched my house and took $12,000 in cash. They told me I was going to lose my house and scared me to death. They took me to the bank and searched my safety deposit box, but they didn't arrest me.

After the law enforcement did all of this to me, I was a total wreck. They left me at my house. They didn't want anyone to know they'd been there. They wanted to scare me so I'd do what they wanted me to do. With the charges they had, I was looking at fifty years in prison. That night I asked the Lord to help me. I had no Christian people to call for help. I didn't know anyone who was a Christian.

Then I began dealing with the stress of the police wanting me to set up the guys I had been buying drugs from. I would have to go wired into the places where the people were selling drugs. If the people selling drugs had caught me with a wire, I'd have been dead. I didn't know what was going to happen with me with my family and prison. My family was finding out what kind of person I really was. On top of all of this stress, my plant was getting ready to shut down. When my bosses announced they were closing the plant, I was forty-nine years old. To retire I had to be fifty years old with twenty-five years of service. I had twenty-seven years in. I was so close to retirement that I had suicidal thoughts. I thought, "Just get it over with." Because the insurance plan at the plant covered mental disorders, I took one week off work.

I went for counseling to a psychiatrist who asked, "Have you ever had suicidal thoughts?" I said, "Yeah." He locked me up at a medical center. It was the same day that I was supposed to be wired for the first time. I just couldn't handle the stress. They called Sue and told her not to come to visit. She could only bring me clothes. After four or five days, I was let out as an outpatient. The psychiatrist gave me Prozac for depression and something to help get me off drugs. Those drugs really helped me. From the time I first went in wired to buy drugs until the sellers were busted took one year.

From the time the police busted me until my trial took five years from September 1995 until August 2000. I plea bargained. I lost my citizenship. Through all of this, I'd quit drugs and drinking. I asked the Lord to forgive me and save me. I know he did. I prayed a lot. I asked the Lord to see me through. He did. The plant stayed open one month until after my birthday. That was God's hand. I got my retirement.

Sue and I got back into church when Sue's mom died. The people at the church were so good to us. We had been coming a short time when the Evangelism Explosion (E.E.) team came to our house. This was one year after I had been busted. That night I really accepted the Lord as my Savior. My life changed completely. I believe that it was through the grace of God and the prayers of the people at church that I just got six months intensive probation and two years of regular probation with a $2500 fine.

In five months it's been miraculous to see what God's done. I'm active in E.E., the choir, the men's group called the Victors and church planting. Now God's put me in the Christian Motorcycle Ministry. Through this organization, I'm able to use my E.E. training to lead many to the Lord. It's great to see them walk through the door to accept the Lord. When I'm on a motorcycle now, I'm on a mission trip. This time I go to the same places I used to go to and take His Word.

One night, for example, I met a 300 pound man in leather. When I shared the truth with him, he began crying like a baby. I was able to lead him to the Lord. Now when I'm with the Christian Motorcycle Ministry in Daytona, Florida, we have a church service every morning at 9:00 a.m. Then we go in cell teams all over the town. Some people work in booths; some walk the streets. We use stickers that say, "This bike has been blessed that God will keep you safe" in order to witness.

So many people are hunting a way out and don't know how. That was me as I used to be. Now I can help others get the Lord in their life. When they get the Lord in their life, the drugs and other things will go. I just thought I had friends when I was doing drugs. I thought I'd have to give up my friends if I gave up drugs and drinking. Now I've got so many friends it's unreal. Now I have real, true friends. God put my marriage back together. He's been good to me in my marriage. She's stuck with me. Now the Lord's using me to help others. I'm blessed that He's given me a giving heart.

In church I've found that people often want a new Christian to fit a certain mold. I've learned that a person should not try to fit the mold of other people. Instead, a person must wait upon the Lord for his direction and stay in the Bible. He'll direct your footsteps at your speed, not someone else's. God is so good. Even when I was on probation and couldn't leave my home after 6:00 p.m., the E.E. group would come to our home for training so that we could participate. I have found that, indeed, "those who wait on the Lord shall renew their strength. They shall mount up with wings like eagles. They shall run and not be weary. They shall walk and not faint" (Isaiah 40:31). As I have waited on the Lord, He has renewed my strength and blessed me mightily.

Coleen and Paul Kennedy

Bless the Lord, O my soul, and forget not all His benefits: who forgives all your iniquities, who heals all your diseases. —Psalm 103: 2-3

Coleen and Paul Kennedy have seen God's healing hand numerous times in their lives. One night they were attending a camp meeting in Ashland, Virginia, when Paul became so excited in the Spirit that he began dancing in the Spirit for the first time in his life. He had two growths on one of his eyelids. One had been bothering him. The next morning when he woke up, the growths were gone.

Coleen had a cancerous thyroid tumor in her throat that was causing her to have difficulty swallowing. One doctor took two biopsies of the tumor. Several doctors agreed with him that according to the slides, there was a big possibility that the tumor was most malignant. At this time she went to Dallas, Texas to visit friends who worked printing Bibles. They took her to a prayer meeting where one man gave a word of knowledge: "Thou will live and not die and declare the works of the Lord."

She was not healed and went to a number of places for prayer. She changed her diet to one with healthy foods and took nutrients. A Magnetic Resonance Imaging (MRI) showed a picture of a very large tumor. She continued praying. Meanwhile she and Paul joined Brother Wallace Heflin at the Ashland Camp Grounds on his trip to Israel. Again she was not healed as she expected.

After many months, she went to Philadelphia to a doctor who was highly recommended by the wife of her cousin's pastor, Reverend Harold Berrian. She knew that he would only do surgery if he felt he had no other choice. He told her that she needed surgery. She had felt the Lord telling her that something would take place in her hospital room, yet she still needed surgery which she had when she returned from Israel. When the doctor came out of the operating room. He said that he had found no cancer. Coleen said, "I was praising the Lord. I believe that God did the work."

Shortly after that, Coleen continued, "God showed me that I should go back to the hospital room I had been in. My daughter, Nancy and I went and asked if we could pray for the lady in the room whom the doctors could not help. She said, 'Yes.' When we prayed, her medical situation turned around. The doctor didn't know what to think. Indeed, as God had said, something did take place in my hospital room. I continued contact with her for awhile. She was amazed at what God did."

Another time Coleen was taken to the hospital unable to move. The doctors said that she would not leave the hospital without back disc surgery. Her mother and brother had already had disc surgery. The Lord showed her in the Word to call for the elders of our church of which Paul was a member. The elders did go and anoint her with oil. As the elders prayed we could all feel the Presence of God in the room in a mighty way. God healed her body. She walked out of the hospital without surgery or pain.

On another occasion, four doctors and Coleen's gynecologist diagnosed her with a uterine tumor the size of a grapefruit. All of the doctors recommended surgery. Lots of people were joining her in prayer. She went with a friend to a prayer meeting where the pastor asked any who desired healing to go up front. Coleen remembers: "I put my hand on the open Bible while he was praying a healing Scripture. He said, 'That tumor's shrinking.' Immediately, I knew in my Spirit that it was done."

"Paul said, 'You need to go back to the last doctor and have him check you out." In the meantime I read a negative story in a magazine about tumors. The enemy was trying to tell me that the work wasn't done, but I knew that God had done the work. I went to the doctor. He started to stutter. He brought in another doctor. Then I told him the story of the prayer I'd had. He said, 'Well, you won't have to have the operation now.' Another time when I was hemorrhaging from fibroid tumors, a friend suggested that I drink Aloe Vera juice. God took care of the tumors. They left. God is wonderful!"

Indeed, for Paul and Coleen the words of Psalm 103: 2-3 could be their testimony. They will never forget His benefits as He has healed their diseases: eyelid growths, thyroid tumors, uterine tumors and fibroid tumors. He is our Jehovah Rophe, our Healer who is the same yesterday, today and forever. Each time as Psalm 107: 20 says, the Word was sent forth through prayer healing them and delivering them of all their destructions. Praise be His Holy Name! They praise God for the many answers to prayer. Praise God!

Coleen and Paul Kennedy

Oh, give thanks to the Lord, for He is good! For His mercy endures forever. Let the redeemed of the Lord say so, whom He has redeemed from the hand of the enemy. —Psalm 107: 1- 2

My husband Paul took me to the pool for water therapy because of back surgery I had had in Mocksville, North Carolina. The doctor had told me to have the therapy. While I was in the YMCA pool, Paul went to the ATM at the CCB bank near the shopping center close to the YMCA.

When Paul pulled up to the ATM and got out, he forgot to put the car in park. The car started to roll down the hill across the road and hit a tree. Paul ran after the car and slipped and fell. When the car stopped, he drove it back across the street to the bank.

Someone saw that he was bleeding and called an ambulance to take him to Davie Hospital in Mocksville. At the hospital, he was examined. He had hit his head and cut himself under his eye and knee. His finger was dislocated. Three doctors tried unsuccessfully to put his finger back in place, so he was taken to Baptist Hospital. Three more doctors worked on his finger there. Finally, a bone specialist came who was prepared to operate if the doctors couldn't put the finger back in place. The surgeon worked on this finger which was shaking from Parkinson's disease until finally the finger was back in place.

Two weeks later I noticed that Paul's big toe was away from the other toes. He had an X-ray done which showed that his toe was fractured. A piece of bone was chipped, and the tendon was pulled away. The foot doctor said that he could do surgery, but it would be painful. He suggested that Paul either tape the toe to the other toes or do nothing. He decided to tape the toe and to have a shoe insert made which was helpful.

A policeman told Paul that the road where the car had gone across the street was a street with heavy traffic. He said that cars go faster than the speed limit on that road. He told him that he was fortunate to be alive. He has a lot to be thankful for. We are also thankful that no one else was hurt because of the accident.

Coleen and Paul Kennedy

Those who sow in tears shall reap in joy. He who continually goes forth weeping, bearing seed for sowing, shall doubtless come again with rejoicing, bringing his sheaves with him.—Psalm 126: 5, 6

In 1965, just before the Communist coup in Indonesia, God began to pour out His spirit on the island of Timor. God impressed Christians to pray, and the country was spared. Immediately, teams of laymen began traveling within Timor and the surrounding islands sharing the Gospel. Miracles such as people had only heard of in the Bible began following the evangelistic teams. God later sent one of the team members, Mel Tari, to the West to share the awesome stories of God's work and to deliver a message to the Western church: "Back to the simplicity of the Word of God."

The Kennedy's lives were forever changed when they met Mel Tari as they learned the truth of Psalm 126: 5 and 6. The Kennedys had first learned of the Indonesian revival from missionary friends, the Bustins. (See the appendix for more information on his ministry.) Before Reverend Bustin spoke at the Kennedy's church, Paul had already read his book about the revival. He had gotten the book from Brother Bustin previously at the church. He had felt compelled to write Mel Tari whose photo was in the book.

As they continued to correspond, Paul learned that Mel would not come to the West at any man's invitation, only at the direction of the Lord which happened in 1970. Of course, the Kennedys wanted Mel to visit them while he was in the United States; but, again, Mel would only come in God's timing. When Mel went to the Indonesian Embassy for his passport, his requests were denied. He prayed and went back to the embassy where a different person was in charge and granted him permission for departure.

He left for the United States with only fifty cents in his pocket and faith that God would meet all of his needs. The week before he was to leave, God had laid it on the hearts of someone in the United States to purchase Mel's airline tickets and express mail them to the airport. Mel did come to visit the Kennedys. They took him to the Indonesian Embassy in Washington, D.C. Coleen remembers that, Mel and I went in a Washington drugstore, and he danced around singing *Jesus Loves Me*. Everyone enjoyed him so much. He had a shine on his face—a great example for Jesus and a blessing in our home. He saw his first snow in our home. We took him to many places and meetings. Mel came to our home three different times. He called me Mamma."

Coleen continued, "Paul was an elder at our church and told Mel to speak for a week. He did, and at the end of the week God said, 'Tell the people everything that happened during the revival in Soe, Indonesia,' where he was raised. The revival started in Soe on the island of Timor and spread as many young people went out in teams to witness. Many miracles took place. Water was prayed over and turned to non-alcoholic wine. People were raised from the dead. So many were healed. Many, many miracles took place." Mel later documented God's mighty work during the Indonesian revival in his book, Like a Mighty Wind.

"At the time of the revival, a coup took place. The Communists were trying to take over. A friend of mine, Lois Fitzgerald was a missionary for the Christian Literature Crusade out of Fort Washington, Pennsylvania. While she was in Indonesia, she could hear the Communists digging graves behind her house for the missionaries."

"Instead, they took five non-communist generals and cut them up and put them down a well. General Suharto got away and later became the President of Indonesia. When the people heard of this atrocity, they went in a rage and killed everyone they suspected of being a Communist—over 500,000 people. They threw them in the river, and blood ran down the river. During the time of the coup, there was lots of prayer, and the revival changed things. Glory to God from whom all blessings flow."

"Mel held many meetings in the United States. One day I said to Mel, 'I don't see anything happening in my life. I wanted to win souls for Jesus. He laid hands on me and prayed. Soon after I was praying in my room about my salvation and sanctification; and while praying, I was filled with the Holy Spirit for sure. The next day, I told Mel what words came to my mind while I was praying. He said, 'That's Indonesian. I have an Indonesian dictionary. I'll show you.' I had spoken Indonesian."

"Shortly after that the Lord told me to pray for a lady who we knew wasn't well. That Sunday in church I testified. Then I had Holy Laughter. Now I was seeing the Lord use me. I was so excited. He showed me many things to do and told me to go many places. I saw people get saved. What excitement to know He was using me!"

"One night while Mel was in our home, we took him to a meeting in Baltimore, Maryland to speak. The school was so full that we couldn't find a seat. We met a lady named Jessie Smith and her son. She said, 'My son, Gary, will move and you both can sit here by me.' We did. We became close friends. She and her son lived on faith. They were precious Christian people. Her husband had died. Jessie and her son were such a blessing to us. God always supplied their needs."

"At the time of this meeting, Gary was weak and mentally ill. He could hardly talk and could not work. God healed Gary. We had seen him before and after the healing. We saw the transformation of his life before our very eyes. It was a miracle! Now he's very strong, able to hold a conversation with anyone, can drive and has a job."

"As Mel was preparing to return to Indonesia, Paul felt like he wanted to go back to Indonesia with Mel. We had land on the bay that we had tried to sell and couldn't. Mel prayed with us about this and said that if the Lord wanted Paul to go with him, the land would sell giving Paul the money to go. Well! It went up for sale again. It wasn't very long before the land sold. Now Paul had the money to go and five weeks vacation that he could use."

"Paul worked at the Philadelphia Electrical Company in Philadelphia, Pennsylvania, where he was working on a settlement with a representative from Arco (Atlantic Refining Company). When Paul told him that he was going to Indonesia, he said he'd send a letter of introduction to Bill Prindibile, the manager of Arco in Jakarta, Indonesia. In the letter he asked Mr. Prindibile to take Paul out to the oil fields over the Java Sea. Well, God had all this planned ahead of time to show Paul he was in control and would take care of him."

"As Mel and Paul traveled to Indonesia, they stopped for meetings along the way. In Hawaii, they stayed at a Nazarene pastor's home on the ocean. It was so beautiful. After Mel spoke in Hawaii, they traveled on to New Zealand, to Australia, to Bali in Indonesia, to Timor in Indonesia and to Jakarta in Indonesia."

"When Paul arrived in Jakarta, there was a blackout. Paul didn't know any Indonesian. The man from Arco had told Paul to go to one of two hotels in the city. When he asked for a room at the Hotel Indonesian, the desk clerk in his broken English told Paul that there were no rooms. When he asked about Mr. Prindibile, he learned that he was in a meeting."

"Finally, the clerk told me that Arco keeps a room in the hotel for the geologist who looks for oil. Since he was in the Selebes Islands looking for oil, Paul was able to have his room for two nights. So Paul had his room. Isn't Jesus wonderful to prepare a place to stay in during a blackout way ahead before even leaving home? He knew all and took care of Paul."

"The next day an Arco representative took Paul on a helicopter out to the oil platform in the Java Sea. The other people Paul was with had already taken care of places to stay. Paul was beginning to think that he had not taken enough money with him. Before he had left home, I had told him that I didn't think he was taking enough money. Paul didn't plan anything, yet along the way, places were given to him to sleep. When he arrived home, he had money left. Praise the Lord."

"When Paul was in Soe, Indonesia, it was awful hot in the daytime and cold at night. There were no toilets, only a hole in the ground. No matter the circumstances, however, God took care of Paul."

"When Paul and Mel went to Pontianak, the capital of Borneo, they stayed in a missionary's home where they found huge rats in the bedroom. The cats were called in to chase them out. Paul went to sleep. If that had been me, I wouldn't have slept all night."

"One day in Borneo, the team left Paul at the equator while others went into the interior. He got very, very ill with a high fever. He was told that the water he had drunk was from the water that ran down a canal by the street. The people brush their teeth, use the toilet and wash in that water. Well, he sure did get sick. Before Paul left for Indonesia, Paul had said to me, 'If I die over there just leave me there.' What a test that was as 'he felt like he would die at the time."

"While he was sick, the police came and took him to the station to ask him questions about why he had been to the generating station asking questions. Of course, he was interested because of his job; but they wondered if he was a rebel or a Communist. Finally, they let him go."

While Paul was in Indonesia for three weeks, God was also working mightily in Coleen's life. She stayed with their children at Penns Creek, a school and a Christian Camp. During that time the book, God's Chosen Fast, came into her possession and she felt led to fast."The Lord truly helped me as this was no chore at this time for me," Coleen said. "I fasted until the Lord let me know that I could stop." She fasted ten days with only water and saw things begin to happen in her life.

During this time, God impressed the words from Psalm 126: 5 and 6 on Coleen's heart. In her life she would learn the lessons of this Psalm personally just as she had already seen them demonstrated in the lives of the Bustins and Mel Tari. She would continually see that as she would sow the gospel message in tears, she would bring fruit with her filling her with joy.

At this time the Lord told her to sow seed by going door to door in Penns Creek, Pennsylvania as He guided her. Coleen and her son Tom would pass out tracts. One day she was impressed to share the gospel with two ladies who were sweeping the sidewalk. Another time she went to a home where the parents could not hear or speak. They used sign language. Coleen pointed to the heavens for Jesus, crossed her arms across her chest for love and pointed to them. These people all got saved. She continued to help them in their walk with the Lord through correspondence.

The three weeks that Paul spent in Indonesia were a blessed time for both him and Coleen. As she says, "I praise our wonderful faithful Lord for He's so good. God showed me with the Holy Spirit what to do during this time. I was blessed to have this opportunity for the Lord! "

The Kennedy's friendships with the Bustins and Mel Tari and their experience with the Indonesian revival have deepened their faith. They have seen God's power to heal, to perform miracles, to provide salvation, to baptize with the Holy Spirit, to guide their footsteps, to provide for their needs, and to fill them with joy. They have seen that as they, the Bustins and Mel Tari have sown the gospel in tears, they have reaped the harvest in joy. As they have borne seed for sowing, they have come again with rejoicing bringing sheaves with them. Praise the Lord from whom all blessings flow.

Coleen and Paul Kennedy

Great is the Lord, and greatly to be praised;—Psalm 145: 3a

We lived in Green, in Aston Township in Media, Pennsylvania. Paul had been praying that God would let the first person who came along buy our home. We had put our home up for sale by owner. Just before we sold the house, we found termites in our breezeway. The first people who came had never before ridden down our street. We told them about the termites. They said, "We'll take care of them. We want to buy your home." God had answered Paul's prayer.

Not long after that Reverend R.G. Flexan, a godly evangelist we knew personally came to our church. Paul went to the altar to pray for sanctification. He loved the church and thought he was saved. That day at the altar, however, God showed him that he was not saved. Paul testified of this and prayed through to salvation and sanctification with the pastor. Praise God that He loves us enough to continue to draw us unto Himself until we completely make Him Lord and Savior.

Later Paul served in this church as an usher, treasurer, deacon and elder. When the minister was away, Paul often preached for him. As Psalm 145: 3a says, "Great is the Lord, and greatly to be praised.

Coleen Kennedy

The eyes of those who see will not be dim. —Isaiah 32: 3

On September 19, 2002, I had cataract eye surgery on my left eye by Dr. Gillis in Statesville, North Carolina. The surgery went well. I did not feel anything during the surgery.

Two weeks later, the right eye was operated on. During this surgery on October 3, 2002, I knew something was different. I told Dr. Gillis a number of times that I could feel him working on my eye this time. While he worked, he talked to me explaining what he was doing.

After surgery, he told me that my eye got hard as a rock; the pressure in the eye went up very high. Dr. Gillis said that he was within seconds of inserting a needle in the white of my eye when all of a sudden my eye became soft again. He said, "I don't know what happened. I told him, "I had prayer, and God did it."

The next morning I had an appointment to see Dr. Gillis again. He told my husband Paul, his assistant and me what had happened the day before. He explained what he thought might have happened but said that he was really not sure. He told me that my eye could have hemorrhaged and that I would have been blind today in that eye. I told him again that God made my eye soft again. I asked his assistant if a record of this had been put on the computer. She said, "No, but Dr. Gillis would have put it in his surgical notes."

It was prayer that made the difference. We had prayed prior to surgery. While I was having surgery, Reverend Benjamin N. Black came into the office and prayed with my husband. I believe that the Lord heard all of the prayers, and I give him all of the glory for answering the prayers. What a glorious God we serve! I can't praise Him enough.

Coleen and Paul Kennedy

When thou passest through the water, I will be with thee; and through the rivers, they shall not overflow thee: when thou walkest through the fire, thou shalt not be burned; neither shall the flame kindle upon thee.—Isaiah 43: 2

Isaiah 43: 2 had been a favorite verse for Paul and Coleen Kennedy for many years when they agreed to participate in a missions trip to the Bahamas. They had no idea that the words of this verse would become reality for them both literally and spiritually.

One day at the Kennedy's church, a missionary from the Bahamas shared their ministry and need for workers to help construct a small building to complement the missions church. Sister Kennedy and her cousin Edith agreed to help in the kitchen at the mission's center in Nassau while Edith's husband, Thurman Short and Paul helped with the building. While they worked, they were amazed to hear the services of several local churches by microphone.

They met another missionary family there from Andros Island who invited them to visit their island. They agreed to fly with him to their home at the end of their work. When they were ready to return to Nassau, Paul decided that he would prefer to take the mail boat instead of flying. Coleen and Thurman were neither one comfortable with his decision because there had been a storm the night before; however, they agreed to join him on the boat anyway. Coleen told about what happened this way:

"I said to my husband that I'd had a premonition that something was going to happen. Just before we left, I saw a scripture on the wall of the home of the missionary. It was Isaiah 43:2. I told everyone that something was going to happen. I had never had anything that strong before.

"As we got on the boat, my cousin, Edith and I passed out tracts all over the boat. The four of us were on the back of the boat. We were singing hymns about the water. I went into my cabin to rest. When I began to feel sick, I returned to the back of the boat and felt better. The boat was rough. Thurman said to Paul, 'This boat's not going to make it unless it slows down.' The water was rough. The boat was made of wood and was old.

"A Bahamian man and woman with children joined us in the back. He said, 'I want to be back here with you Christians.' I told him of my premonition. He'd been on the water many times but had the same feeling. We shared our lives and talked about the Lord. He was backslidden. His father was a preacher.

"Paul decided to walk to the middle of the boat where the motor was. The young man who was supposed to be watching the the fuel in the barrel fell asleep. When the fuel ran out; the pump cut off, and the boat started taking on water. When Paul saw what was happening, he ran quickly to get life preservers for all of us. Everyone got theirs on but me. Paul had to come help me. He asked the captain to call for help. He wouldn't because he'd had trouble the last time he was out and had called for help. They finally found more fuel, but the pump still wouldn't start.

"Meanwhile the people had had time to read the tracts we had passed out. Many people were screaming. Some had gathered in the back of the boat with us to pray. While we were praying, Thurman gave his heart to the Lord. All of a sudden we could hear prayer all over the boat. It was really something. Then the Bahamian boy got saved. Then others began to get saved.

"Finally, the captain called for a bucket brigade to get the water out of the boat. Suddenly, after all of the prayer, the motor started. There is no doubt in my mind that the boat got under control because of all of the prayer. Praise God from whom all blessings flow.

"When we got back to Nassau, I still had my preserver on. Shortly after we returned, we learned that the boat had gotten burned up. When we shared the trip in the church, Edith said, 'I didn't know what to do. Where we were was one of the worst places for sharks.' That was one time when people found out if they were ready to meet the Lord.'

"I hate the idea of drowning but felt I was ready. We didn't have much time to think of ourselves. We were praying. God was so good!

We can really praise His holy name! If it weren't for Him, we wouldn't be here today! God had His hand on everything.

He had it all under control. That was His way of getting to Thurman and the Bahamian boy. Since this time Thurman has remained a Christian. In fact, Edith had prayed for thirty-seven years for Thurman's salvation.

"Before we returned home, I went to the straw market and gave tracts out while I talked with people about the Lord. When we got on the plane, I continued to give out tracts. I'd never done that before on a plane. We had a terrible ride coming home. Now we were in trouble on the plane. It got pitch black out. We couldn't see out because of the storm, and it was day time. The pilot was having trouble because of the storm.

The stewardesses were not supposed to show that they were concerned, but we could see that they were very upset. They showed it very much! I know prayer works! It brought us out. There's no doubt in my mind that the Devil was mad. God was the Victor! Praise His name! If I ever knew that God is so wonderful, I really saw it in this experience as God brought us safely home.

Indeed, the Kennedys found that when they passed through the troubled waters, God was with them. Because they trusted God and prayed, God saved their lives. He did not allow the rivers to overflow them on the mail boat. His hand stayed the burning of the boat until they were safely ashore. While they were working on the mission field, the truths of Isaiah 43: 2 became their reality literally and spiritually. Prayer did work bringing them through the waters and the fire. God is the Victor yesterday, today, and forever.

Coleen and Paul Kennedy

But He was wounded for our transgressions, He was bruised for our iniquities; the chastisement for our peace was upon Him, and by His stripes we are healed. —Isaiah 53: 5 ...by whose stripes you were healed. —I Peter 2: 24b

When our daughter Nancy was five years old, she came down with Spinal Meningitis, a rare disease. She had a high fever of 105 degrees. She threw up and was delirious. We took her to one doctor who said that she had a virus. We went to a second doctor who said the same thing, but we just knew that something else was wrong. When I'd lift her up, I'd put my hand under her neck; and she'd cry out. We decided on a third doctor who was a children's specialist. Right away he felt that Nancy had meningitis and put her in the hospital. By this time, her neck had started to pull back.

We were so thankful for all of the prayers of people in our church and that we did not stop with the first two doctors' diagnoses. The Lord has been so good to us. We thank Him again and again for all He's done for us. Nancy could have been crippled, but God had other plans for her future. She's fine today, and we praise Him.

Also, when he was young, our son, David, grabbed a bone out of a dog's mouth. The dog bit David. The bone was sticking up out of David's finger. The specialist who did the surgery on David's finger didn't expect David's finger to ever grow right since his tendon was cut. We prayed.

We later went back to the doctor who took X-rays of David's finger. The doctor called the nurse in to look at the X-rays because he was so surprised to see David's finger growing normally. Isn't God good! What a mighty God we serve! Indeed, as I Peter 2: 24b says, it is by His stripes that David was healed.

Coleen and Paul Kennedy

For in the righteousness of God is revealed from faith to faith as it is written. "The just shall live by faith —Romans 1: 17

Paul worked for the Philadelphia Electric Company in the Real Estate division. For years he traveled to many court houses. In later years, he worked in the office going out on jobs when needed. He was happy when his boss gave him the job of negotiator. He bought property to build transmission lines and substations for the electric company. He was given his own company car. He enjoyed meeting the people. Lancaster, Pennsylvania, was one area where he bought land from the people some of whom were Amish.

After Paul was saved, the Lord let him know He wanted him to discontinue the negotiation job. Paul was honest, and that is what the company wanted; yet Paul did not feel comfortable when the electric company assigned values for properties where the transmission lines would go through the land. People who held out longer sometimes received more money than those who did not hold out as long.

A formal appraisal was not done on the land, rather the supervisor assigned the value. He told Paul that the value he had assigned could not be changed. At times Paul would feel that people should get more money than allocated to them. This bothered Paul, and he prayed and asked the Lord to help him tell his boss that he could no longer do this job. Paul's boss told him to take the company car and ride around for a week and not work. Paul did just that. Then he went back and turned the car in.

The enemy told him, "You'll lose your job," but Praise the Lord, that never happened. The negotiating job was not filled for a long time. We wondered if they thought Paul would change his mind, but he didn't. He wanted to obey the Lord.

Paul was given another title with a conveyancer, and his pay was never cut. God is so good. If we obey Him, He'll always see us through any situation. Paul retired after forty-four years with the electric company. He had been hired after high school graduation when he was eighteen years old.

After he had been there one year, we married. Paul worked in the day time, and at night he attended Temple University in Philadelphia, Pennsylvania, where he studied business law and real estate law. As of July 27, 2002, we have been married for fifty-five years. God has been so good to us. We have learned the truth of Romans 1: 17 that the just do, indeed, live by faith.

Bill Krider

In My father's house are many mansions; if it were not so, I would have told you. I go to prepare a place for you.—John 14: 2

Ever since I was born, I have gone to church. I remember when I was saved. The preacher said that if I would just put my trust in God, my name would be written in the Lamb's Book of Life. In John 14: 2, Jesus said,

> In My father's house are many mansions; if it were not so, I would have told you. I go to prepare a place for you.

I'm so glad that I know today that He's preparing a place for me because my name is written in the Lamb's Book of Life.

Going to church has always been second nature to me, yet I really didn't realize what a personal relationship with Jesus was until I was in service. I started going to different churches. When I was in Alaska, I found a holiness church, a Church of God. It was different, and I knew I wanted what I found there. My life has been so much richer since that day. I look forward to every church service. I want to be in God's house.

One day in 1966, I became very ill. I thought everything was all right until suddenly I began throwing up blood. I had emergency ulcer surgery. After the surgery, the tube in my throat filled with blood. The doctors took me back into surgery. When I had this operation, the doctor said that there was a good chance I would not pull through, yet a tremendous peace came over me. I knew that I was in God's hands. If He wanted to take me home, it was o.k. with me. I was losing so much blood, and the doctors couldn't figure out why. Friends lined up at Fifth Street Church of God to give me forty-three pints of blood.

This time the surgery caused a stroke, and I was in a coma for a week or two. The doctor told my wife that I had died during the surgery. My heart had stopped for three minutes. I remember waking up and hearing someone saying, "I see his eyes movin'." Everyday I grew a little stronger. There were lots of people praying for me. There was a time while I was in the hospital that I was so discouraged, but Jasper Farmer and Pastor Benny Black came to visit me. It is so important that we visit each other in our church family when one of us is in need. It made such a difference in my life.

When my pastor visited me, he said that there were three Criders in the hospital at the same time. I thought that was strange because none of them were related to me. Had it not been for the prayers of God's people, I would not be here today. I know that God cares about His people. I know that as Isaiah 53: 5 says, it's by His stripes that I was healed. God's been good to me. When I had my stroke, I lost my job at the post office. They tried to hold the job for me; but I was out of work too long; and they had to replace me. I prayed, and God opened a door for me at Celanese where I worked for thirty-three years.

I've been through some difficult times in my life, but my God has always been faithful. I know that I can stand on His Word, and that what He says is true. There are many mansions in My Father's house, and He has gone to prepare a place for me. Revelation 21: 27 says that no one will enter heaven whose name is not written in the Lamb's Book of Life.

John 6: 47 says, "Most assuredly, I say to you, he who believes in Me has everlasting life." I'm glad I know that I have everlasting life and that my name is written in the Lamb's Book of Life.

Judy Kuehneman

...that their hearts may be encouraged, being knit together in love, and attaining to all riches of the full assurance of understanding, in the knowledge of the mystery of God, both of the Father and of Christ.—Colossians 2: 2

I thought the best thing in my life was being saved, and it was; but something better happened. Although I've been saved, have attended church regularly, and have witnessed, I have always felt like something more was ahead for me. Also, like so many others, I was just taking life and being born again for granted. I'm sharing my testimony so that, as Colossians 2: 2 says, you may be encouraged as I have been by the Lord.

Well, one day I began not feeling well. I prayed, for Psalm 55: 17 says,

> Evening and morning and at noon I will pray, and cry aloud, and He shall hear my voice.

I prayed, yet something kept leading me to a specialist, and fast! I didn't think it would be serious. After all, that happens to everyone else, especially not a Christian! Wrong! Very wrong!

I had cancer! Throat cancer! I was smoking at that time; but I had asked Jesus to take the addiction to cigarettes away from me. He did. I have not had withdrawal either! As Matthew 7: 7 says,

> Ask and it will be given to you; seek, and you will find; knock, and it will be opened to you.

In two weeks, I was scheduled for surgery—extensive surgery. The doctor told me that he was going to cut me from ear to ear in order to remove all of the cancer and skin graft the incision back together. He also told me that I'd never be able to swallow again, or at least it would be highly unlikely that I'd ever swallow again. He said that I would be on a feeding tube through my stomach.

I was failing fast. I lost from ten to twelve pounds or more in one weekend. Altogether I went from 125 pounds to 92 pounds. I was very devastated. I was scared; and then again, I wasn't! My thoughts were turning to, "I'll be o.k." I began to get courage, and calmness set in. I was being comforted by the Holy Spirit. What a great feeling! Indeed, as Psalm 22: 24 says,

> For He has not despised nor abhorred the affliction of the afflicted; nor has He hidden His face from Him; but when He cried to Him, He heard.

Well, I went into the hospital. I was lying on the gurney waiting to be operated on. I kept saying and singing quietly over and over to myself, "Take my hand, Lord Jesus. Take my hand." I went under anesthesia and came to eight or nine hours later. I had tubes in my throat, nose and stomach. I was in pain. I couldn't talk or move my body at all. I was swollen two to three times my normal size. The doctor came in. He said that at one point he had lost me.

Well, during that lost time, I was with Jesus! I saw Jesus! He was standing along side the road, about twenty to thirty feet from me. He didn't stretch His hand out. No, He smiled!! Now, I can't tell you what He looked like except that He was dressed in blue. I felt His peaceful warmth and His smile! I was safe, and He was guarding me and leading me back to my family. I was not afraid. After all, Psalm 145: 19-20 says:

> He will fulfill the desire of those who fear Him; He also will hear their cry and save them. The Lord preserves all who love Him, but all the wicked He will destroy.

Well, it's been nine months since my operation. I've been through radiation treatments; and I had to learn how to hold my head up, to raise my arms and to talk. I'm still weak, but I've come a long way. I still can't swallow and probably never will; but I'm not depressed or sad or mad. I'm o.k. I'm not alone because Jesus is still with me, and I saw Him! What a blessing! I wouldn't change that for anything. I'm so glad that God loves me and that Jesus died for me. He's my Savior every day! Praise the Lord!

Debbie Lambert

And we know that in all things God works for the good of those who love Him, who have been called according to His purpose. —Romans 8:28

Leaving a church family is one of the most difficult decisions to make. That is why in 1993, I didn't understand the Holy Spirit's prompting to attend Landmark Church of God. I loved the congregation I was a part of, and there were no problems to prompt such a move.

I began praying for understanding and God's guidance. During such a time of prayer, the Lord spoke to my heart and told me that He wanted my family to be a part of Landmark and the work there. He also told me that my husband would rededicate his life to God at Landmark because it was Roger's childhood home church.

In April, my brother-in-law invited us to attend revival services. After the services, there was not a doubt in my mind that this was where God wanted my family. My daughters and I began attending. On the last Sunday in October, my husband came with us. He rededicated his life to the Lord that day.

In April, I had not understood why God was leading me away from the church family I had come to love. I was sad to leave my close friends there. Seven months later, I was able to proclaim that God had indeed worked for my good.

Roger Lambert

There is, therefore, no condemnation to those who are in Christ Jesus, who do not walk according to the flesh, but according to the Spirit. For the law of the Spirit of life in Christ Jesus has made me free from the law of sin and death.—Romans 8:1-2

There was a time when I went to church, but I got out of going even though my wife continued to go. To put it plainly, I had backslidden. There'd be days when I'd feel differently. For example, I'd feel really irritable, and then the next day I would feel maudlin. One might say I was experiencing extreme mood swings. This roller coaster ride would always lead to the thought or sense that I needed God in my life again. During this time my brother asked how I felt; he was referring to spiritual matters." I feel as though I have lost the most precious thing a person could ever have," I replied.

The emotional strain went on for some time until one day it occurred to me that someone might be praying for me. I had heard someone say once that if you want to make a backslider miserable, just pray for him. I knew how the Church of God people prayed for the sick, needy and lost by anointing and praying over handkerchiefs or cloths. I knew how the person requesting prayer for their loved one would go and attach the anointed handkerchief to the person's pillow or place it beneath their mattress—just some way to establish contact between the person they had prayed for and the handkerchief. With this in mind, I would search the house for such items. I vividly remember making the bed up and looking for anything that might resemble a prayer cloth. Once I inspected my pillow closely. I would go so far as to say that I looked straight at a prayer cloth but didn't see it. Years later, Debbie showed it to me.

About three years passed. During those years, my wife continued going to church. Every Sunday, she would get our daughters ready, and off they would go. I suppose her dedication and continual praying caused me to feel sorry for her. It wasn't until she began attending the Landmark Church of God that I decided to go with her. I went about three times and found the services uneventful. The morning of October 31, 1993, proved to be different.

The choir was singing a song in which the phrase "My heart sings His praise again. Hallelujah! Praise the Lamb" was repeated several times. I remembered how I used to raise my hands and with all my heart praise God. I thought how wonderful it would be if I could raise my hands, look toward heaven and with all my heart praise God again. This memory and desire began to prick my heart, which by the way, had become very cold and hard toward spiritual matters.

The straw that broke the camel's back came when my mother entered the pew and sat down beside me. I was totally surprised to see her. An understanding smile and a soft pat on my forearm was her only response. The music, the memories, and Mother being there really softened my heart. I began to cry; I couldn't stop. I believe at that moment God was adjusting my attitude. There I was, a full-grown man, crying like a baby; and I didn't have a handkerchief which I desperately needed. I felt embarrassed about my condition. Mother handed me a handkerchief, and I was truly grateful. In my soul I could hear the words, "Did I not say I would provide for all your needs?" I knew it must have been the Holy Spirit.The thought of God providing something as simple as a handkerchief touched my heart.

The church congregation was really beginning to worship God. I could sense His presence.The Holy Ghost began to speak through someone, and Pastor Williams gave the interpretation. I don't remember the whole message, but a part I'll never forget is, "I did not leave you.You left me." In my heart I knew the message must be for me. I prayed and asked God to forgive me for leaving Him and asked Jesus to come back into my life.

Pastor Williams began giving a general altar call. I didn't want to go. I tried to make some excuse and remember praying, "God, if you want me in the altar, you'll have to send someone to ask me." Ten seconds may have elapsed when I noticed a man approaching me. The gentleman asked, "Would you like to come to the altar and give your life to God?" I was enthralled and really amazed at the rapid response to my prayer. At first, I was reluctant to go, but I had made a deal with God. He had kept His end of the bargain. "I'd better keep my part," I thought.

At the altar I asked for God's forgiveness. I didn't feel any great emotion but just believed the scripture, Romans 8:1-2. The law of the Spirit of life in Christ Jesus had made me free from the law of sin and death. By January 1994, I was singing in the choir and still am today.

In December 1996, I dreamed about my mother. I dreamed we were in a large place filled with thousands of people. I didn't know if we were in church or in heaven, but I knew for certain that we were in God's presence. People were standing up and thanking God for healing them. Mother stood up holding a white handkerchief and said, "I want to thank God for healing me of throat cancer." I thought, "Momma hasn't been sick." The next day I felt disturbed about the dream and wondered what it meant. Three days later the meaning became apparent.

Friday evening Momma called and told me she was having problems breathing. I arrived at her home; her throat was swollen really big. Debbie drove us to the hospital. At the hospital, a doctor performed a tracheotomy on Momma. He informed me of a large mass in her throat that was making it difficult for her to breathe. The next day, Debbie and I were informed by a throat specialist that the mass was malignant. It was cancer! For the next eight months, Momma fought the dreadful disease. I remembered the dream of momma thanking God for healing her of throat cancer. The memory gave me peace.

Finally, the illness wore her down.The family sat beside Momma's bed as she was dying. Without warning one of the devil's imps began to mock me. I could sense a dark hateful evil thought flowing into my mind. A cold sarcastic voice seemed to scream into my ear, "I thought you had a dream where God healed your mom of throat cancer." For a few moments, I felt really beat up. "I'm not going to be defeated," I thought. I reached over and took momma's hand and said to her, "Momma, I want you to do something for me when you get over there. I want you to stand up and thank God for healing you of throat cancer."

I felt a boldness I hadn't felt before. The evil spirit was gone; a sweet, peaceful spirit was in the room with us now. A few moments later, Momma was gone. I believe God sent the dream to help sustain me during this difficult time. He gave me peace and strength to go through this valley.

The day I recommitted my life to the Lord, God took a tear, turned it into a river and washed away a hard heart. Now, I do not feel condemnation any longer. I am free from the law of sin. Walking according to the Spirit has given me a peace that passes all understanding and enables me to feel His strength in difficult times.

Three times God has used handkerchiefs in my life—the one Debbie sewed to my pillow during the time she prayed for God to soften my hard heart, the one Mother gave me the day I rededicated my life to Christ and the one Mom held in her hand in my dream. I've often wondered what all of these handkerchiefs mean. I wonder if the common thread in all of them might mean surrender. Debbie had surrendered her life to the Lord and prayed fervently for me to do the same. As I wept rivers of tears, Mother gave me a handkerchief as I surrendered my life to the Lord. Finally, as my mother completely surrendered her life, God healed her of throat cancer and took her to heaven to live in peace with Him. Now all of us are free in Christ Jesus.

B.J. Larson

And my God shall supply all your need according to His riches and glory. —Philippians 4: 19

Struggling with finances has been a lifelong thing for B.J. Larson. Throughout her life, she has stood on the promise of Philippians 4: 19 believing that God would, indeed, provide for her. She accepted Jesus Christ as her Lord and Savior and was baptized at the age of twelve. As she would learn, this was the most important decision that she would ever make.

When she was seventeen years old, her stepfather kicked her out of the house. Her mother did nothing to stop him. "God has literally been taking care of me since then," she said. "When he kicked me out, I had no money. A friend came and got me and took me to the home of Jack and Helen Laws to live. From this early age, I've depended upon God and His mercy to take care of me. Even though I have often not known where my next meal would come from or where I would lay my head, I have just always known that God would take care of me."

From this early age until now, B.J. says that her life has been like a roller coaster going up and down. Like seasons, there have been good and bad times. As Ecclesiastes 3: 1 says,

> To everything there is a season, a time for every purpose under heaven....

For example, she had a good job working in various positions with Eastern Airlines. Then the company went bankrupt leaving her with no insurance. Life seemed bleak. It looked as if there would never be enough money to pay the bills or buy groceries; yet God provided for every need including extra for some pleasures.

God's provision would often come so unexpectedly. "Once," she said, " I found $20.00 lying on the ground in a grocery store parking lot. One winter, I put my hands in the pocket of my coat where I found money I did not know I had. Without this money, I would have been unable to buy gas. Many times God has burdened people's hearts to give me money. One time, for example, a person gave me $100.00 and said to me, 'God told me to give you this.' I remarked, "But you don't know anything about me." Then I heard, 'But God told me to do this.'"Once again, God had provided for B.J. according to His riches.

Prior to the bankruptcy of Eastern Airlines, her husband had passed away leaving her with a child to raise. She received widow's benefits which enabled her to stay at home with her daughter, Nicole, until she began school. "We didn't have a lot," she said; "but it seemed that anytime we lacked money, someone would invite us for dinner. Often it would even be our favorite meal."

One time B.J. needed to have both of her hips replaced. She had no money, no insurance and no way to pay for the surgery. God opened a door through the North Carolina Rehabilitation Center which paid for her surgery (each hip cost $100,000), her rehabilitation and her retraining for a job to accommodate her limitations. When she couldn't drive, neighborhood people would take her to the doctor even though it meant driving from Cape Carteret to Raleigh. They would even buy her lunch.

The Center paid for her to attend Mitchell College and Lenoir Rhyne College to prepare for a teaching career. There were basics for which she still had to borrow money, however. Many times though when she needed money for items like textbooks, "Someone would just hand me money," she continued. They would say something like, 'I just thought you might need this.' Again, God was supplying our needs according to His riches through Christians He put in my path."

Recently, God provided the money for B.J. to pay off her $10,000 loan in a most unusual way. Her fifty-year-old stepfather who had kicked her out at the age of seventeen called her at 8:00 p.m. one evening and asked her to come to his home immediately. He told her that he had cancer. The doctors didn't think he would live long. He told her that he had decided to change his will. "God changed his mind," B.J. said. "He had originally left everything to his cousin.When he died, I learned that he had left me his house which I was able to sell, a car that I gave to Nicole who had just turned sixteen and $10,000 in cash."

In addition to the financial blessing, B.J. had the opportunity to ask her stepfather if he were saved. Before this time, she could have never asked him this question. She led him in prayer for assurance of his salvation. "All these years I had stood on God's promises," she shared. "I knew these blessings had come from God."

Jerry Long

Beloved, let us love one another for love is of God, and everyone who loves is born of God and knows God. He who does not love, does not know God, for God is love. —I John 4: 7-8

It is hard to believe that I grew up in the church, attended regularly and participated in many activities; but I was lost. Finally at age fifty-six, I had an encounter with God that changed my whole life. Church was a haven for me where people treated me nicely and made me feel as though I were important.

My home life was very difficult growing up with a father who constantly belittled me and often told me that I wasn't worth anything. Even later, he told my son, his grandson, those same things about me. Often he would run through the house yelling at me. "College boy, you think you are something." Later in life, my aunt, his sister, told me that I was the unexpected arrival that kept my Dad from fulfilling some of his goals—playing professional baseball, a career offered by the St. Louis Cardinals or going to North Carolina State University on an athletic scholarship. I never remember my mother being very happy or smiling.

Later I realized that my Dad was a reflection of his Dad. He would often talk about what he would find wrong that day as his father would walk out the road towards Dad's farm.

Life was hard, but my Dad never physically abused me. I grew up on a dairy farm, the only son, milking thirty-five to forty cows twice a day. Between the ages of thirteen and twenty-one, I got up at 3: 45 a. m. and handled a grade A dairy herd.

My mother and father could leave me for a week and head to the beach knowing everything was in good hands. With my help, he was able to get to the field early and stay late. This was necessary because he and I were the only workers on this farm. Even when I asked if he missed me while I was off in college, he just said that I did nothing. I don't regret all the hard work because it taught me the necessity of discipline in order to be successful in life.

I obtained a college degree in history and later a masters degree in counseling. For thirty-five years, I taught as a teacher or served as a high school counselor. During those years, I still participated in churches, usually teaching Sunday School classes or singing in the choir. I was even elected as a deacon. Early in my first church, I was baptized, urged on by Miss Erma, a wonderful junior teacher. In the process, the Lord provided for me a wonderful Christian wife who stuck with me through the difficult times that I had.

At a church I attended before my present church, I was astonished at the genuine love I felt from many of the members. Finally my attitude towards them was somewhat haughty because I thought that most of them were quite ignorant and backward. I felt that no one could be that happy. I started comparing what I had attained or achieved educationally with what they had obtained. To be successful, I was a driven compulsive worker on my job, but the Lord started chiseling away at my hardness.

He began with a truck driver at a men's retreat who gave me a Christ-like bear hug. I could feel the power of Christ in him, and it shook me. At a revival later that year, everyone seemed happy but me. I said, "Lord, where is my happiness?" He said, "You have no happiness because you don't know me." Yes, I knew Him from the Bible, but I didn't have a relationship with Him.

Three days later, the Holy Spirit was striving with me at a religious retreat in Gatlinburg sponsored by that church. With no music or stained glass windows, and even before the afternoon conference started, at 4:00 p.m. on January 27, 1996, I heard a voice saying, "NOW! NOW!" I looked around and didn't see anyone, but I knew the voice calling.

To the back of the room I moved and called two church leaders to come to a self-made altar where I poured myself out to the Lord. Heavy hot tears streamed down my face as I told the Lord that I came as a child to ask Him to forgive me of all my sins and to make Him Lord of my life.

The Lord said, "I want you to give your testimony before the evening assembly." I told the pastor that the Lord wanted me to give my testimony. Before I started, I asked the pastor to pray that what I would say would be hidden behind the cross and would glorify the Lord. For about fifteen minutes, the most awesome testimony flowed forth naturally.

My walk since has been focused on the Lord, and He has provided me with a different spirit of love. Even my father is loved by me because I am able to love him through Christ's love. One week before a stroke placed him in a nursing home, for the first time ever my Dad told me that he loved me. He was seventy-seven years old. On February 1, 2002, I lost my Dad whom I had learned to love dearly.

The Lord continues to bless me daily. He protected my wife and me in two car accidents in which neither my wife nor I were hurt despite a high speed on the interstate. The Lord's promises are yes and amen. Bless His holy name!

Jean B. Loudermilk

The effective fervent prayer of a righteous man availeth much.—James 5: 16

When I was a small child, at the age of ten months, I experienced a tragedy in my young life.

One afternoon, while my mother was sewing, she placed me in a baby swing. In those days, the swings were attached to the door frame of the bedroom and swung freely in the doorway. While my mother was busy sewing in another room, visitors arrived. My cousin, who was several years older than I, came bursting through the doorway pulling at my swing and letting it fly with me in it. My swing flew back and forth knocking me against the door frame and an iron bed which was nearby. I sustained severe head trauma which resulted in a stroke.

My parents rushed me to specialists who did not have good news for them. My grandmother, who was a Church of God prayer warrior, took me in her arms and prayed constantly for me. The stroke left me blind in one eye. I was unable to walk until the age of three. God was with me, however, and sustained me.

He is an ever-present help in times of trouble. He saw the frail, little body and heard the prayers of the righteous. The Bible tells us in James 5: 16 that the prayers of the righteous availeth much. I am a living testimony of that. When I could have lost my life, He held me up. In fact, Dr. J. Christine Dean said of my healing that I am a walking miracle.

God has been gracious unto me and has blessed me through the years. I am now seventy-five years of age, and God blessed me with a loving Christian husband for forty-four of those years. He has also blessed me with four wonderful children who adore me and are all Church of God members. Some are ministers and others are teachers and singers; but, not only that, I have lived to see my children's children minister in the Church of God. As for me, I was called of God to be a teacher in His church, and I taught Sunday School for many years.

God is still with me; and as Psalm 46: 1 says, He is "my very present help in trouble."

Bonnie Malboeuf

As thy days, so shall thy strength be. —Deuteronomy 33: 25

Bonnie Malboeuf has seen many twists and turns in her life. There have been times of great joy and happiness and times when she had no idea which way to turn next. In Deuteronomy 33: 25 in Moses' final blessing on Israel, Moses' prayer and blessing for Asher was that, "...As your days, so shall your strength be." He was blessing Asher saying that as long as you live may you have strength. Deuteronomy 28: 1-2 says,

> And it shall come to pass, if thou shall hearken diligently unto the voice of the Lord thy God, to observe and to do all his commandments which I command thee this day, that the Lord thy God will set thee on high above all nations on the earth: And all these blessings shall come

on thee and overtake thee, if thou shall hearken unto the voice of the Lord thy God.

These blessings of long life and strength were contingent upon Asher's submission to God's authority and commandments. Likewise, as Bonnie has continued to put her trust in God, He has continued to be faithful to her to provide strength for every trial and to bring joy out of despair.

The youngest of twelve children, Bonnie grew up on a farm with wonderful parents who took her to church. As a teenager she loved to sing *The Green Cathedral* in the Glee Club and as she walked in the woods. She especially liked to sing these words about getting close to God in nature:

I know a green cathedral, a hallowed forest shrine where leaves and love join hands above and arch your prayers and mine.

During an old-timey revival in a little country church, she heard a missionary sing, "Turn your eyes upon Jesus. Look on His wonderful face." Bonnie was twelve years when she responded to the altar call and accepted Jesus as her Lord and Savior. In an all day affair, she joined others who wore robes into the Catawba River to be baptized as they sang, *Shall We Gather at the River* and *It is Well With My Soul*. After her baptism, she would often go to the woods to spend time with God. Bonnie remembers saying, "Jesus, hold my hand," and He would hold her hand.

In 1950, at a Billy Graham Crusade in Charlotte, she recommitted her life to God as an adult."I went every night," she said."When Billy Graham gave the altar call, I couldn't wait to go up. I'll never forget Grady Wilson holding my hand and saying, 'All the angels in heaven are rejoicing.'"

At age sixteen, Bonnie had left her parents' home to marry a man she had met in school. "He was so handsome and so fair," she said. "I went straight from my parents taking care of me to living with him and his parents. They were so good to me, but he was moody and shy. He brought out the mother instinct in me. I was attracted to him, yet, I also felt sorry for him. He was very jealous of me, and I mistook his jealousy for love. I lost my innocence and girlhood."

When Bonnie's husband was abusive, she would cry and cry. One day when her husband left her, she found herself with three babies and one on the way. She had no job skills and certainly wasn't prepared to be a single parent. It seemed that all of her props had been knocked out from under her; yet, God had foreseen all of her trials. Prior to the breakup of her marriage, He had given Bonnie three dreams to sustain her through the times that were ahead.

One time she dreamed that she was in the country, and it was snowing in rainbow colors. She saw two glowing angels in the middle of the snow who looked as if they were glowing from the inside. Their feet were not on the ground but a few feet above the ground. It was as if all her senses were involved. "It felt as if a current were going through me. I could feel wonderful sensations and see so much beauty," she recalled. "I remember thinking if I'm asleep, I don't want to wake up."

Another time in a dream, Bonnie felt such comfort as she saw three angels walk away from her. One time she dreamed that she had just gotten her son Danny on the school bus when the sky began to become cloudy.The sky became so dark that she wondered if they were going to have a really bad storm. All of a sudden, she looked out the window and saw one pinpoint of light in the darkness. Then as she saw thousands of angels going back and forth to the light, she heard a voice say,"Woe unto the inhabitants of the earth." She immediately came out of bed and fell with her face on the floor. "It was such an awesome experience," she said. "If we could really fathom what it means that Jesus is coming, we wouldn't be able to stand on our feet. We believe it but don't really understand it."

When her husband left, Bonnie's mother came to stay with her and encouraged her saying, "God gave you these children. Trust Him. He'll help you." Still, it was a most difficult time, and she continued to get more and more depressed. In the midst of her discouragement, however, she wrote the first verses of her poem, *Testimony*:

What am I living for, why am I here?
Why does my life seem so empty and drear?
What can the reason be—is it all just a game?
I searched for an answer, but one never came.

I opened my eyes, and I looked all around.
I saw others shackled and tortured and bound
By the chains of envy and hatred and pride,
And seeking a refuge—but no place to hide.

I opened my ears, and I heard everywhere
The sighs of the lonely—the cries of despair,
The sobbing of children, the groaning of pain,
And seeking relief, but it seemed all in vain.
I opened my mind, and became more confused
At the way some folks prosper, and others abused.
The lies and the cheating, the homes torn apart,
And searching for peace with unrest in the heart.

With eyes dimmed by tears and naked and cold,
And ears that but echoed the pain in my soul,
This road was so rocky that I walked upon.
My load was so heavy I could not go on.

Bonnie wasn't prepared to do anything to make a living. Her husband's debts were hanging over her. One day as she was reading the Bible, she turned to I Corinthians 7:15 where she read:

> But if the unbeliever departs, let him depart; a brother or a sister is not under bondage in such cases. But God has called us to peace.

When she went to bed that night, God gave her such peace about letting her husband go and gave her the remaining verses of her poem, *Testimony:*

Then a Light shone on me—as if from Heaven,
And a voice said, "Ask, and it shall be given.
Knock, and I'll answer; seek and you'll find.
I'll give you Joy to your heart, and Peace to your mind.

"This is my Promise—hear, and believe.
It is in Giving that you shall receive.
Sometimes it may seem you have nothing at all,
But your Gift is recorded, no matter how small.
Remember the widow who gave her small part—

"Yet her gift was the greatest—that came from the heart.
Give bread to the hungry, a coat to the cold.
A prayer for the lonely, a smile to the old.
For the young, understanding turns night into day.

"To the lost, give a lamp to help them find their way.
The Key I have given, the rest you must do.
And unlock your Heart so my Love can shine through
Giving as you have received from above
The Heavenly Gifts of Peace and of Love."

I opened my Bible and began to relive
The Life of my Lord, and I cried, "God, forgive!"
I opened my Heart, and His answer came through.
"Take my life, Dear Jesus. I'll live it for you."

Many times God kept Bonnie from death."When my husband, Tommy played music in clubs; I knew better," she said, "but he was my husband, and I went with him. Tommy would drink and drive. I never felt good about the places we went. From a young age, Mother drummed Christian values and the Word into me. A person with that kind of teaching who does bad things will never feel good about his or her actions. Proverbs 22:6 says,

> Train up a child in the way he should go and when he is old, he will not depart from it.

Bonnie shared that her mother never raised her voice. "She'd get us together and say,' You must be good. God wants us all to be in heaven together.' Through the years, when there seemed to be no way to get through another day, He always made a way for me, and He will continue to do the same."

"For a long time," Bonnie said, "I couldn't pray for my husband. Then with God's help, I began to pray for God to spare him and to bless him. I know it would mean so much to the children to know that he was saved."

One of the most difficult times in Bonnie's life was when her mother died. Before she passed away, she had lost her sight from macular degeneration. "She was truly an amazing woman," Bonnie said. "Even after she lost her sight, she continued to crochet quilts for all of her children." In 1991, she began to have mini strokes. One day when Bonnie's sister could not wake their mother up, she took her to the hospital where she had a massive stroke the next morning.

When Bonnie arrived at the hospital, the nurse told her that her mother would not look like herself. When she advised Bonnie to stay and talk to her mother, Bonnie was confused. The nurse said that her mother might need comfort, but her mother was in a coma and hard of hearing. The nurse told her that even in a coma patients hear what people are saying in the room. "My mama was everything to me," Bonnie said. "Every time I'd say, Mama, we're o.k. I love you,' the monitor in her room would jump. She was hearing me. God was so good. He did not allow mama to suffer. She just went into a deep coma and didn't linger."

When Bonnie's mother died, it was as if every bad dream she could imagine had come true in one day. "Mama was my comfort," Bonnie said. "I didn't think I could go to the funeral home, but it seemed that I had been given a natural anesthetic. It was as if I were watching overhead while the body of my little momma was there. I thought, 'How am I doing this?' It was like someone whispered the words from I Corinthians 15:55 into my ear,

> O death where is thy sting? O grave where is thy victory?

I knew where my mother was. I know that's how I was able to get through that."

Later, Bonnie wrote a poem called "Rock Me To Sleep," that is a testimony to the bonds and strength of a mother's love:

> Tonight my thoughts drifted, as thoughts often do,
> Back to my childhood, when cares were so few.
> All play worn and weary, at night I would creep
> On Mama's knee, and she would rock me to sleep.

My days were all sunshine—my nights were sweet dreams.
And Mama was there when I called her, it seems.
And each little tear I shed, each fear so deep
Would all go away when she rocked me to sleep.

Sometimes when my load gets too heavy to bear,
And my heart is broken or filled with despair,
You may think me foolish, but I long just to creep
On her knee and hear once more, "I'll rock you to sleep."

Come to my dreams, Mama, say, "It's all right."
Brush every tear away—just for tonight.
Your child is so weary and would no longer weep
If once more, just once more, you'd rock me to sleep.

When Bonnie tried to find a church, she met another challenge. It seemed that everywhere she went people would give her a cold shoulder because she was divorced. "It hurt me so bad," she said. "I thought that I couldn't stand it, but something kept saying, 'Don't give up.' Denise Yount kept saying, 'I wish you'd come to Landmark.' I bit the bullet and came. Bea McGimsey met me at the door and gave me a big kiss. I felt like I'd come to a big family reunion. I thank God everyday for my church. As Andre Crouch says in his song, *Through It All*: I've learned to depend on God. I trust Jesus and depend on His Word as the truth I stand on. I know that neither God, nor Jesus, nor His Word will ever let me down.

As Bonnie says, "God has been good to me. He gave me four wonderful children with tender, soft hearts. I know exactly why each child was given to me. God knew that out of this broken marriage, heart and home my children would be blessings for me. God knew my heart. He gave me a baby so I could cope with what was coming. So many times I felt so alone. I know that God in His mercy and grace allowed me to see the angels in the dreams I had so that I would know that I was not alone. I have learned the truth of the words to Vern Jackson's song, *He Giveth More Grace*, when he says:

He giveth more grace when the burdens grow greater.

He sendeth more strength when the labors increase.
To added affliction He addeth His mercy.
To multiplied trials, His multiplied peace.

When we have exhausted our store of endurance,
When our strength has failed ere the day is half done,
When we reach the end of our hoarded resources,
Our Father's full giving has only begun.
His love has no limit,
His grace no measure;
His pow'r has no boundary known unto men.
For out of His infinite riches in Jesus,
He giveth and giveth and giveth again!

Bonnie continued, "Every day He's given me strength. I see people hurting and want to scream out, 'I know how to get past that. I go to bed and put it all in His hands. Some thieves steal physical things. Others steal your joy if you allow it. One day while I was working at the Tea Room at Iredell Memorial Hospital, I saw a lady who must have been in her eighties. I knew that she was having a hard time. I said, 'I' 11 be praying for you.' She took my hand and said, 'You remind me of my mother. You have such a sweet, gentle spirit.' I felt as if someone had just poured warm honey on me. Those things, you know, are gems God sends our way to strengthen us. People will never have such strength to draw from as adults unless they have the Word and Christian values put in them as children."

God has taught Bonnie that if she will trust and wait on Him, He will enable her to renew her strength, to run without growing weary, to walk without fainting and to mount up with wings like eagles (Isaiah 40:31). As Bonnie said in one of her poems,

I have forgotten how to cry—
But the sky remembers,
And sheds its healing tears
That experience and years
Have taught me to discipline, and dry.
The sky and I

Have an agreement about pain.
And I love rain.

Bonnie has also learned that it is not what happens to her that is important. It is how she allows it to affect her that is important. Although she can't control the way others treat her, she can control the way she reacts. She sees her life explained through the following words of Grant Colfax Tullar's poem, *The Weaving*, which Corrie Ten Boom often quoted:

My life is just a weaving
Between my God and me.
I do not choose the colors
He worketh endlessly.

Oft times He chooseth sorrow
And I in foolish pride
Forget He sees the upper
And the underside.

Not 'till the loom is silent
And the shuttles cease to fly,
Will God unroll the canvas
And explain the reason why

The dark threads are as needful
In the Master's loving Hand.
As the strands of gold and silver
In the canvas He has planned.

God has, indeed, been faithful to bless Bonnie with long days and with strength for each of them. She has known times of great joy and happiness as a child growing up in the country, as the mother of four children and as she spends time in the presence of the Lord. She has known loneliness, discouragement and sadness in the loss of her dear mother, in the breakup of her marriage and in times of financial difficulty as a single parent.

God gave her dreams to sustain her. He gave her grace and mercy to see her through the trials. Through the gift with words He had given her, she was able to express her feelings through her poetry in order to encourage herself and others. He gave her peace and joy in the midst of each storm and always made a way for her.

He taught her to give and to forgive and to have compassion for the hurting. She learned to trust in Jesus and to depend upon His Word. She learned to love the rain as it reminds her of the healing God has brought through her tears. She has learned to allow God to weave the fabric of her life and to trust Him, knowing that, as her days are so has her strength been, and so shall her strength be. What He's done for Bonnie, He'll do for you if you will just put your hand in the hand of the Savior.

Irene Mattingly

And we know that all things work together for good to those who love God, to those who are the called according to His purpose. —Romans 8: 28

There have been many situations in Irene Mattingly's life that God has used to build her faith and to teach her that, indeed, "all things work together for good to those who love God," and "who are...called according to His purpose."

"I am paralyzed; consequently, I have to depend on the Lord more than others," Irene said. "For example, if just one part of my wheelchair does not work properly, I can't do anything."

She was raised Baptist and did not know much about healing. In 1981 when she had the accident that paralyzed her, her mother and sister prayed believing that she would walk again. She hasn't walked yet but is still believing for a miracle.

While she was in the hospital, she began to get really close to the Lord; but when she left the hospital, she returned to her old lifestyle in Louisville, Kentucky. She went back to the world's way of living to drugs, bars, and drinking. Her children were nine and eleven years old. "It was easy to be in the world, even in a wheelchair, " Irene shared. "Friends would come and get me and bring me home. I didn't have to get up the next morning."

One day a lady came to her house and applied to be her attendant. When Irene asked her why she was no longer with the lady for whom she was working, the lady responded, "She went to be with the Lord." As Irene said, "That struck me. I thought, 'I want to be with the Lord.' I didn't hire her, yet she would come and get me for Bible study. God is so good. The first time she came for me, she couldn't lift me into her car. Just then a man stopped by who was willing to help. As I continued to go to Bible study, I began to learn about the laying on of hands.

I also realized that I could not continue to live with the man I'd met in the hospital. Although he was an alcoholic, he was everything to me—my attendant and my boyfriend. It took about four months for me to give everything up including pot, alcohol and my boyfriend; but I did. Then I began trying to be the person I knew I should be."

As Irene would listen to people in her Bible study share their testimonies, she began to believe for her healing. One day she found a lump in her breast. She had never had anyone lay hands on her before and said to those who were praying, "Don't pray for me to walk. I don't have faith for that. Just pray for the lump." One man said to her, "Faith comes by hearing and hearing by the Word of God" (Romans 10: 17). As soon as people prayed for her lump, Irene knew that it was gone. Of course, she could not check to be sure at church; but when she got home, the lump WAS gone! God worked this situation to good because now she had a testimony to share.

Three months after Irene found the lump, she developed kidney stones that were discovered when she had a physical. When she made an appointment to have them removed, she was told that she would have to stay overnight in the hospital. People had prayed with her. "I didn't take clothes to stay overnight with me," she said. "I just knew that the stones were gone.

After the doctor examined me again, he came back with a look of shock on his face. 'I don't know what you did,' he said,'but they're gone.'" Once again God had healed me and given me a testimony. Since then I have believed in the laying on of hands. Now I depend on God for everything. See, 'All things work together for good to those who love God.'"

In 1987, Irene needed transportation and began to pray for favor in this area. In Louisville, she had bus service to take her anywhere she needed to go; but once she moved to Statesville, she had no means of transportation. She didn't have people to help her; and when people did try to help, it was difficult to get the wheelchair in and out of their cars. She moved to Statesville in September of 1987; and on Thanksgiving Day, she was given a van.

God had laid it on someone's heart to give her a brand new van. She shared at a Bible study she had begun attending that she did not know how she was going to pay the taxes on the van. She said, "The devil would say don't pay your tithe; pay the taxes. I didn't agree. I don't believe God works that way." Once again, God laid it on the heart of a lady in the Bible study to give her a check. "Since then," Irene said, "God has continued to provide for all of the needs of the van." God had again worked things to good for Irene.

In 1994, Irene's kidneys were not functioning properly. She was in the hospital three times with I.V.s and very depressed. One night, she just did not want to go to the hospital again. The infection would not leave, and her fever was 102 degrees. A friend came over and prayed with her and believed with her for new kidneys. "Both of us in our spirits," Irene said, "could see the new kidneys going into my body. My temperature returned to normal and the infection left. The doctor couldn't believe it. He thought something was wrong with the machines because the documents showed such improvement in my kidneys. I didn't have to have antibiotics for five years after that." Again, God had provided healing for Irene.

"This year," Irene said, "the doctors at the Veteran's Hospital (V.A. Hospital) in Augusta, Georgia found bladder cancer. They gave me the option of chemotherapy or surgery to remove the bladder. I chose surgery. The Lord had to sustain me because the nurses had to call the Code team four times. I got a staph infection. For six weeks, I was unable to eat or drink. I lost forty-five pounds. I was in intensive care for three weeks. They almost lost me several times. I was told that one morning at church Pastor Hudson just stopped the worship service to have prayer for me. God honored that prayer because I was able to be taken off the respirator and started to recover. I was taken out of intensive care. The power of prayer is so powerful. I know that friends of mine had been fasting and praying. So many people prayed."

When Irene's doctor performed surgery, he forgot to hook her kidneys back up. She knew something was wrong because she knew her body. She was so sick. The doctors would tell the nurses to give her morphine but would not try to find out what was wrong. Poison was backing up in her system. Finally, the doctors took X-rays. When they saw that the kidneys were not hooked up, they took her to emergency surgery. The surgery lasted eight hours. When the surgeon explained the mistake to her, he just shrugged his shoulders and said, "That happens."

As Irene said, "It was very difficult to deal with the pain. It was even more difficult to deal with a doctor who did not seem to care. I just did not think that I could ever forgive what he had done to me; but finally, as I was watching Christian T.V. one evening, the Holy Spirit showed me that I had to forgive. I cried out to God, 'Please help me to forgive! I don't know how!' Because the Holy Spirit helped me, I did forgive the doctors and nurses. Such a burden lifted off of me. I had not realized that I was so clogged up with bitterness and anger. Forgiveness really frees a person."

As Irene believes, "God has brought so much good out of all of these situations in my life. He uses me to minister to others in the V.A. Hospital. He has given me a best friend who is paralyzed as a prayer partner. I have learned that I can minister even in a wheelchair. God has given me the opportunity to witness of His power to my family, especially to my brothers. As they have seen my tears and what God has done, I have begun to understand God's purpose for the things that have happened in my life."

Irene remembered, "One time my grandson was looking for his momma to come pick him up at my house. As he kept looking out the window for her, I thought that we should be like that with the Lord—always looking for Him and for His purpose in our lives. In my life all things have worked together for good for me because I do love the Lord and am called, "according to His purpose," as Romans 8:28 says.

Bea McGimsey

Be anxious for nothing, but in everything by prayer and supplication, with thanksgiving, let your requests be made known to God.—Philippians 4: 6

A number of years ago, I was very concerned about the health of my husband Donald. He was going for tests because the doctor suspected cancer. There was a history of cancer in his family. I had been praying and crying out to God, "God, you know he's all I've got."

That Sunday I went to church and sat in my usual place on the left up near the front. At that time there was no screen for the choruses. I was listening to the choir where Donald was singing and looking at the stained glass window when suddenly it seemed as if I were seeing smoke that looked like a cloud floating there. I rubbed my eyes thinking that I must be tired and not seeing correctly, but the cloud did not go away.

As I prayed, God showed me that this was the Holy Spirit like the cloud that God sent to guide the Israelites. Suddenly, I was filled with peace and knew that everything would be all right. Philippians 4: 6 says,

> Be anxious for nothing, but in everything by prayer and supplication, with thanksgiving, let your requests be made known to God.

I was anxious; but as I prayed and let my request be made known to God He answered me in such a special way and filled me with His peace. Today I am praising Him and thanking Him because He did also take care of Donald.

Donald McGimsey

Confess your trespasses to one another, and pray for one another that you may be healed. The effective fervent prayer of a righteous man avails much.—James 5: 16

In 1992, when Reverend Eddie Williams was the pastor at Landmark Church of God, I got up one Sunday morning to get ready to go to church and just didn't feel good. My wife, Bea, saw me looking out our bedroom window instead of getting ready for church and realized that something was wrong. She took me to the emergency room where doctors examined me. I thought it was just a routine exam.

There was a family with a little boy in the room next to me. Bea and I could hear the doctors asking if they could move them. "This guy's getting ready to have a heart attack," they told them. I saw the doctors bring in a defibrillator. Dr. Lai examined me and said that my heart was not beating right. The doctors took me up to a room where Bea and I prayed. Bea went home to get some things I needed for a hospital stay. On the way home, she stopped by the church and told Pastor Williams. He had the church pray during the service.

Dr. Lai arranged for me to have a heart catheterization on Tuesday. On Sunday night, Jack Moore came to the hospital. He put his hand on my chest and prayed for me. The nurse asked me if Jack were my pastor. I said, "No, just a good friend." When I asked why she wanted to know, she said that she was watching the heart monitor and saw my heart beat become regular while Jack was praying. Dr. Lai said that it was just the medicine. He still thought that I had blockages in my arteries.

When Dr. Lai did the heart catheterization on Tuesday, he found nothing wrong. He said that it was probably just the medication working. After six hours he discharged me from the hospital. Dr. Lai can attribute the healing to the medicine if he chooses, but Bea and I know where the healing came from. Dr. Jesus healed me!

When I had the catheterization done, Brenda Coley came and stayed all afternoon with us; and she prayed. What a blessing it is to have a church family with friends who are there when you need them. That is something none of us should ever take for granted.

This miracle in my life was not the first time Bea and I had witnessed the power of prayer. There were so many things that happened while I was in the army in Korea. I am sure that had I not had a praying wife at home, I would probably be dead now. We have learned that, indeed, the "effective, fervent prayer of a righteous man avails much" (James 5: 16).

Daniel McGinnis

The steps of a righteous man are ordered of the Lord. —Psalm 37: 23

Since I was born, my parents have always taken me to church. I have always gone to Sunday School and Children's Church. I went to my uncle's church where he was the pastor. There I went to the altar and gave my heart to God. I was five years old. At that time I really didn't understand what it all meant; but I knew I loved Jesus, and He was real. God started to move in my life when I was eleven. I came from a Christian heritage. My grandfather was a Church of God minister. I remember him preaching and singing about God. He really had an influence in my life. He was always happy and whistling.

One thing that happened to me that made an impact on my life was when I was in the seventh grade. I started having these blackout spells where my eyesight would go. I would blackout for a few seconds; then I'd be o.k. The doctor said I was having some type of seizures because this showed up on the test. We prayed, and my parents and I trusted God. I was a little scared because I didn't know what was going to happen. My parents seemed to be calm believing that God would help us, and He did. One day I realized I hadn't had another seizure, and have had none since. I KNOW God healed me!

Phill Greene had a good influence on me, and I learned a lot from him. I was sad he had to leave, but I understood. God had a work for him in Alaska. In a service two weeks after Pastor Tracy came, I received the Baptism of the Holy Spirit. After that, I went to youth camp. That has made a big impact on my life. It was there that God spoke to me and told me He had a calling on my life but that He would let me know more about it later. Then during the 2000 Camp He did. He told me to be a youth pastor, so I'm trusting Him about what's next. Psalm 37:23 says, "The steps of a righteous man are ordered of the Lord." I know that He will continue to direct my steps and my life.

My youth group has been my rock and support. We not only have a good time together, but we share the love of God. I'm looking forward to see what else God has for me.

Bobby Messick

For God so loved the world that He gave His only begotten Son that whoever believes in Him should not perish but have everlasting life.—John 3: 16

John 3: 16 represents my life because if it had not been for Jesus, I would not be here today. Instead, I'd probably in a cemetery somewhere. The kind of life I was living when I was between twelve and fourteen years old was a life on the streets. I was called the black sheep of my family. My three sisters and mother were Christians who were living good lives. My dad had been saved but had gone back on the Lord.

I was fighting and struggling with God. I wanted no part of God. I wanted to drink. I looked for trouble. I think my middle name should have been trouble instead of Paul. I got in with the wrong crowd. I was easily coerced, but my mom would pray. I would hear my mother saying, "Protect Bobby wherever he's at." I didn't want to hear about God.

My sister Shirley had friends—Dorothy and June McDaniels. They invited her to church. Dad let her go once. He didn't let the girls go anywhere much. Shirley invited Pastor Black and his family to visit. When they came, I hid. I'd been around church people. I just didn't want any part of it. I was peeping out, however, while Brother Black was talking to Dad. "Yes, I've got a son, Bobby," Dad said.

My mother and Brother Black walked into the den where I was, and Brother Black invited me to church. I thought, "Right!" I was afraid of church and what it meant. I knew it'd be the end of my fun. Dad told Shirley she could go to church if she took me. He knew I was hardcore and wouldn't go, but she begged me, and she cried. After a while, I said I'd go just to shut her up. We went on a Wednesday night. I thought, "It's not really so bad."

The next week there was a revival with J.H. Baity. We called him Robot. He was a tall, huge guy who wore big, black wide rim glasses. I was hanging out with the other teens until we had to go in. It was cold outside and was spitting snow. He preached on the blood of Jesus Christ that was shed on the cross for my sins. It seemed as if he looked only at me every time he mentioned the blood. I felt fidgety.

Then he turned the service over to Pastor Black. He asked for people who wanted to accept Jesus as their Savior to come to the altar. He asked everyone to pray. He said, "I believe there's someone here who needs to give his heart to Jesus. Pastor Black came to me and said, "Bobby would you like to come tonight." I said, "No." He stopped and came back to me. He said the Lord told him to come back and ask me a second time. He was almost to the pulpit when he came back again. He pulled me into the aisle and said, "This way goes to hell. The other way goes to heaven.

I think the pew I was sitting in must be indented to this day with my knuckle marks. Finally, I decided to give Jesus a try. At the altar tears were streaming down my face. I was amazed at the change that came in my heart. I had a hunger to know Him. One night I received the Baptism of the Holy Ghost. It was after midnight and snowing. Only the Blacks and my sister were with me. I felt weak-kneed and was afraid Dad would be angry because it was late. When I got home, he was asleep. Mom was excited.

Life was rough at times. Then the time came when I was to get married. I had backed off some from the church. My wife, Rose, was a Christian. I knew she was leading a good life. I was getting ready to go into the military. In the end I didn't go. I was going into the military to get away from God. I didn't know that I couldn't get away from God. God touched my life again.

I met Rose at a horse show. I was smoking cigarettes when I saw Rose. I put them in my pocket so she wouldn't see them. When I put them in my pocket, I thought the fire was put out; but they burned my skin. Then I realized the fire was not out and hit my pocket to put it out. I passed this off with an excuse.

Rose and I dated for a year. We got married at Southview Baptist Church. Brother Black prayed a special prayer that we'd walk hand in hand to the sunset together. Every year we look at the video of our wedding, and we remind each other of this prayer. Prior to our wedding, Rose had asked Pastor Black to pray a prayer that would last for eternity. We've said to our kids continually that one day we'll all walk hand in hand to the sunset meaning the Rapture. We believe that Jesus could come at anytime. We often hear our kids say to their friends, "When we have children, we'll walk hand in hand to the sunset together."

Every one of our children was an answer to prayer. Rose had difficulty getting pregnant. We prayed about the names of our children. When it was Israel's time to be born, we weren't expecting a boy. I'd had a dream three years earlier about a boy. In the dream I was told to name him Israel, "For he shall save his people from his sins." The doctors, however, kept telling us that the heartbeat sounded like a girl. Rose had also had a dream several years earlier that we'd have a boy who would be bald and look just like a girl. In the dream everybody said, "He looks too pretty to be a boy." It happened just that way. Today Israel has an influence on people. I think that when he gets his life together, he will win many to the Lord. We're trusting God for him.

When Michael was born, I had heard the name of the artist, Michaelangelo and liked it. We took his name from the artist's name. The doctors had told us that Michaela would be a boy, but she was a girl. We had another name picked out for her, but two weeks before her birth we saw the name Michaela and liked it; so we changed it.

God has intervened in my life and protected me and those I care about numerous times. One time I was working at Kewanee. The job was stressful because everything was being changed at work. One day I was having to move shelves.When Rose got up that morning to get coffee, she wanted to pray. As she began to pray, the Holy Spirit began to pray through her in tongues. When I came home from work, I told her that shelves had fallen on a woman and cracked her skull. She was hurt but was alive and would be o.k. God had protected me from this accident by having my manager ask me to drive a truck just before this happened.

Another time I was working with my uncle Bill Moose on the garbage truck. We had been talking about the Bible. I had asked him what he thought about death. He said that if he knew he was going to die at a certain time and place, he'd go three or four blocks out of the way to bypass the area and to keep from dying there. At the time he was on high blood pressure medicine. He had quit taking his medicine because his doctor had said he was better. I asked him how he was. We had worked together for fifteen years.

That afternoon it was cold. As we were going down Broad Street, God brought the thought to me, "What would you do if he had a heart attack." I thought, "The main thing would be to stop the truck." He did have a heart attack and fell down on the accelerator. He ran up on a curb. I thought he was mad at me for some reason because he hadn't spoken to me. I jumped off the truck and saw him slumped over. I thought, "God what am I going to do?"

I jumped off the truck and stopped the oncoming cars and van to avoid an accident. At the curb, I jumped head first through the window on broken glass and grabbed the air lock. I was still trying to reach the brake when we headed toward an oak tree. We were headed toward the house where the mayor and city council were meeting. They ran out of the office. The truck stopped two feet from the house. My uncle was still breathing. They called 911; but because of the snow, the ambulance couldn't get there quickly. He'd stopped breathing when a fireman saw the accident and gave

CPR. When the ambulance did arrive, the paramedics shocked his heart until it began beating and took him to the hospital.

I drove the truck back to the city garage and went home. I got in my car and went to the hospital. I called my mother. My uncle lived two months in a coma. I was talking to another uncle, a preacher, about how the Lord took care of me during the accident. I said that I didn't know if Uncle Bill was a Christian or not. I asked the Lord to give us a sign that he was hearing us and was saved. All of a sudden without speaking, my uncle sat up in bed and lay back down. Up until that point, he hadn't moved.

While Uncle Bill was in the emergency room, my dad came in and asked, "How is Uncle Bill?" I said, "He's in a coma." My dad said, "I used to say I'd give my heart to the Lord on my death bed. I may have made a mistake." We'd prayed for Dad. We planted a seed. He hadn't lived for the Lord for thirty-five years. A couple of weeks later in Brother Black's Sunday School class, he gave his heart to the Lord.

Later Dad broke his hip, and we had to put him in a nursing home. One day my sister Cookie had been to see him and said to me that Dad didn't know anyone. One time Dad grabbed Rose and said, "Can't you see? Isn't it beautiful?" Then he said to me, "Bobby, can't you see? Look how beautiful it is! Look at the flowers. Look at the streets of gold. Look at the water. How beautiful it is! Look at all the people coming. There was a smile on his face.

Then his tone changed. He said, "Last night there was a storm. I was so scared. I started to call the nurse. Then Jesus came to my bed and said, "Don't be afraid. I'll be with you to the end." We prayed with Dad, and he started speaking in tongues. He began singing in the spirit, "I'm going home. I'm going home." Dad had never spoken in tongues before, and he never could sing. I knew I could believe what Dad was telling me because my Dad had never lied to me.

I told Pastor Williams this story and asked, "What do you think about Dad going home?" He said that God had told him that I was the reason Dad was staying here. He said, "I know it's hard, but you need to tell your Dad that it's o.k. to go home." I did that, and Dad smiled. Such a peace came over him. The day before Christmas

Eve, I had Daddy on my mind. We were going to take his gift to him early, but he died. He breathed a deep breath and was gone. His passing was so easy and peaceful. Daddy had made me promise I wouldn't cry when he died. We had knocked heads together when I was young; but as I got older, we became closer.

One night I had a dream that Dad was leading me in a building. I know God was letting me know that Dad's o.k. One time I said, "God, I'd like a sign that Dad's o.k. I walked outside the church fellowship hall and saw a balloon come down outside. The balloon just sat on the pavement not moving. On the balloon there were smiling animals and a message, "Having a great time. Wish you were here." I know God answered my prayer letting me know that Dad was o.k.

Through the years God has taken care of our family. If it hadn't been for a praying mother and a pastor with determination I wouldn't be here. I praise God that God did love the world enough to send His son to die for me. I know that because I have placed my faith in Him, I do have eternal life and will one day see my Dad again. What a blessed hope!

Rose Messick

If we confess our sins, He is faithful and just to forgive us our sins, and to cleanse us from all unrighteousness.—I John 1: 9

From the time God gave Rose Messick I John 1: 9 as a scripture for her to stand on, her life has not been the same. As a little child, Rose remembers that even though her family didn't go to church, they somehow knew that there was a God. When she was twelve years old, she went to a tent revival with her mother, brother and sister. (Her father would never go to any kind of church service.)

She remembers, "I wanted to go forward when the altar time came, but I was afraid of getting lost in the crowd. I raised my hand. I had no intention of going forward, but someone behind me touched my shoulder. I went forward like an automatic reflex to accept Jesus as my Lord and Savior.

"The Lord impressed the scripture, I John l: 9 on my heart. As I confessed my sins, I found that, indeed, He was faithful to forgive me of my sins and to cleanse me from all unrighteousness. After I was saved, I was given a pamphlet and materials explaining salvation. People prayed with me and tried to explain salvation to me. I took the pamphlets and went home. I put them in my Bible and started trying to live the best life I could."

Rose continued, "Things seemed to be very, very hard. It was almost like one person was trying to teach me to do good while another was trying to teach me to do bad things. Things got so bad that I was thinking of committing suicide.

"As I was standing in my room thinking of how I was going to take my life—knife, drugs or a gun—I began to feel like there were two beings over or behind my left shoulder and one over my right shoulder. In my left ear, it seemed as if they were telling me, 'Go ahead and take your life. Nobody loves you or cares about you. End it all. You'll be better off.'

"Then I began to notice so strongly in my right ear someone telling me, 'They do love you. What does God's Word say about this?' I felt so strongly that someone was there that I turned to see who was there. Then I decided to see what God's Word did say about suicide.

"I believe that the being on the right side was God's angel that overpowered two of the devil's demonic beings and saved my life. That's when my real relationship with God began. I began to pray and ask God to help me understand His Word because I was a poor reader. Sometimes I would read the same verses three or four times and pray for understanding. During that time, I learned that God does answer prayer. He took away the horrible nightmare dreams that I'd been having."

Many times when Rose has gone through difficult times in her life, she has stood on the promise of I John l: 9 remembering His faithfulness. This verse especially helped her when she lost her baby. She began to feel guilty and blame herself for what had happened.

Finally, after a long time and during a study of of Kay Arthur's book, Lord Heal My Hurts, in Freida Gilberg's class, she began to understand that she was going through a spiritual battle. She recognized Satan as the enemy who was trying to cause her to feel guilty. Rose continued to quote this scripture when the enemy would attack her so strongly. God delivered her from these feelings of guilt as she stood on His promise.

One time as a child before Rose was saved, her family was in a very dangerous situation. She prayed from her heart for God to keep them safe. Obviously, God heard her cry. Her family had gone to Ohio to visit an uncle who was dying from cancer. On their way home, they crossed a very long bridge that began to shake as they drove across it.

Rose described the experience this way: "It was so scary that I couldn't talk. Even though I didn't know God, I was praying in my own heart for God to keep us safe. My sister would say something to mom about the shaking. I'd tell her to be quiet. I didn't want it to happen. We got across the bridge safely and came home. When we got home, we heard on the radio that the bridge had fallen in shortly after we crossed it. I became very emotional and began to shake." In Matthew 19: 14, Jesus said,

> Suffer little children, and forbid them not, to come unto me: for of such is the kingdom of heaven.

As Rose learned, God is especially attentive to the cries of children as He draws them unto Himself. Rose saw God work powerfully in her life shortly after she and Bobby were married. It was her first year in the Church of God. She was just beginning to learn about divine healing and the teachings of the church.

She said, "I wanted to live for the Lord and to do what He wanted me to do. I was hungry to learn. On one occasion, I had a terribly bad cold. It was the worst I'd ever had. Of course, there's no cure for a cold. I was so upset because my newborn nephew was in the hospital, and I couldn't go to visit him.

"On Wednesday night at church, the teacher had taught that we must pray until we get an answer. He said that we must continue to go through doors until we get where we need to be. He said that we must not give up.

"One day as I was reading the Bible and praying that God would heal me, I remembered what my teacher had taught. I went back to my knees and prayed every Bible story I could think of from the beginning of the Bible to the end. Determined not to stop praying until I received an answer, I prayed everything I knew to pray. Suddenly, I felt a chill start at the back of my neck and go down my spine. I blew my nose one time, and the cold was gone. Thank you Lord for the divine healings. It was a time when I knew that I knew that I knew God had touched me. Nobody could take that away from me."

Another time in Rose's life, she was wrestling with hatred and anger toward her father. My sister-in-law, Shirley gave me Philippians 4: 8:

> Finally, brethren, whatsoever things are true, whatsoever things are honest, whatsoever things are just, whatsoever things are pure, whatsoever things are lovely, whatsoever things are of good report; if there be any virtue, and if there be any praise, think on these things.

As she prayed, she began to realize that although her earthly father was rarely there for her when she needed him, her heavenly Father was always there for her. As she recalls, "This verse has helped me in many situations. I'd learn to see the good instead of the bad in things that would happen.

"Then my dad got saved. I can remember that just before he got saved, somebody took the time to continually go just to be with him and to teach him and be by his side. Shortly after I learned that he'd gotten saved, my sister got saved. I will never forget and shall always be grateful for one preacher who continually took time to go to my dad's house to have Bible study with him and to explain things to him."

When Rose was saved, she had no idea of how meaningful I John 1: 9 would be in her life. As she confessed her sins, God was faithful to forgive her and to cleanse her of all unrighteousness. As she continued to pray and to fellowship with the Lord, God honored her prayers and saved many of her family. Now I John l: 9 has meaning for the rest of her family.

As a small child, God heard the cry of her heart for him to save her family from a disastrous accident on a shaking bridge. He not only saved all of their physical lives, but also their souls. As Rose has continued to study the Word and to commune with the Lord, He has also taught her the power of the words in Philippians 4: 8.

He has taught her to forgive and to overcome anger, hate and bitterness so that her life can be a living testimony to God's love—a love that helps his people daily to live lives built on a solid foundation of truth, honesty, justice, purity, loveliness, good reports, virtue, and praise. What God has done in her life, He'll do for anyone who will take the time to seek Him!

Jack Moore

O Lord, I am oppressed; undertake for me! What shall I say? He has both spoken to me, and he Himself has done it. I shall walk carefully all my years in the bitterness of my soul. O Lord by these things is the life of my spirit; so You will restore me and make me live. Indeed it was for my own peace that I had great bitterness; but You have delivered my soul from the pit of corruption. For You have cast all my sins behind my back. —Isaiah 38: 14-17

Jack Moore began his testimony of God's power of deliverance in his life by recalling how many years these issues had plagued him—"a long way back—1984." The following are his words: "I had been serving in the capacity of Assistant Supervisor in the Health Department. Our supervisor retired around the first of May.

Everybody thought the Director would move me up to that position, but he didn't. He brought in a man who had hardly three years experience. I had thirteen. He had no experience in a supervisory capacity. He was just a line person. The Director put him over me and the rest of the department.

"I never got over that. I prayed from time to time. I got used to it except when he'd criticize my work or whatever. Sometimes I'd visualize or fantasize hurting him physically or mentally to retaliate. The bitterness and unforgiveness I had are not good attributes for a Christian, so I'd hide my feelings. This problem persisted for sixteen years.

"There was a black pastor from Charlotte, Larry Jackson, who spoke at a Promise Keepers Rally I attended. He said the Lord would rid our houses of our enemies, but not our friends. If we had allowed enemies such as false pride, bitterness, unforgiveness or lustful thoughts to become our friends, God would not cast these "friends" out without our permission.

"He reminded us that we often have friends such as these who are not good friends. It's just like some of our personal friends who have bad habits. We don't like their bad habits, but we still keep them as our friends because we don't feel that we can treat them as enemies even when we know that their company is not good for us. He said that if, however, we will treat false pride, bitterness, unforgiveness or lustful thoughts as deadly enemies, the Lord will get rid of them; and He did when I laid it all on the altar.

"The next week, I talked with my supervisor. We'd recently had some controversy over leave time that I felt I'd been unjustly charged with. When I went in, he probably expected an uncomfortable confrontation. I told him that after all this time, I was getting ready to leave and retire. I said that I'd like this to finally be over. I asked him to forgive me for anything I'd done against him and for the feelings I'd harbored against him. I put my hand out to shake his, but with tears in his eyes, he said, 'May I have a hug instead?' We hugged each other. Now my burdens were lifted. I'm free! God took away the enemies of pride, bitterness and unforgiveness. Now I feel like He can use me to be an instrument of peace and forgiveness."

Just as God's promise of healing brought joyful relief and a totally revived spirit to King Hezekiah according to Isaiah 38:17, God's deliverance has filled Jack's life with forgiveness, peace and joy. God has restored him and made him live afresh with a renewed spirit.

What a Change in My Life

I

I wandered along the downward road in sin and darkness,
My soul was lost and I was sinking in despair;
But kneeling one day in humble prayer down at the altar,
My life was changed and I've had joy beyond compare.

II

The storms may come and winds may blow but I'll not waver,
The captain is Jesus, He's the Master of the sea;
No longer I sail in doubt for I know where I am going,
My life was changed and I've had joy beyond compare.

III

One day we shall see the Lord return in clouds of glory,
The graves will burst and all the dead in Christ will rise;
My body will then be made like my Lord's glorious body,
And with the angels we'll go sailing thru the skies.

Annette Moose

Therefore if any man be in Christ, he is a new creature; old things are passed away; behold, all things are become new.
—II Corinthians 5: 17

What a Change in My Life

God gave me back my tomorrow because before I was saved, I did not want to see tomorrow come.

When I was two years old, God answered my prayers and my life was spared. My mother had five children. My younger brother was sick. He had bronchitis, and my mother had a pot of boiling water for him. I don't remember if it was on the floor or the table. She had it for him to help him breathe. My older sister and I were playing around, and my foot got tangled up in the cord. That hot water poured over on the left side of my body. I had third degree burns on my chest and upper legs.

I went into the hospital for about thirty days. The doctors told my mom that they didn't think I was going to make it because I had gotten pneumonia. But God had a plan. My mother called her prayer partners together, and the prayers were answered. My life was spared.

I always remember growing up as a child that I had a praying mother. My mother was spirit-filled, and my dad was the total opposite. He said it was foolishness. He would not let my mother take us children to church. On occasions when he would be out of town working, she would take us. I remember going to Fifth Street and Troutman Church of God the few times we got to go, but at home my mother put the Word into us. She read the Bible to us and taught us a lot.

My dad had said that when my younger brother turned sixteen, he would leave. He did. As children we all went our separate ways.

My mother eventually met Roch and remarried and moved to Kings Mountain. I didn't really understand what she had to make her so strong in the Lord, but I knew it was real.

Years later, my two older sisters were saved. Deep in my heart, I knew that my time would come, but I continued to be stubborn and to go my own way.

I married Darrell and had Lindsey two years later. I wanted to bring her up knowing about God, and Landmark Academy had just opened. I wanted to put her in the pre-school part-time to prepare her for school. I started coming here on Sunday mornings in order to bring her. I continued to come. I felt that I was doing something good because I had my child in church. Darrell wouldn't come with me, but he urged me to come. He wanted Lindsey in church.

I remember so many times trying to hold back the tears and swallow that lump in my throat. My mother and sisters were praying, and I was running from God. I felt that I had to wait on Darrell to get saved with me. I was living two miserable lives. On the outside things were great, and on the inside I was the most miserable person on this planet.

Six years later Krystal was born. I had two beautiful children, but inside I had nothing. I had no peace and no joy in my soul. I believed in God, but I didn't know Him. My mother was always asking me, "Annette, are you saved? Do you not know?" I would tell her, "No, I don't guess I am."

But one day I will never forget, my Lindsey looked up at me and said, "Momma, are you saved?" It struck my heart. I couldn't be untruthful to my child. I said, "No, honey, I'm not." She looked at me, and she said, "But momma, that makes me sad." I really was in trouble then.

Three years ago on February 16, 1997, Darrell suggested that the girls and I go to my mother's and spend the night. I knew that if I went, I'd have to go to church and to Sunday School because I knew my mother went. Sunday School was some place I had never been. We went, and I thank God we did. Little did I know what he had in store for me.

The Sunday School lesson was about a place called "hell"—some place I had heard about but not thought about. Fear gripped my heart. I knew that I had to get out of there and get to the altar. The time had come. I had come to the end of the road. I could run no longer. I knew that it was time to run to Jesus.

I sat there on the pew, and weakness came over my entire body. I felt as though I was going to pass out, if I didn't get to the altar. I heard God say loud and clear to me, "Who are you going to serve?" I said to Him, "I surrender my life to you. Take it, Lord." I looked over at my mother, and I grabbed her hand, and I said, "Will you go with me?" I fell at Jesus' feet, and I heard Him say, "Annette, I love you. Give it all to me." I felt the load that I had carried all those years come off of me. As I stood up, I knew that I was a totally new creature of Christ.

I came home busting to tell Darrell. I looked at him, and I said, "I have something to tell you." He said, "I already know." No one had called him and told him. He just knew. He continues to be very supportive of me, but he's not ready. He says, "I'm proud of you, but I'm o.k." Deep in my heart, I know where Darrell's at. God knows, and He has a plan. I know He will give me the desires of my heart and save my family.

I compromised with this world for a lot of years. I wasted a lot of years, but I know it's never too late. I am no longer going to compromise. I am a new creature in Christ Jesus. I have new desires, and I long to be with Him. I'm growing every day. I now have a church family which I dearly love. I thank you all for your prayers and for the love which you have shown me and my family. What I have now is priceless. I have so much to be thankful for.

A couple of months after I was saved, I knew there was more. I needed what my mother had, and in April I received the Baptism of the Holy Ghost. That made it complete. It freed me from this world. Now I understand what mother had. God does answer prayer.

Barbara Myers

Forever, O Lord, Your word is settled in heaven. Your faithfulness endures to all generations.—Psalm 119: 89-90

I was raised in Gastonia, North Carolina, in a family with four sisters and one brother: Donald, Virginia, Helen, Laura and my twin, Betty. My dad taught us to go to church, and I was saved when I was ten years old. In 1952, I married James Myers with whom I had four children three of whom are married: Jimmy and his wife, Linda; Shelia and her husband, Paul Cook; Michelle and her husband, Tim Dehart; and Jerry. When we were dating, James always went to my Baptist church with me; but when we got married, James insisted on going to the Church of God.

At first, since we were of different denominations, we tried staying home from church; but it didn't work. I decided to go with James to the Church of God. It took me about two years to really understand the teachings of the Church of God. In 1956, in a tent revival I received the Baptism of the Holy Ghost.

We were living in Salisbury, North Carolina, when our son Jimmy was born. Our faith was severely tested when, as a baby, his stomach valve closed up. Everything he ate came back up. The doctor said that he would have to operate and that Jimmy might have a fifty/fifty chance of living through the surgery. It seemed that everyone thought that he would die, but we had people praying. I knew that God could heal him, and God did heal him.

The doctor was amazed, but we weren't surprised. We knew that we served a big God. Jimmy's healing was truly a big miracle in our lives. I know that God saved Jimmy's life for a reason. It was hard to see my baby suffer, but God brought me through. I have learned that His "Word is settled in heaven. (His) faithfulness endures to all generations" (Psalm 119: 89-90).

I have stood and prayed for all my children because I know that as I John 4: 4 says, He that is in me "is greater than he who is in the world." We have to claim our children. As I have stood, I have seen God do a mighty work in the lives of my children.

A number of years ago, I faced cancer which I knew could have meant death. When my doctor said that I had cancer, I remember saying, "You're kidding?" I just couldn't believe it. I had never expected to be faced with cancer. I had surgery, and the doctor wanted me to have radiation. I'd seen my husband suffer through cancer and radiation and said to the doctor, "I'll have to pray."

One morning I was praying and said, "God, I've got to have an answer this morning. The deadline for my decision is today." All of a sudden I began laughing and crying. I said, "Well, Lord, I trust You more than I do the radiation." People were praying for me. Now I'm not against following the advice of doctors or against radiation if someone needs it, but the Lord showed me that I didn't need it. It's been ten years, and I've had no other signs of the cancer. Just as God healed Jimmy, he healed me. I know that God saved my life for a reason. Once again, God had brought me through. God has also healed me of tendinitis, back pain and spurs on my feet. I remember just dancing in the spirit when He healed my feet. As Isaiah 53:5 teaches, Jesus shed His blood for our salvation and for our healing. It is through His stripes that I was healed.

God has not always, however, spared my loved ones from death. My husband James passed away in 1983. It was so hard. My boys were grown, but my girls were only thirteen and sixteen years old. I thought, "Lord, I can't handle this." We had done everything together. We had made all of our decisions together. I thought, "I can't make decisions alone. I just can't make it without him." I truly thought that James would be healed. I didn't want anyone around me who expressed doubt that he would be healed. Finally one day I said, "God, not my will be done, but yours." Within fifteen minutes he was gone.

It was amazing to me that when James died, I began quoting Psalm 23. When I called our pastor, Nathan Ridgeway, he also began quoting Psalm 23. In spite of my grief, God did give me peace like a river. He showed me the truth of Psalm 23 that though I was walking through the valley of the shadow of death, I did not need to fear because His rod and staff would and did comfort me.

I don't know why God took James. I really wrestled with that question for a time, but once again God saw me through. Most of us never think about death. When it comes, we have to learn, as I did, that it's all a part of God's plan. Perhaps God saw the future and knew that trials lay ahead that he would not be able to handle. I don't know, but I trust God and know that His plan is best.

James had had the vision for Landmark Church of God. When others thought that our little church on Fifth Street couldn't possibly expand its vision for a church the size of Landmark, James was able to believe God. It was so sad to me that he never got to be in church at Landmark. I'm so thankful for the thirty years that we had together.

I have learned that God never closes one door without opening another. A number of years after James died, I met Bob Purkey. We dated and were dear friends for ten years. One day he was at my house helping fix my well when he fell over. I saw the look on his face and knew that this was serious. I called 911. We had just had a nice dinner together. His death was the last thing I expected. I believe that God in His mercy and grace had been trying to prepare me. Just the week before he died, we had talked about death. We had agreed that neither of us wanted to ever be a burden to anyone or to live on a machine. I believe that God honored Bob's request.

It's been hard since Bob died, yet God has seen me through. We always went bowling together. Every Friday and Saturday we went out to eat together. Right after Bob died, I thought that I just couldn't sit in church where we had always sat together. God's hand was in that situation. Just as He has been with me throughout my life, He was there. In His mercy He understood. It seemed that every Sunday there'd be someone sitting there. God is so good.

I have also lost my parents to death. When they died and when James died, God was with me filling me with peace that passes all understanding—peace like a river. Each time I felt the Spirit leaving their bodies. I could feel the Holy Spirit with me. I praised God that they had made it home. We're still striving to get home to heaven, but they've made it. That's what life is all about.

Each time I lost someone close to me, my church family as well as my immediate family and their friends have been there for me. It is so special to have a wonderful church family. I honestly don't know how people make it in this world without knowing the Lord and without a church family.

God has shown me that we've got to be ready to meet our Maker. We just don't know when our time will come. I've learned that we can lean on Him. He'll never fail us. When we hide the Word in our hearts, the Word never leaves us. Each time I have lost someone precious to me, as I have wept and grieved, peace has filled my heart. I have learned that, indeed, "Weeping may endure for a night, but joy comes in the morning" (Psalm 30: 5). I have also realized that we must cherish each moment we have. God has shown me that we must always thank Him for our blessings.

I have come to understand how special our families are. In addition to my children, God has given me seven wonderful grandkids who have helped me to fill my time when I have been alone. My daughter Shelia says that she sees Jesus in me as she watches me stand on the Word through every situation. I often think of married couples who take each other for granted. I want to say, "Wake up!" If they could just see! No one knows what tomorrow will bring.

Through all the things I've gone through, I have found who God is. He has always been with me through death, heartaches, troubles and sorrows. I know that His Word is settled in heaven and that His "faithfulness endures to all generations (Psalm 119: 89-90)." He has been faithful to me. I know that as Psalm 118: 8 says, it is always "better to trust in the Lord, than to put confidence in man" (Psalm 118: 8). As I have trusted in the Lord and stood on His Word, He has always seen me through.

Betty Oates

For I know the plans I have for you declares the Lord, plans to prosper you and not to harm you, plans to give you hope and a future. —Jeremiah 29: 11

I am a sixty-eight year old woman. I live in Gastonia, North Carolina. My husband is Glenn Oates. I have two daughters and sons-in-law, Cindy and Van and Terry and Sonny. I have six grandchildren: Franklin 21, Kristen 19, Jett 18, Jami 14, Cathy 4 and Kaitlyn 2. I have three step grandchildren and four step great grandchildren. I have three sisters, Helen, Virginia and Laura; one twin sister, Barbara Myers and one brother, Don.

I became a Christian when I was about eleven years old. My uncle, Reverend Craig Rhyne, was pastor of Stalling Memorial Baptist Church in Salisbury for twenty-five years. He came to Gastonia to hold revival services at Beech Avenue Baptist Church where his brother Reverend Marshall Rhyne was pastor. This is where I gave my life to Christ.

The Lord has always been with me to help me through many trials. I always enjoyed helping other people. I would pray for them, and God would direct me and show me what to do for them.

In 1997 my time for needing help came. A mammogram showed something suspicious. The doctor thought it might be scar tissue since I had previous benign biopsies. They decided to do a biopsy. The nuclear radiologist tried to point to the spot but could not find it. I kept praying, "DEAR LORD IF IT IS CANCER, LET THEM FIND IT." The nuclear radiologist asked if she could go to the operating room with me. The surgeon said if it had not been for the nuclear radiologist, he would have missed it. He was getting ready to close the surgery when the radiologist saw it behind some scar tissue. Thank God for the miracle. I had some tissue and thirteen lymph nodes removed. The cancer was not in the lymph nodes. I had thirty-three radiation treatments.

In July 1999, I found that I just couldn't seem to get my energy back after the treatments. I kept asking the doctor for a check-up and blood work. Finally, he decided to check my blood and give me a physical. I felt tired all of the time and had to push myself to go. I wanted to sleep a lot and had infections. The blood work showed I was anemic. Two days later my doctor died. Another doctor took over my case. All he was doing for me was checking my blood work in another month. I prayed that the doctors would find out what was wrong with me.

I asked another doctor in the group if he would see me. He looked at my blood work and said he was sending me to a cancer doctor. I saw the oncologist, Dr. Forest Thompson. He did a lot of blood work and a bone marrow biopsy. When he got the report back, he called me back in. By this time, I needed blood and platelets. He told me I had Mycoldysplastic Syndrome which is a blood disease of the bone marrow which causes the red and white blood cells and platelets to be low. My counts were preleukemia with a twenty-five percent cancer blast in transformation. About thirty percent of the people with Myelodysplastic Syndrome go into leukemia.

Dr. Thompson called Dr. Bayard Powell, the director of leukemia at Wake Forest University Medical Center. They had previously worked together for five years. When I saw Dr. Powell the next week, he said that he was going to put me on oral chemotherapy for preleukemia. He gave me blood and platelets and a choice of two kinds of chemotherapy. He told me to go home and think about it. He would call in a couple of days for my decision. I prayed that the doctors and I would make the best decision.

When Dr. Powell called, I told him that I was getting weaker and weaker and thought I needed another bone marrow biopsy. I did not know much about leukemia. Something just made me say that. He saw me the next day and did the bone marrow biopsy which showed ACUTE MYEOLOGENOUS LEUKEMIA with thirty-five percent cancer blast. This is the fast acting kind of leukemia. This was in November 1999. He told me to go home that weekend and enjoy Thanksgiving with my family. He said I would be in the hospital from four to eight weeks. They would start chemotherapy right away.

I was admitted to the hospital on the floor reserved for patients with leukemia and Hodgkin's Disease. Thirty-six of us had leukemia. We all had private rooms with special air filtration systems to keep out germs. I was in isolation to keep me from getting germs. Only the family could come to see me. The doctors put a catheter line in my chest to give me chemotherapy, medicines, blood, platelets and another line to take my lab work.

I was given three kinds of chemotherapy continuously for seven days. All of my counts went down as the chemotherapy killed the cancer cells. I was given blood and platelets about every other day. My white counts also bottomed out, so I got a lot of infections. I was given a lot of antibiotics. Some gave me a lot of fluid. They gave me Lasix to get rid of the fluid. I was allergic to the sulfa compound in Lasix. I had a severe reaction and broke out all over and turned red and itched real bad. By this time all of my hair had come out. I was some sight. I looked like a lobster and was bald. All I could do was laugh at myself.

After two weeks they did another bone marrow biopsy. It showed I still had some cancer cells. The doctors did another round of chemotherapy for five days. With all of my counts already low, this was really hard on me. I could not eat. I drank a lot of Boost. I continued getting more infections and diarrhea. Because all of my counts were really low, I was getting platelets and blood every other day and shots to build up my white count.

All I could do was to pray. I CRIED, "DEAR LORD, HELP ME!" I felt as if the Lord put His arms around me and gave me peace. My husband, daughters, brother and sisters were such a comfort to me during this time as they visited me and stayed with me.

I had so many people praying for me. People in my church, Crowders Creek A.R.P. Church in Gastonia, and other churches were praying. People at Landmark Church of God where my twin, Barbara, attends had a special prayer service for me. Barbara stood in for me. I received so many cards and inspirational books and verses which meant a lot to me. My walls were covered with cards.

My counts started going up after seven weeks. I had to spend Christmas and New Years Day in the hospital. I went home on January 24. I was still weak and had to avoid crowds. I was able to go to church in May. It was such a spiritual blessing to be back in church. I wanted to cry. I held on to every word, to every song and to every prayer. Everyone told me what a glow I had. I was able to attend my grandson Jett's Eagle Scout Award in May. I was so happy for what the Lord had done for me.

I still had to get blood once a month. My platelet count was still low but not low enough to get platelets. I was still not in remission. I continued to see Dr. Thompson and Dr. Powell once a month. I could do all of my work and help my husband in his business. I enjoyed every day. I enjoyed my children and precious grandchildren. I still could not be around them if they had a cold or a virus.

In November 2000, I started getting weaker again. I had to get blood and platelets again because my counts had started dropping. Another bone marrow biopsy confirmed that leukemia had returned with a thirty-five percent cancer blast meaning that thirty-five percent of the cells in my bone marrow were cancerous. Again Dr. Powell told me to go home and enjoy my family for Thanksgiving.

I was again placed in isolation on the leukemia floor at Wake Forest Hospital. Doctors put another catheter in my chest for chemotherapy. This time the chemotherapy was stronger. My hair came out again. Again I broke out from reactions to the medications. Again I was red and bald. The medical students would come in and look at me. They said I had one of the worst reactions they had seen. I still had to laugh at myself even though I was miserable.

I had to get blood and platelets frequently. After two weeks of chemotherapy another bone marrow biopsy showed that there were still some cancer cells. I started another round of chemotherapy for three more days. All of my counts started dropping more. Again, I could not eat and drank Boost. I had more diarrhea and infections. I started getting weaker and could not concentrate. I was really low. My heart stopped beating a couple of times. My family called friends and people in churches for prayer. Barbara said she stood in again for me in prayer. My counts slowly started coming up again. I was able to go home on January 6. After six weeks in the hospital, I had again spent Christmas and New Years Day in the hospital.

When I came home, I could not walk or stand without help. I had to keep the catheter in my arm for eight months for my blood work and blood. I had to get platelets for about three months and blood for six months. Then the doctors started me on Procrit to build up my red blood cells. A Home Health nurse came out once a week to change the dressing on my catheter and to take vital signs to avoid me getting an infection at the catheter site. I could not understand why I could not walk.

My family, church friends and neighbors brought food. My daughter Terry would come over at lunch from work and flush my catheter and fix my lunch. My husband Glenn had to work. He would cook breakfast and help me with my bath. Cindy, my other daughter who lives in Asheville, would come once or twice per week. Barbara came once a week. I would not have made it without them.

The Home Health physical therapist came out three times per week for four months to help strengthen the muscles in my legs and feet. I could not understand why I had no balance. Dr. Powell sent me to an E.N.T. (Ear, Nose and Throat doctor) at Wake Forest who told me that my nerves had been damaged in my middle ear by an antibiotic gentamycin. This had caused me to lose my balance on both sides. I kept praying, "Lord, help me to learn to walk again and to wait on myself.

I went through six months of physical therapy. My sister Helen and her husband Tommy took me to physical therapy three times a week. I did exercises at home five times a day. I went from a wheelchair to a walker to a cane. Now I can walk and do my housework without a cane. I have to use a cane to go outside. I can't drive, but praise the Lord! I can walk and wait on myself and sometimes others.

I can also help my husband with the bookwork for his company. I am enjoying my family. I never thought I would see my youngest grandchildren, Kaitlyn and Calley, grow to be two and four years old. Now Jami is fourteen and in high school. Jett is getting ready to graduate from high school and go to Appalachian University. Kristen is a sophomore at North Carolina State University. Franklin is a senior at the University of North Carolina.

Last September, I talked with my doctor about the possibility of stem cell transplants in older people. This is a new procedure which only a few people have done. The doctors said that there was only a fourteen percent chance of someone at my age with my type of leukemia making it through this. At Wake Forest all six people over the age of sixty who had this procedure died.

I knew that the leukemia blast cells could start up at any time, and I could have a relapse. Even though my brother was a match for this procedure, I knew that I had already gone past the six month time period when the relapse usually comes back. I prayed to God to help me and the doctors make the right decision. Others were also praying. When Dr. Powell called me for my decision, I told him that I just could not say yes. He told me that I had made a wise decision.

In November 2002, it had been three years since the doctors diagnosed me with leukemia. I had the fast growing kind of leukemia. My doctors said I wouldn't live for more than three months without treatment. At my age and with the kind of leukemia I had, I had only a four percent chance of living for three years. It has now been two years and four months since my last treatments. My platelets are still low but not low enough to get platelets. My white count is forty percent germ fighting cells. At this time I no longer get Procrit injections every two weeks for my hemoglobin and red blood cells. I am overall feeling all right. I am what they call coasting.

Thank the dear Lord. I would not have made it this long without the Lord and without the prayers and support of family, friends and people in the churches. Dr. Thompson and Dr. Powell are such great doctors. They and their assistants Susan and Karen have helped me tremendously. My pastor, Reverend James McLurkin, has also been such a comfort and inspiration to me with all his visits and prayers.

I CANNOT EXPLAIN THE INNER PEACE AND THE CLOSENESS I HAVE WITH GOD. I FEEL HIS SPIRIT WITH ME. THROUGH THIS I HAVE LEARNED TO TAKE ONE DAY AT A TIME AND TO ENJOY EVERY MINUTE OF IT THAT I CAN. OF COURSE, THERE ARE BAD DAYS, BUT HE WILL SEE ME THROUGH THEM. People still say I have that smile and that glow. I don't know when God will decide that my time is up on earth; but I know I will be at peace with it for as Jeremiah 29: 11 says:

For I know the plans I have for you declares the Lord, plans to prosper you and not to harm you, plans to give you hope and a future.

God has given me hope and a future. Thank You dear Lord!

Nancy Parsons

I can do all things through Christ who strengthens me.—Philippians 4:13

I grew up in church all of my life. As a child, I remember going to the altar many times. I saw every little thing I did wrong as sin. When I first married, I always took our children to church whether my husband, Ron, went or not. Throughout my life, God has always been faithful. I have learned that as Philippians 4: 13 says, "I can (indeed) do all things through Christ who strengthens me."

I was so disturbed that two of my children and my husband were not living for the Lord that I sewed anointed prayer cloths in my husband's pillow and my children's mattresses. My son had abused alcohol and cocaine for ten years. God faithfully brought him back to Himself. Today he is filled with the Holy Ghost and loves the Lord. One of my daughters tasted of the world and found that the world wasn't the way she wanted to go. Now she's fallen in love with Jesus. My other daughter gave her life to the Lord as a child and never went through life in the world as did my other two children. She saw the life of rebellion lived by her siblings and didn't want that for her life. She didn't want to put her parents through that.

At one time my husband was filled with the Holy Spirit; but when our pastor and his wife divorced, he was so disappointed that he left the church. For many years our marriage was a struggle. There were times when I would want to leave and other times when he would want to leave the marriage. My husband was often so critical and mean to me. I, on the other hand, was addicted to credit cards and overspending. My mother had taught me to always look for a bargain. I spent every spare minute of my life looking for a bargain. God showed me that I had had as much a part of causing bitterness and hurt in our marriage as Ron had. All my husband wanted was to be out of debt.

One Wednesday night, God showed me that I had to repent of my addiction and ask the Lord to forgive me. I stood up and told the congregation that I had an addiction to spending much like an addiction to alcohol. I said that I knew that this behavior was not pleasing to God. It had caused a rift in our marriage. When I was willing to stand in front of my peers and repent, He took away my desire for spending.

Ron and I refinanced our home to a lower payment. God showed me that I was to put an extra $ 100 a month from my income toward our bills. My husband and God saw that I was willing to right the wrong. Now when I need something, I go to the store. I don't spend all of my time looking for bargains. I do not believe that most Christians see overspending as a sin; however, God has shown me that what I know to do and do not is sin (James 4:17). God also took away my addiction to chocolate.

Throughout the years, God gave me the strength to endure a difficult marriage. " I can do all things through Christ who strengthens me" (Philippians 4: 13). Recently, Ron recommitted his life to God. Now God has brought peace back between us. He has brought forgiveness to us for each other. What an awesome God He is!

When the Lord filled me with the Holy Ghost, He also birthed in me a praise and worship ministry through song and dance. I am so grateful that He continually leads me to a higher level in Him. I have learned to praise Him in the midst of my heartache. I have learned that His timing is perfect. Indeed, He has always been faithful to me. Praise the Lord!

Sue Parsons

I can do all things through Christ who strengthens me.—Philippians 4: 13

I grew up in a Catholic family. My parents always fought, argued and yelled at each other. I never heard the word "LOVE" as I was growing up and certainly had no idea about the true meaning of love. I thought people showed love by hitting me on the back with a spatula, by pulling hair (My mom had a good grip on my long hair.) or by hitting me with a hickory stick.

One time she hit me so hard that it broke the stick. One weekend we were sick. My mom made us kids go to church twice the next week. I didn't learn a lot and certainly couldn't pronounce the words I heard. I never understand what the priest was talking about. I just thought it was boring to sit for an hour. I couldn't wait for the day I could quit going to church. I did not know that I could have a personal relationship with a Savior who would strengthen me and love me just as I was.

When I was older and able to move out on my own, I quit going to church and began living in the world. I'll admit that I did enjoy it, or so I thought. I loved to go to bars, dance, get drunk and come home late. I also liked smoking pot because it would make me eat (I had an eating problem). Smoking pot was the first thing I did every morning.

Then I got married to a man who always put me down. I was wrong no matter what I did. He criticized my body and called me stupid or dumb. I had no self-esteem. You see, at the time, I thought I was in love; but I was just young and naive. Finally, I decided that I shouldn't be treated this way. I had been treated like dirt for too long. One day when I came home, I found some unexpected company in my bed with my husband. He told me that I was wrong for coming home. I said, "NO! I was right for coming home!" This relationship had gone on for ten years when we moved to North Carolina. The kids and I moved out.

Even though I had ended this abusive relationship, I was still out partying it up. I met this guy. We dated for a year. Then we decided there wasn't any sense paying rent on two places, so we moved in together. When I talked with him about how irritable he always was with the kids, we realized that kids weren't for him. We had been together for two years when I left with the kids.

I was working for a car wash and wondering what I was going to do. I had sold all of my household belongings when I moved in with him. I was scared and lonely. I did not know how I was going to make it. Well, I bought a mobile home. I'm not sure how I did it especially with the bad credit my husband had left me with. The mobile home dealer put my kids and me up in a hotel for two months until our land was cleared and my trailer was moved.

It was during this time that we started going to church in Clemmons, North Carolina. We had only been going for a couple of weeks when the church had a revival.The evangelist said some stuff that I knew was directed toward me. I thought to myself, "How did he know that? I've never told anyone those things." I had goose bumps even though I wasn't cold, and the air conditioning wasn't on. I didn't know what was going on. When he asked everyone to bow their heads, he said, "If anybody here doesn't know the Lord and would like to and if you feel this message was for you, please raise your hand." I did. I meant it. My hand was raised as high as I could raise it.

On that day in June of 1998, the Lord came into my life. I found out later that my daughter, Amanda had also raised her hand. Neither of us knew the other one had done that. When I left there that day, I could feel a change in me. It was as if I were a new person. I had peace and joy. I didn't feel lonely anymore. It was like I was filled up on the inside. I was so happy and didn't know why. I was grinning from ear to ear and could feel so much love. I realized that my language, my selection of television programs and my choice of friends had changed. I was still drinking and smoking cigarettes and pot, however.

One Sunday in August 1998, I was running late to church and smoked my last cigarette on the way. I'd planned to buy another pack of cigarettes on the way home; but when I got out of church, I didn't desire any more cigarettes, pot or alcohol. The Lord had delivered me from those bad habits. You see, when you first ask the Lord into your heart, he might not change you right away; but in His time. He will. I thank the Lord every day for my deliverance. As I John 4: 4 says:

> You are of God, little children, and have overcome them because He who is in you is greater than he that is in the world.

As a single mother, I was still working at the car wash. The children had a dead beat dad, yet all of my bills were paid. We were not rich, but we had some extras. My mobile home had tables, a couch, beds, dressers etc. I learned that the Lord would provide for me if I put my faith in him.

My co-workers saw a change in me. They didn't believe that the Lord had delivered me from smoking cigarettes and pot. They teased me about listening to radio station 94.1 FM. They would say, "You're the devil. You're the devil." They would say that my friends were Satan worshippers, but their behavior just drew me closer to the Lord. I prayed for each and every one of them every day. I did not have any friends. I got rid of all of my old partying friends. That was o.k. because I had the Lord to talk to and laugh with. I just went to work, worked hard and read my Bible. I didn't mind leaving my Bible around at work because I knew nobody would touch it.

One day I started praying for a husband. Someone had told me to be specific. I wanted a man who would treat me as a lady should be treated and who would love my kids as his own. I mean I really got specific, right down to the height. Of course, God didn't answer my prayer overnight. Two months later I met Ronnie. He was such a special man that I fell in love right away with him. I prayed and prayed, "Lord, I'm tired of getting hurt. Please let me know if this is the man you have in store for me." I didn't want my kids to get attached to him only to have us dump each other. Well, Ronnie asked me to marry him. I know the Lord was in on this because it was perfect timing. You know, the Lord is SO GOOD! If you ask him according to his will, you'll receive.

The Lord has changed the lives of me and my kids. When we first started attending Landmark, they were not respectful. Now they are respectful, and I know that I couldn't have caused that change. I just praise God for what He has done in their lives. I can see God's peace, joy and love in them as well. I thank God for dying on the cross for my sins and for saving me from bondage. I know I have eternal life and that I will go to heaven. God is so merciful. I love Him and appreciate Him so much even when He pulls me out of my comfort zone.

I have learned that Jesus is love. He loves me and each and every one of us so much. We just can't explain that kind of love. I wish that I had come to know the Lord earlier in life. I could have been so much happier than I was. But, I know Him now.

According to Nehemiah 8: l0b, "...the joy of the Lord is your strength." His joy has been my strength especially since I received the Baptism of the Holy Spirit in September of 1998, during a revival service. So yea! I'm full of Joy! We serve a big God who is, indeed, greater than he who is in the world. I know that I can do all things through Him who strengthens me and fills me with an exceeding, great joy!

Nick Pennell

For He shall give His angels charge over you in all your ways. In their hands they shall bear you up, lest you dash your foot against a stone.—Psalm 91: 11-12

Once while helping a good friend of mine build a landscape/ irrigation business in Mooresville....

I was mowing a very nice yard on a big walk-behind mower (the kind that you stand on a platform with wheels, and the mower pulls you behind it) when for no reason at all I "broke" the pattern I always mowed in and went several yards out of the way just to make a circle around a tree. Then I went back to my usual mowing pattern. This was something I almost never did—break a mowing pattern; but for whatever reason, I did. I had just completed my circle around a very large, very healthy and very alive oak tree when I felt something brush the back of my neck.

I immediately stopped the mower thinking that my friend had snuck up behind me to simply aggravate and play with me by brushing me with a little twig with leaves. Instead, to my utter dismay, as soon as I turned, I saw that a large limb had crashed to the ground just a few inches, at the most, behind my heels! My jaw dropped! I looked around half bewildered. No one was in sight—there was no wind blowing—and as I said earlier, the tree was alive. This limb had fallen from about thirty feet in the air, ramming several branches deep in the ground when it landed. Had it hit the back of my neck or head, it would surely have done major damage to me or even resulted in death.

I'm not at all in favor of the way we (...people collectively) have gone "angel crazy" with a "cazillon" books and little childlike figures everywhere we look. It has come to seem like angels are being worshiped. Even people who don't claim Jesus or have any relationship with Him will many times, however, tell you about their "Guardian Angel." Well, I happen to know that Jesus dispatches the true angels in heaven to do things here on earth, and I also **know** that Jesus sent one to protect me that day. As Psalm 91: 11-12 says,

> For He shall give His angels charge over you in all your ways. In their hands they shall bear you up, lest you dash your foot against a stone.

I fell to my knees alone in the backyard of this home, raised my hands and gave praise and thanks to God right there. I was SO excited about what He had just done for me! I just laughed and rejoiced right there in that yard. I left the limb lying there and finished mowing the yard singing various songs to myself—a little louder. HA! HA!

I think one of the reasons I was so excited was that the intervention God had just provided was so incredibly clear. I understood it because I knew that at this time, God was in the midst of "molding" me and preparing me for some ways He wanted to use me! I AM's plans ARE!!!! It isn't as though He had the obligation to prove Himself to me, but that day He proved to me that His plans will not be thwarted in my life!! Hallelujah!

Marge Puffenberger

And He said to me, "My grace is sufficient for you, for My strength is made perfect in weakness." —II Corinthians 12: 9

From the time Marge was just a little girl, she was always in church with her parents. She helped lead the Praise and Worship and remembers knowing from a young age that God would hear and answer her prayers. One time, for example, she prayed that her father would not loose his vision, and he didn't.

Through the years, Marge has continually seen God's hand in her life and in the lives of her children. She has seen the sufficiency of God's grace continually. One Sunday, she returned home with her children from teaching Bible School. Her husband had promised to fix lunch while she showed a neighbor the horse they wanted to sell. While she was outside, the grease caught on fire. Her husband grabbed the pot to dump the grease accidentally splattering the grease on their youngest daughter and oldest son.

Their daughter, Nancy was in shock and so critically burned that she was not expected to live. For six days, the doctors could not bring her temperature below l05 degrees. Marge prayed for her daughter to live only under one condition. She asked for grace to be the kind of mother Nancy would need for spiritual guidance and for a painful and lengthy recovery. God answered her prayer. After forty-five skin grafts, Nancy was able to attend college and graduate with a teaching degree. As Marge has watched each of her children become professionals with a desire to reach out and help others, she has seen God's hand in their lives.

During the time her children were small, Marge's husband divorced her refusing to support the children. He was not a Christian and ridiculed her for going to church. He had no skills as a husband or as a father and no desire to acquire any. He did not want the responsibility of a husband and a father and became involved with a lady at his workplace. "I prayed for a miracle," she said. "I wanted to see my marriage healed. God didn't do that. Instead, he delivered me from the physical and mental abuse. It took a while for me to grasp that my husband had free will which God also had to honor."

Marge was terrified that she would be unable to make ends meet working for a vet. Again, as she prayed; God prepared her for what was yet to come in her life. She accepted a second job in a factory, but the money still was not enough. Through a friend, she found a better job with a railroad and was able to give up the factory job. She continued the railroad job for ten years and was able to see all of her children graduate from high school and all but one graduate from college. (He didn't want to go to college.) It seemed that her life was going well, but the railroad downsized eliminating her position. Her mother would have said, "This, too, will pass."

She could only find minimum wage jobs and followed a relative's advice to move East. She found no jobs. Finally, a children's home in Huntersville hired her only to close the campus six weeks later. She found her strength to be made perfect in weakness through His grace. She accepted a position with Barium Springs Home for Children where she remained three years.

Nancy, the daughter who had been burned moved to North Carolina to teach and live with Marge. Her youngest son moved to Statesville and also lived with Marge until he married. Her oldest son moved to Atlanta and became a chiropractor. During all of this time, however, Marge just knew that God had something He needed her to do beyond what she was doing.

Indeed, as God used Marge at Barium Springs in work with counseling children and families, He prepared her for the work she began in 1990 as a volunteer working with battered and abused women. She witnesses of Jesus Christ and helps them to get their lives back on track. She goes with the families she counsels to church to help them become established in the church of their choice. Today, God uses Marge to minister to others from the lessons she has learned from her own pain. Through her pain, God has taught Marge to see that people can only do what they know to do. Her mother-in-law was burned and died when her husband was only five years old. At seven years old age, his father developed polio and became an invalid. Marge's husband controlled their children through manipulation. That was all he knew. As a Marine, he had learned to be tough. In Marge's words, "God's allowed me to see the process. He couldn't love. He had never felt it.

"When we divorced, the children were angry with their father and didn't want to see him. I told them that one day they would want a relationship with their father. As the children have healed and matured, that has happened." As Marge continued, "God has given me wisdom I couldn't have gotten any other way than through the pain. It took me a long time to laugh again. I felt guilty for what had happened to my family; but when joy came, it was here to stay.

"I prayed for my husband's salvation for fourteen and one-half years, from the time of our marriage until our divorce. He has been saved and has remarried."

Marge is grateful that when she moved to North Carolina, she found Landmark Church of God where she has found such love and can be fed herself in the midst of helping others.

In 1987, God helped her with her finances so that she could purchase a home near the church. As she says, "I'm often overwhelmed at all of what God's done for me. In the most difficult circumstances, I've always known that man can't change God's will. I have more to thank Him through than others. I've been through tough times, but those, too, have passed. I can't wait to go to heaven. I'm so thankful for the peace and joy He has given me.

I thank God that I have that spiritual edge some people can't seem to grasp a hold of. You see, it's grown from childhood. It's incredible to think of the physical and mental abuse my children and I endured and to see the way my children are now. Look how we've been able to touch people! I'm so grateful to God for His grace that has been sufficient for me. I know that He is going to work in other lives so they will receive something from my pain and suffering.

Bert and Shannon Rogerson

If I ascend into heaven, You are there; If I make my bed in hell, behold, You are there. —Psalm 139: 8

The truths of Psalm 139: 1-3 have been borne out in the life of Bert Rogerson. Indeed, God was acquainted with Bert when his marriage was in trouble; when he was wrestling with anger, bitterness, hatred, and prejudice; when he was struggling with the cruelty of the drug world; when his life was in danger; and when he sincerely recommitted his life to the Lord, Jesus Christ. God hedged him behind and before and laid His hand upon him (Psalm 139: 5) through it all and brought him out to serve Him with a greater devotion than ever "in the way everlasting" (Psalm 139: 24).

Bert was raised around people who hated people because of the color of their skin. His family told him to respect people regardless of their race, color or creed. His grandfather would also talk of the need to remain separate in marriage from people of other races, colors or creeds just as robins and cardinals roost separately.

In 1984, while he worked as a bodyguard for a White Supremist group, he saw first-hand the hatred that could ensue from such prejudice. Being a bodyguard was dangerous work. He wore a bulletproof vest, yet he had to be willing to die to protect those he guarded. "These were mean people," Bert said. "One of the overseers is now serving four life sentences in prison because he killed a good friend of mine whom we called Cecil. He was my sister's boyfriend." But even in these situations, God's hand was leading Bert (Psalm 139: 10).

One weekend there was a big Klan rally in Stone Mountain, Georgia, with many different varieties of Klan organizations represented. A preacher was preaching from the book of Deuteronomy. "I had seen people of different races commit horrible atrocities against one another that caused me to hate people based on skin color." As Bert related, "Some of what I heard that day didn't add up. I understand that they were saying what they were saying because of the way they had been raised, but I was believing it. Unfortunately, out of this kind of hatred and rebellion, people in our society do things every day that they regret in the long run. Our children suffer for it."

Bert continued, "I had prayed and asked God to help me overcome this hatred. About this time I met a black man named Bobby. We became good friends. We talked about prejudice. He knew right from wrong and didn't want pity. I started going to the Church of God in Fairfax, Virginia, near Manassas, Virginia, where I was working as a security guard for a mall. God showed me that this hatred was wrong, and I walked away and got more in church." God turned the darkness in Bert's thinking to light so that with God he was able to say, "Depart from me...you bloodthirsty men" (Psalm 139: 6: 19).

In September 1990, Bert's daughter Amanda was born handicapped. "I wasn't perfect with my wife, Michelle," he said. "It was hard on Michelle. Amanda was handicapped, and I was working sixteen hours per day. I would go to church on Sunday and spend the rest of the time at the hospital with Amanda. I believe that God gave me Amanda. No one else can care for her. Without her, I'd be wild.

"When Michelle and I began to have problems, I was discouraged and walked away from the church. When I moved to Statesville in 1992, I didn't mess with any church. I'd go see my mother and stuff. You know how mothers are. They inquire. I always found excuses until I started working at Wal-Mart where a friend told me about Landmark. I began coming in 1995 and turned my life back around again and started dating Shannon and once again quit going to church. We were married in 1998."

Shannon and Bert saw God's ever faithful hand upon their lives in a mighty way only five days after they were married. Amanda was due for another surgery when three men came in with guns to rob them. Bert just knew they'd kill him and pleaded with God, "Lord, please don't let them kill Shannon and Amanda." He heard them click the safety. One said, "Shut the kid up or I'll kill her." On the floor he remembers himself saying, "Lord, please don't let them kill us. I'll change." Yet he knew that he probably would not change. It was Amanda that made the difference as Bert related, "When Amanda cried to God, God honored it."

Bert continued, "At first racism rose once again in me. I would have spared the man who spared Amanda, but I was determined to find the others and hang them on a fence post. God knew that I had enough hate and connections that I could have gone on a round of more destruction, except that Amanda cried to God. I wouldn't do anything to hurt her. I remember Shannon saying, 'They're gone.' They took my guns, but our lives were spared." As Psalm 139: 11 reads,

> If I say, "Surely the darkness shall fall on me," Even the night shall be light about me.

Darkness did fall, but once again God hedged them behind and before and laid His hand upon them.

In 1997, even before he and Shannon were married, his problems with drugs began and continued until May of 1999 when the State Bureau of Investigation (SBI) came to his house and indicted him for the selling of marijuana and cocaine. By the time he was indicted, he had already walked away from the drug scene and was wanting to return to church which he did shortly thereafter. He told the agent that he would go to jail for marijuana but not for cocaine of which he was not guilty.

Fortunately, the agent believed him. His wife Shannon moved out. As Bert says, "Rumors flew that I was only in church to get out of my mess, but I was sincere. Satan began throwing a lot of fiery darts my way. I knew I had to stand strong. I couldn't ride on the edge. I really had to pray. Satan tried and still tries to bring thoughts of where He's brought me from. I have to fight every day to stand against Satan.

"When my court case came up, many people were praying. Every way I turned, there seemed to be no place for Amanda to go if I went to prison. The pastor prayed with me and said that he didn't see anything bad happening. My lawyer said that I could expect to pull a minimum of five years in prison and a maximum of forty years. Shannon and I were back together. I knew that I shouldn't worry, but I was concerned about my church activities. I knew that I couldn't be in the cantata if I were locked up."

"I knew that any worrying I would do should have been done before I got into trouble. Besides I know that I can't worry about things over which I have no control. A lot of people are looking to see if you'll mess up; but also many want you to make it, so they can cross over."

"There were big time drug people involved in my case. I was incorrectly portrayed as a big time drug purchaser. The SBI knew, however, that I was the smallest person involved. My phone had been tapped. The SBI knew my bank account. I was indicted but not charged with the purchase of five kilos of cocaine, yet they knew that my lifestyle gave no evidence of such. I wasn't driving Porches and living as one with lots of money. When I went before the judge, the SBI never asked me to turn state evidence. They knew I was done with drugs."

"At first the lawyers had told me that I was facing twenty years to life in prison; then the term changed to ten years to life and finally to five years to forty years. Through it all God continued to have me pray for the SBI agent who had indicted me. In the end he helped me more than anyone else did. The day of my sentencing, I was tried last. The Attorney General asked for a sentence of three years house arrest and eight years in prison. The judge opened his huge book of guidelines and quickly closed it. He gave me two years of supervised probation."

Psalm 139: 19 says, "Surely thou wilt slay the wicked, O God." God rewarded Bert's honesty about his actions and his contrite heart with favor and confounded the counsel of the ungodly by sending the man who lied to prison. He further gave Bert favor when he blessed him with a Christian to conduct his pre-trial investigation and a Christian probation officer. He has no restrictions on when he has to be at home as do many who are on probation. He simply has to complete a monthly report.

There are no conflicts with his church work. He has a good job with income to support his family. What an awesome God we serve! Once more God beset Bert behind and before and kept His hand upon him. As Bert concluded his testimony, he contrasted his life when he walked with the bloody men and the wicked spoken of in Psalm 139 and now as he strives daily to walk with God echoing the words of Psalm 139: 17-18:

> How precious also are thy thoughts unto me, O God! how great is the sum of them! If I should count them, they are more in number than the sand: when I awake, I am still with thee.

"There was a time in my life that if I had not learned to stand on the Word of God, I could have been on the most wanted list. I was so cold-hearted that I could see death and not be bothered by it. I've been in places where I had to crawl among the trees with branches falling to dodge the bullets that were flying knowing that it was just a matter of time before they made contact with me. I have run with rough people including some of the toughest bikers. I've been with Hell's Angels although I was never a member. We take so many things including life for granted. I could name so many times that I could have been dead.

"Once I was hit on the side of the head with an axe handle. I have driven cars over 130 miles per hour. One of those times I just made it into my grandmother's yard with no brakes. What stopped me? You tell me. Another time as I approached a train track with a train coming, I lost my brakes. Just as I hit the track, my car stopped. Who stopped me? You tell me. Once I was working on a Cadillac car when it caught on fire as I opened the hood.

"I heard a comment the other day. How long will it be before I quit the church? I desire to be more involved than ever before. I know my weak side. There are so many things out there in the world. Growing up I saw my parents fight violently. Shannon and I don't fight. I don't believe children should see their parents fighting. I love my family, but today I stay away and keep my distance from the danger zone. I know the things that can rob me of my salvation and I avoid them.

"Yes, every day I have to stand and fight for my faith and walk with the Lord. At one time in my life, I was one of the worst judgmental people; but I've learned that if I can't say something good about someone, I just won't say anything." Today Bert can say with Paul:

> I know whom I have believed and am persuaded that He is able to keep what I have committed to Him until that Day
> —II Timothy 1:12

Bert has learned how true the words of Psalm 139: 7-8 really are:

> Where can I go from Your Spirit? Or where can I flee from Your presence? If I ascend into heaven, You are there; If I make my bed in hell, behold You are there.

No matter his circumstances, Bert could never run from God. God was always there.

Bert has seen God put his marriage back together and give him a most special daughter for whom his love knows no bounds. He has watched God deliver him from the spirits of bitterness, hatred and prejudice. He has seen God deliver him from the drug world and from prison. He has seen God save his life so many times. He knows that Jesus Christ is real and that his faith is real! He knows the power of prayer and of the Word of God. When he sincerely recommitted his life to the Lord, Jesus Christ, God did, indeed, change his life and make of it a new creation. He'll do the same for you! Psalm 139: 1-8,10-12, 17-19, 23 says:

> O Lord, You have searched me and known me. You know my sitting down and my rising up; You understand my thought afar off. You comprehend my path and my lying down, and are acquainted with all my ways. When I awake, I am still with You. For there is not a word on my tongue. Oh, that You would slay the wicked, O God! But behold, O Lord, You know it altogether. You have hedged me behind and before and laid Your hand upon me. Such knowledge is too wonderful for me. It is high, I cannot attain it. Where can I go from Your everlasting Spirit? Or where can I flee from Your presence? If I ascend into heaven, You are there; If I make my bed in hell, behold,You are there. Even there your hand shall lead me, and your right hand shall hold me. If I say, "Surely the darkness shall fall on me," Even the night shall be light about me; indeed, the darkness shall not hide from You, But the night shines as the day; the darkness and the light are both alike to You. How precious also are Your thoughts to me, O God! How great is the sum of them! If I should count them, they would be more in number than the sand; When I awake, I am still with You. Oh, that You would slay the wicked, O God! Depart from me, therefore, you bloodthirsty men. Search me, O God, and know my heart; try me, and know my anxieties; and

see if there is any wicked way in me, and lead me in the way everlasting.

Conrad Sells

Therefore I say to you, whatever things you ask when you pray; believe that you receive them, and you will have them. —Mark 11: 24

I had been having pains in my heart off and on for the last year or so. I finally went to see my family physician, Dr. Chang Lieu, in Mooresville, North Carolina. Dr. Lieu was my father's doctor up until my father died on May 22, 2002.

I have had diabetes since 1991, and diabetes is linked with heart disease. Dr. Lieu ran an electrocardiogram (EKG) on me. According to the EKG, it was highly possible that I had a light heart attack and didn't know it. The next stop was a nuclear stress test and a treadmill test at the Sanger Clinic in Mooresville, North Carolina.

Dr. Koehler also told me that I had a single artery or maybe two arteries that were blocked. His recommendation was for me to have a heart catheterization. With this procedure in mind, I began to call on the troops, who are my brothers and sisters in Christ, my family and friends and other churches whose heartfelt prayers went up all over Iredell County to Almighty God.

I went to Mooresville two days ahead of the scheduled heart catheterization to have a chest X-ray made at Lake Norman Regional Hospital. As I got into Mooresville, I stopped at the gas station to put gas in the car. After getting gas, I went inside the store to pay for the gas. Inside the store, I recognized a young lady with whom I had gone to church several years back. Her name was Michelle Miller. She is a health nurse who privately works in homes of different people. God called Michelle to the office of Prophetess. The Lord honored our prayer that I would be healed as we agreed in prayer together inside the gas station.

As we were getting ready to go our separate ways, the Holy Spirit rose up inside of her to tell me that I had no blockage. I told Michelle that I willingly received what God had told her. I let my family and hospital know that they would not find anything wrong with my heart.

Now Dr. Sugarman, who was an associate of Dr. Koehler, did the procedure. I was awake during the entire procedure. Even though my family and the hospital staff were skeptical, I made the statement, "On this, you will know that I serve the God of Abraham, Isaac and Jacob." I also spoke healing scriptures over myself.

When the procedure was almost over, Dr. Sugarman put his hand over his mask; and I saw an unbelievable look in his eyes. He said, "Mr. Sells, you have a perfect heart, and you have no blocked arteries." then I made the statement to all of them that, "I could have told you that before you rolled me in here."

I was rolled back to my little room. The good report was made to my family and my pastor, Doug Smith, of First Wesleyan Church. After going for so long without food because of this being done and having to lie flat and not move, I was blessed by my brother who fed me the greatest bowl of Cheerios I have ever tasted and eaten.

I give all the praise, honor and glory to God for healing me and watching over me. Hallelujah! What a mighty God we serve!

I Need Thee Every Hour

I need Thee every hour, most gracious Lord.
No other voice but Thine can peace afford.

Chorus
I need Thee, O I need Thee.
Every hour I need Thee.
O bless me now my Saviour.
I come to Thee.

I need thee every hour. Stay Thou near by.
Temptations lose their power when Thou art nigh.

I need Thee, O I need Thee.
Every hour I need Thee.
O bless me now my Saviour.
I come to Thee.

I need Thee every hour. Teach me Thy will,
And thy rich promises in me fulfill.

I need Thee, O I need Thee.
Every hour I need Thee.
O bless me now my Saviour.
I come to Thee.

I need Thee every hour Most Holy One.
O make me Thine indeed Thou blessed Son.

I need Thee, O I need Thee.
Every hour I need Thee.
O bless me now my Saviour.
I come to Thee.

Conrad Sells

Let everything that has breath praise the Lord.—Psalm 10: 6

Recently, I've looked back over my life at some of the things that have happened to me. I know that it's just through God's grace that I'm even here. I've had so many accidents in my life. I have to say that it's just because of God's grace and His breath that I even lived through the accidents I suffered.

For example, I remember the time I'd gone swimming and climbed on top of the high diving board. I slipped and fell and went down sideways. I landed on the concrete instead of in the water. I got up from having fallen twenty feet on concrete and walked away without a scratch.

Then there was another time when I had a little AMC Javelin sports car. A man behind me was driving too fast and hit me from behind knocking me off the side of the road. I went airborne about forty feet in the air. The car came back down in a nose dive straight down. The car hit with an incredible impact when it landed, yet I walked away again without a scratch. Both accidents happened before I knew the Lord.

Later, I joined the youth choir at the church I was attending. I was asked to sing, I Need Thee Every Hour, the first solo I'd ever sung. It was the first time I'd ever performed in front of people. After this, I began to play with a country rock band. Every place we played was in a different town staying in a different motel. I was totally miserable and very lonely.

Finally, I met a lady who invited me to her house. She witnessed to me about Jesus, and that night I became a Christian. After I became born again, the Lord spoke to me and let me know that my calling was going to be that of a Psalmist and a praise and worship leader. I was to work to bring denominations together into one body. I was to go into the field of evangelism to do praise and worship seminars.

Since that time, Jesus appeared to me on three different occasions. Now I want to tell everybody that we have breath in our bodies because He gave it to us. There have been so many times when I should have been killed or badly injured but walked away without a scratch. It is only by His grace that we have breath to live; consequently, every word we speak and every song we sing should magnify the Lord and be used only for that.

Think about breath, the air you breathe. Just to be able to breathe at all is a gift. He created breath so that we could praise and worship Him in spirit and in truth. We must not take that breath for granted. We must confess with our mouths that the life of God is in us just as He first breathed life into Adam. He says in Psalm 139 that He knew us before we were even in our mothers' wombs. Since our breath came from God, let us use it every day to praise the living God. As Psalm 150:6 says, "Let everything that has breath praise the Lord."

David L. Shangle

I will lift up my eyes to the hills—From whence comes my help? My help comes from the Lord, who made heaven and earth.—Psalm 121: 1-2

My wife and I were in a bad accident in 1994. According to the police, we should have been dead. They don't know how anyone survived that wreck.

My right leg was broken in eight places. The doctors called it a "popcorn break" because the bones resembled popcorn. There were broken ribs, torn ligaments in my left leg, head injuries and other minor damage.

We were both in a wheelchair, walker and crutches for the better part of a year. We were both also taking therapy during that time. I don't know what we would have done if one family hadn't taken us under their wing. For over six months they did everything for us—shopping, washing and cleaning. They even built a ramp for us so we could get in and out when we were able.

As with many injuries, arthritis set in both of my ankles. I was in constant pain whenever I was on my feet. It became something I had to live with. I took pain medicine when the pain got too bad.

Shortly after we started coming to Landmark Church of God, it was announced that there would be a "Foot Washing." I had heard about "Foot Washings" but had never participated in one. It was an emotional experience. The Holy Spirit came down on me but only lightly, and I forgot about it.

The next day my wife and I went shopping at Wal-Mart. As we were walking from the parking lot to the store, I stopped suddenly. My wife asked me what was wrong. I told her that I didn't have any pain in my legs. After living with it all the time, I didn't realize that it was gone right away. I haven't had any pain since then. I am giving this testimony in the church on November 26, 2000. It has been two years since our accident. PRAISE GOD from whom all blessings flow. God is good—all the time!

Dr. Eric Shapiro

Be anxious for nothing, but in everything by prayer and supplication with thanksgiving, let your requests be made known to God; and the peace of God which surpasses all understanding will guard your hearts and minds through Christ Jesus. —Philippians 3: 6-7

I was born to Jewish parents in Roanoke, Virginia. When I was six months old, my parents split up. My mother took my older brother and me to her birthplace in Silver Springs, Maryland, near Washington, D.C., where her parents lived. My dad stayed in Virginia where he was born.

I lived in a depressive and uncomfortable environment. My dad didn't come around very often. When he came, I always wanted to go back with him. When I stayed with him during summer vacation, I always hated to return to my mother's house.

When I was in the fourth grade, we moved into a house in Chevy Chase, Maryland. Without God, my mother tried to find happiness in other ways. For example, she was a compulsive shopper. One day my brother went to live permanently with my Dad. My mother, however, kept custody of me.

It was really tough when my brother left. Life was extremely difficult. My mother worked a lot of overtime after which she would go shopping. In the eighth grade, I finally went to live with my dad thinking that the grass would be greener. Dad had a new wife with a chemical imbalance who had been married four times previously. Not only was I now living with my brother, but I also had a stepsister living with us. This, too, was a most difficult situation. My dad was self-centered and unable to show affection or love to us. When he didn't want to deal with life, he would just shut us out and keep to himself.

I tried to get his attention by asking a lot of questions. He'd say, "If you don't have good questions to ask, don't ask." My stepsister and brother were often in trouble. That was definitely not a great environment. It was a hornets' nest.

Whereas my mother treated us with acts of commission against us, my dad treated us with acts of omission. When I went to live with my dad, it was difficult. In school I was the new kid. All the other kids had known each other all their lives. I rebelled and was always in trouble in school. At the end of that first year with my dad, I had two choices—military school or returning to live with my mother. I chose to return to live with my mother.

When I went to live with my mother, I was in the tenth grade. We moved into an apartment in Rockville, Maryland, where I began to attend a new high school. I was still miserable. Now my dad was absent from the picture. He didn't want to deal with me. My home was a war zone. I was very angry and had a lot of rage. I was filled with bitterness and had thoughts of suicide. I saw no way of escape. I felt that I was living in a prison. I had no nurturing. I felt that I was a monster.

My mom had always dealt with the finances, and her name was on my account. I had always been a saver; and when I got a job, I saved most of my money. I had built up a good account. One day when I was eighteen, I found that my money was no longer there. I confronted my mother. She became very defensive and threw me out.

I went to a friend's house and called my Dad. I didn't know if he would come or not, but he did. My mother dumped off my clothes and everything belonging to me at my father's house. I had a job and had been accepted into college. In the fall, my mother put the money she had taken back into my account. I entered college at the University of North Carolina at Wilmington. I did not make good grades because I was drinking and partying. I had difficulty with relationships. Meanwhile, my stepmother left my father. I was driven to succeed and was very afraid of failure. I put most of my energy into school leaving very little time for anyone else.

When I received my degree, I moved to Statesville. God was working even though I couldn't see it. I became a student intern and passed my chiropractic board exams. To people on the outside, it looked as if I had it made. I had a good job contract and a family; but I was miserable. I was severely depressed. It was scary. I had little confidence in myself and was working in a high volume practice.

One day a patient came to me for treatment. I found out that he played basketball which I enjoyed. I didn't know he was a Christian, but eventually he invited me to church. He came by and picked me up. I'd met the pastor of the church because he lived two doors down from us. This was a pivotal time in my life. God was working. I continued to play basketball.

I was not easily convinced about the Christian faith. I had so many questions and challenges to the faith. For a year, the pastor met every Monday with me. As he educated me, I began to realize that something about this makes sense. Yet, I had a Jewish background. I didn't want to make a decision for Jesus. I didn't feel blessed and didn't have God in my life.

I could support my family, yet I was still miserable. As I was hearing what this Jesus character was about, I was really being convicted. I really challenged the pastor. He said that he learned as much from me as I did from him. What made the difference was that he lived what he taught.

The battle within my soul was becoming more and more intense. I knew that what I was hearing was right, but I was afraid of my family. I had to have scripture to support what I believed. Finally, during the Easter service, I prayed the Sinner's Prayer.

First, I told my stepmother. This began making my decision real to me. She brought my decision to my dad's attention. I experienced such a great peace. All of the clouds lifted. I told my mother that I had converted. By then some of my other relatives had already converted.

I took my mother to a Jews for Jesus service and took her to church. I bought her a Bible. She was offended, yet she said that she had given her life to Jesus. On my grandfather's deathbed, my mother told him that perhaps he should consider Jesus. My stepsister has given her life to Jesus.

Before I accepted Jesus into my life, my life was a mess. I was depressed and unhappy. I was angry and miserable. Now I know the peace of Philippians 3: 6-7 "which surpasses all understanding." Now I choose life, not death. I don't have to be anxious for anything because I know the One who guards my heart and mind. His name is Jesus.

I have learned to control my anger. I have three beautiful children and a growing chiropractic practice of my own. Now when I have problems, I have One to whom I can turn. I have friends who will pray with me. I have learned to forgive my parents so that the cycle can be stopped. I've learned to let go of the bitterness.

Yes, I still have problems. I still get angry. I'm human. I still get discouraged at times like anyone else, and sometimes I worry too much. The difference is that now I have a bright, peaceful future here on earth and an eternal future because I know the WAYMAKER. Not only do I know the God of Abraham, Jacob and Isaac and my heritage, I also know the Messiah. Now as a Jewish person I am complete. What joy and peace!

Let me encourage you. If you do not know Jesus Christ as your Lord and Savior, take time to invite Him into your heart today. You'll never be the same again. As I have learned, you will learn to "Be anxious for nothing." You will find that as you "let your requests be made known to God" in prayer, "the peace of God which surpasses all understanding" will fill your heart and mind as it has mine (Philippians 3: 6-7).

Barbara J. Smith

I will fear no evil.—Psalm 23: 4

Roots of Love: Flowers that Never Fade

"I will fear no evil." In Psalm 23: 4, David the shepherd poet reminds us of our power in Christ. These words were inspirational to me on many occasions but never more so than on a beautiful morning in April of the year 1997. From the beginning of that year, my sixty-six year old mother prayed the Twenty-third Psalm in a most unusual manner. She began to pray the Twenty-third Psalm with a vengeance and at the oddest times.

My siblings and I often wondered if she were losing her mind because when she would go to the part in the Twenty-third Psalm of, "I will fear no evil," she repeated that phrase seven times. When asked about this unusual behavior, she explained that she felt inspired by God to repeat the phrase, "I will fear no evil" seven times. Although this was highly unusual for her as well, she obeyed the directive from the Lord. It was only a few short months later that we understood the purpose for this unusual behavior. God was reiterating to her that His power is immeasurable and available to every believer.

It was very early on April 21, 1997, in Denver, Colorado, when I received a telephone call from my mother who lived in the state of Alabama. "Barbara, your dad is dead. He just died of a heart attack." I could not believe it—not my dad. He was a tower of strength, never sick. He never made appointments to see the doctor. He was always strong and healthy; yet, her words were unbelievably true, and there was no prior warning of this tragic event. I was so shocked and unprepared. He was only sixty-eight years old—too young to die! Words are not adequate in expressing the shock and tremendous grief which engulfed me on that horrible morning.

My mother and father were married when my mother, a cotton farmer's daughter, was only fourteen years of age; and my father, the son of a farmer, was seventeen years of age. At my father's untimely death, they had been married for fifty-one years. In God's faithfulness, He planted Psalm 23 in my mother's heart as a reminder that He knows our future and cares about every detail of every day. God helps us to lean on Him and trust in the strong arm of the Lord at all times. We have power in Him; and in the darkest of times, we can trust Him because He will never fail us and never leave us.

Devastation and despair surrounded me as I flew from Denver, Colorado, to Alabama to attend my father's funeral; yet, I also began to reflect on the roots of love he and mother had planted in my life. They provided a home full of love and acceptance where friends were always welcome—a home where the peace of God's love and blessings could readily be felt. I was reminded of the scripture found in Proverbs 3: 3 (*NIV*):

> Let love and faithfulness never leave you; bind them around your neck, write them on the tablet of your heart.

At that moment I realized that my parents had given me something so much more important than life itself; they had given me an unwavering devotion to God. They demonstrated faithfulness and love of God by their walk of love. They were from a long line of love where their parents had celebrated golden anniversaries together in love. This long line of love had been passed from generation to generation. What a beautiful garden of love that had been passed to me! I am so blessed to be given this abundant treasure—a faithfulness to pass on to the generations that follow me. In the book of Ephesians, God instructs us to be rooted and grounded in love. Such was the case in the home where I was reared—parents rooted and grounded in love, God's love.

"I will fear no evil for thou art with me." My mother was reminded that she had nothing to fear. She had nothing present, nothing past nor nothing in the future to fear. God was her ever present help in time of trouble; and she was reminded to fear nothing for God's power is limitless, immeasurable and present at all times.

In the days following the funeral, I remained with my mother for three weeks. After all, she had never slept by herself since the age of fourteen when she married my father. For three weeks after the funeral, I shared the king-sized bed where my father had always slept.

Often I would awaken in the night to find that my mother was not beside me. Upon searching the large five bedroom home, I always found her praying in her prayer closet. As I approached her prayer closet, I could hear her praying loudly and speaking in tongues as she relied upon the Holy Ghost to get her through the darkest of nights.

Early the next morning, I would inquire of her to see if she were going to be all right; and she always assured me that I had nothing to fear because as she said, "She and the Holy Ghost always worked these things out together, and everything was going to be all right." She had learned to do as God's word instructs in I Peter 5: 7: "Cast all your care on Him for He cares for you."

Mother demonstrated that the way one survives life is by leaning on the strong arm of God, not the arm of flesh. She cast all upon the Lord and found Him faithful. As a flower that never fades, she reminded me of the scripture found in Proverbs 3: 3 (*NIV*),

> Let love and faithfulness never leave you; bind them around your neck, write them on the tablet of your heart.

This never fading flower taught me a profound truth:

> Yea, though I walk through the valley of the shadow of death, I will fear no evil, for thou art with me.—Psalm 23: 4 (*NIV*)

My mother died suddenly and unexpectedly like my father, three years and eight months later. Her death also caught me by surprise; however, I found greater strength through her death because she had beautifully illustrated the way to survive dark hours in life. I learned to *cast my care upon Him, for He cares for me.* She and my father were choice servants of the Lord, and they remain in my life as fragrant flowers that never fade. By their faithful service to God, I, too, am rooted and grounded in love.

Reverend Jerry Smith

Trust in the Lord with all your heart, and lean not on your own understanding; In all your ways, acknowledge Him, and He shall direct your paths.—Proverbs 3: 5-6

Reverend Jerry Smith preached a revival at Landmark Church of God from April 4, 2000, until April 7, 2000. During that time, he shared several testimonies from his life and ministry. He used the following to illustrate a point about God's ability to minister to our every need "exceedingly, abundantly beyond what we can ask or think (Ephesians 3:20)."

"My wife and I," he said, "after leaving the Home for Children, were pastoring the great church in Pine Valley in Wilmington, the largest Church of God in Eastern North Carolina at that time. We had a beautiful congregation, things going great when the Lord said, 'I need you in Raleigh.'

"No, no, not me," I said. "The first thing I did was to get my minute book. I started subtracting. I said, 'No, Lord. I'd have to take a $200.00 a week cut in salary to go to Raleigh. But the Lord said, 'That's where I need you. I need you to go there and to relocate the properties there.' So we gave up the great church in Wilmington, and we went to Raleigh.

"For the first two years there I beat my head against the wall. My gift is not in singing or playing musical instruments, but God has given me a gift to get things done sometimes when it seems there is no other way to do it. So I beat my head against the wall, and I got nowhere. I began to understand why so many pastors had come and had gone because of the frustration that they just couldn't get it done.

"See, in Raleigh you've never seen the resistance of trying to do something for God like you have in the capital city. The devil doesn't want any churches. He wants all the beer halls, the dance halls and the honkey tonks that he can get, but he doesn't want any more churches."

"Keep these dates in mind—June 1994. We were getting ready to go to the Campmeeting. A realtor called and said, 'Pastor, I've found you a piece of land. I've got three acres. It's $175,000 an acre. It'll cost you $500,000 to get it built up so that you can build a church on it.' I said, 'Man, we can't afford anything like that. That's completely out of reason. He said, 'Well, that's the best I can do, and that's the best that you'll do because you're not going to find any land in the city of Raleigh unless you pay high dollar for it.' I hung the phone up and went to campmeeting."

"Monday through Saturday night Tim Hill from the state of Virginia was the night speaker. On Saturday night we were standing after the service. There were about 200 people fellowshipping in the Tabernacle. Tim Hill was getting ready to walk out the door when he ran up and grabbed a microphone. 'Hold it a minute!' he said. 'Everyone stop talking. God has just spoken to my heart and told me to make an announcement from this pulpit. There's somebody in this building who has been trying to buy land to relocate and rebuild a new church. Everywhere you turn the land is too high, but you go home and wait on me. I'm going to do a miracle for you.'

"My wife looked at me as we left the Tabernacle and said, 'That man was talking to you tonight.' We go home and I'm sitting there waiting, God, you're going to drop it right out of the sky right on top of me. But we went for several weeks. On a Saturday night the telephone rang. A man called and said, 'Pastor can you meet me in fifteen minutes?' I got in my car and went over there. He said, 'You see this six acres of land? It's on the tax books for $ 1,070,000. It's gone into foreclosure. If we can raise $200,000, you can buy it for the church for $200,000.' The Lord clicked a light bulb in my head and said, 'Son, this is the promised land. This is what I promised you in the Campmeeting.'

"I'll tell you something church. The devil will try to cloud your vision. He'll try to retard your spiritual growth, but I've come by Statesville to tell you one more time that He's a God of miracles! He's a God of signs and wonders! There's nothing too hard for the lovely Lord to do!

"I rushed home. I could hardly sleep. The next morning I got up to go to church. I showed the plan to my mens' council. 'Oh, yes, preacher that's it.' I could have already told them that. 'We ought to raise the money this morning,' they said. They'd talked about this for twenty years but had never done anything to save any money. They didn't have any money in the bank. 'We can raise it this morning,' they said. I said, 'Oh, no, no, no.'

"They said, 'What do you mean, no?' I said, 'I don't want to raise this money on your emotions. There will be some of you that will tell me you'll give me $ 5,000; but before you get home, you will have talked yourself out of it. We're going to do this thing the way that God tells me to do it. I'm going to talk to God about how we're going to do it.

"I had a meeting the next morning on August 3, 1994. We're scheduled to fly out the next Monday morning for the San Antonio General Assembly. I had a meeting that morning with the man from the bank. I go down. He's sitting there. I walk over. He said, 'Preacher, we can let you have the land for $ 200,000 that's worth $ 1,070,000 on the tax books, but there's one catch.' I said, 'What's that?' He said, 'You've got to raise the $200,000 in the next twenty-eight days. You don't have time to borrow it. If you're really serious, you've got to raise the money.' I said, 'Give me a pen and let me sign the paper for a commitment.' He pushed the contract over to me, and I boldly signed my name as the pastor of the Raleigh Church of God.

"I walked out of McDonalds and got in my truck. Before I got half way home, the anointing left me. I walked in the house, and my wife said, 'What's the matter?' I said, 'I've just signed a contract to raise $200,000 in twenty-eight days.' She said, 'But we're supposed to be going to the General Assembly.' I said, 'No Assembly this year, dear. I've got to stay home. I've got to raise $200,000.' She said, 'How are you going to do that?' I said, ' I don't know. Me and God have got ourselves a problem.'

"I was praying when God said, 'I want you to go to Durham to a car dealer. I got in my truck and was going down Interstate 40, sixty-five miles an hour toward Durham when this crazy nut rushes up on the bumper of my truck. I remember looking in the mirror, thinking to myself, 'He's going to wreck me.'

"I just held to the steering wheel. He pulled up beside me almost metal to metal with me. Then he took off the highway. Then in a few minutes, I saw him again. This time he had slowed down, and my truck was catching up to him. I got to within thirty or forty feet of his automobile. I noticed it was a taxi cab. When I got to within about thirty feet of him, the dome on the taxi cab lit up and said, 'Trust God.' I grabbed hold of the steering wheel. The wise man, Solomon spoke into my spirit, 'Lean not unto your own understanding; but in all thy ways, acknowledge Him, and He'll direct your paths.'

"I'm telling you, God knows where you are. He's a miracle worker. He's a God that can do the impossible for those that believe Him. I get to the car dealer. I walk in and tell the man that I need to talk with him in his office privately. I tell this man my story that the Lord sent me here and told me that you would give me $ 1,000. When I get through telling him that God sent me here, he looked at me and said, 'Preacher, I'm sorry. I can't give you anything. I don't have anything to give you. I can't sell a car. My rental business has gone to nearly nothing. We can't even hardly give automobiles away.'

"I'm confused now. So I get up and I start to the door. I got to the door, and I turned around and said, 'Now sir, let me tell you something. God sent me over here. I'm going to pray all the way back home. I'm going to pray for God to make you sell more automobiles than you've ever sold. I'm going to pray for God to make your rental business the greatest it's ever been. He said, 'I sure would appreciate that.' Then I said, 'But when He does, then I'm expecting that $ 1,000 check in the mail.'

"In a couple of days, his wife called and said, 'We're selling cars like we've never sold them before. Instead of sending you $ 1,000, we're going to send you $2,000.' Church, you hear me! Wachovia may go belly up tomorrow. The Dow Jones may hit $250 tomorrow; but my Father owns the cattle on a thousand hills, and He owns all the gold that's in those hills. He's a miracle worker! He's a miracle worker! Hallelujah!

"I started writing letters. The Lord told me to write letters. I told folks, 'Now, I've got to have $1,000 minimum. You can send as much as you want, but we've got to have $ 1,000 minimum.' We got a stack of letters and poured anointing oil over them, soaked them good. We took them to the post office. God did a miracle. To make a long story short, on August 31, twenty-eight days later, I walked into an attorney's office and laid on his desk a cashier's check for $206,000. Hallelujah! He's a God of miracles.

"We built a beautiful church there in Raleigh sitting on a million dollar piece of property. One night in a service, I called a couple out of the service. I felt impressed of the Lord. I said, 'I want you and your wife to come here.' I handed them a bottle of anointing oil. I said, 'Tomorrow morning I want you to start walking from one end of the lot to another.' We had 1350 feet of road frontage, one and a half football fields long. I said, 'I want you to walk along pouring the anointing oil. They did; and as they walked, they said, 'God we're claiming this land for prostitutes. We're claiming this land for drug addicts. We're claiming this land for broken marriages. We're claiming for sinners, and we're claiming this land for people that need God.'

"The architect came by looking at the landscape. He was doing his final drawing. He pulled up his shoe and looked at me. He said, 'Do I have oil all over my shoe?' I said, 'Yes, but it's not Kendall. It's not Phillips 66. It's not Havoline. It's Holy Ghost oil. Praise God! It's going to make the grass grow and win souls for the Kingdom of God!

"We built the church and completed it for about $ 5,000 under budget. On February 16, 1997 we were going to the church. At the Children's Home, my wife and I had decided that when I became fifty-five years old, I wanted to go back into evangelistic work. Here I was going into the church on February 16. On February 25, I would be fifty-five years old. As of January 1, 1998, I became an evangelist for Eastern North Carolina.

"Things went pretty good from January to June. Then the first week of June, I got a call from the state office. Brother Smith,' We're sorry to have to tell you. We don't have the money to send you to the General Assembly this year. I said, 'O.K. No big deal. I'll just stay home. Well, I got it out of my system.

"Then two weeks later, I got a telephone call. The overseer said, 'I've got good news and some not so good news. We've had a little bit of extra money to come in. We've got enough money to pay for your motel and your meals if you can arrange for your transportation to the General Assembly and back.'

"I hung up the phone and that same light went off again. I took off running up the stairs to my desk. There it was—an airline ticket dated August 1994 to San Antonio, Texas. I got in my car and went to American Airlines to ask if the ticket was any good. The lady said that it sure was but asked, 'Why did it take you so long to make this journey?' I told her that she wouldn't believe it if I told her. There I was with money in my pocket for a motel and meals and now an airline ticket.

"I got to the airport ready to leave out about 4:00 p.m. I heard someone page me. I thought something had happened at home and ran to the desk. The lady said that she had a businessman who urgently needed my seat. She asked if I'd give up my seat. I asked what it was worth to her. Keep in mind I had enough for my motel and meals. I didn't have any spending money. She said, $ 300.00.

"I asked when the next flight would leave. She said, '7:00 p.m.' I said, 'Write me a check.' She wrote me a check and I went over to the ice cream bar. I got me a cone of butternut ice cream. I said, 'God, this is the way it is in the land that flows in milk and honey. You never let your children down. You're a God of miracles and a God of signs and wonders! Hallelujah!

"At 7:00 p.m. I got on the plane and flew to Dallas-Fort Worth. I got off and went to my connecting flight. I laid my ticket on the desk. The ticket clerk said, 'Are you Reverend Smith?' I said, 'Yes, Ma'm.' She said, 'Reverend Smith, we've got a businessman that needs to be in San Antonio early in the morning.' Why me out of 297 passengers? I'll tell you why me! God knew the little sparrow. There's not a sparrow that falls that doesn't catch His eye. There's not one of His children that has a need that He doesn't take care of. 'Would you consider letting us have your seat?' I said, 'No, ma'm. I also have to be in San Antonio in the morning.' So she did what she needed to do to my ticket. I got on the plane and buckled up.

"Then I remembered that I forgot to ask her what it was worth. I asked the stewardess if I could get off the plane. I asked what it would be worth. The lady said, $ 200.00.' Then the next lady said,

'No, you give him $ 300.00.' I'll tell you—first I didn't have money to go anywhere. Then I got the money for a motel and meals. Then I got an airline ticket. Now I had $ 600 in my pocket. He is my God! He's a miracle worker!

"They chauffeured me over to the Hyatt Regency and put me in a king size suite, compliments of American Airlines. That room was as big as this platform. I want to tell you that it wasn't complements of American Airlines. It was compliments of my Heavenly Father who takes care of His church, who provides for the needs of His people.

"The next morning I went back to the airport and laid my ticket on the desk. The lady said, 'Are you Reverend Smith?' I said,'Yes, ma'm I am.' She said, 'Reverend Smith, we've been waiting for you. American Airlines headquarters told us to be on the lookout for you. You have been so cooperative in assisting us with a valued customer that we've been told to fly you first class for the rest of your journey to San Antonio and back to Raleigh, North Carolina. Talk about walking like a peacock with his feathers spread back. I was a King's kid. Thank God I'm a King's kid. I said, 'ma'm, I've never sat in first class. Would you do me the honor to escort me to my seat?' She said, ' I certainly would.' She took me in and sat me down in seat IA.

"I was sitting in 1A feeling so good when one of the men who voted that they did not have the money to send me to the General Assembly walked on the plane and gave me a double take. Well, he went to the back of the plane and ate peanuts. I sat in first class and ate filet mignon. God takes care of His church. God's going to take care of His church. He'll take care of you! I haven't told that man to this day why I was sitting in IA.

"Is this going to happen at the next General Assembly? Probably not. I've tried to save up a little to have enough. If it were to happen, I can still turn to my resource. It's not Wachovia. It's not First Union. It's not the bank downtown. My resource is my Heavenly Father, the God of all creation.

"What do you need? I believe that whatsoever God says, He will do. My uncle once said to me, 'Son, we are going to do the work of the Lord. He will take care of us.' If you will exercise your faith in God, He will do a miracle for you, too. The Holy Scripture says that with God all things are possible. The same God who helped me raise $ 200,000, who gave me an airline ticket, can heal your body. He can do anything you have need of. Indeed, God specializes in signs and wonders for His people. As Proverbs 3:5-6 says,

> If you will 'trust in the Lord with all of your heart and lean not on your understanding and in all your ways acknowledge Him... He shall direct your paths. He will provide for you exceedingly, abundantly beyond all you can ask or think.

"For, as Paul said, 'My God shall supply for all your needs according to His riches in glory" (Philippians 4: 19).

Onnie H. Smith

In the beginning was the Word, and the Word was with God, and the Word was God. —John 1: 1

One Sunday when I was I child, I went to the children's class In Sunday School where all of us children were given postal size cards with pictures on them. I kept the one with Jesus holding a lamb that said, "Come little children. Come unto me."

I was nine years old when I became stricken with a bone disease that would have left my body stiff (not flexible). I laid in bed day after day with the doctor making his visits. He said to my parents, "You will either have to buy a casket one day, or she will be a burden for the rest of your life and her life. I looked to Jesus who was my constant companion and said, "No way," and He said, "No way," back to me. Today I am walking on my own because of my childish belief in that person on the post card. Since then that is the way my life has been—believing and trusting in Him.

I think of others and ask Him to walk with them making their lives comfortable. That's the way I feel and think about other creatures. I ask Jesus to help them too because they also have lives to live. Why kill them? My greatest pleasure in life is to help others to believe and trust wholly and sincerely in Jesus that they, too, may grow stronger in mind and strength.

My experience helping lead others to believe and trust in Jesus continued as I worked with my husband (an ordained Southern Baptist minister) in the brushy mountains of North Carolina. Where we lived no one would choose to go to teach the Bible. We went to show people the way of life taught in the Bible. We worked with people who needed to feel loved and cared for by others. We wanted them to feel free to come into town to fellowship with others. As we loved these people and planted churches, I always shared and stood on John 1: 1:

> In the beginning was the Word, and the Word was with God, and the Word was God.

When my husband died, I was left with two adopted children to raise. That was a challenge. Now I am left with two grandchildren to raise. Raising these children has required the full use of my abilities, energy and resources; but I know that as we continue in childlike faith to believe and trust wholly and sincerely in Jesus, we'll win!

Steven Smith

Yea, though I walk through the valley of the shadow of death, I will fear no evil, for You are with me; Your rod and Your staff, they comfort me.—Psalm 23: 4

My name is Steven Smith, and I'm fighting liver cancer. It's called lymphoma. My problems all began in January of 1982. My stomach hurt for five days, and I had diarrhea. I went to Iredell Memorial Hospital twice and was sent home. I went back a third time and was admitted.

The doctors did a liver biopsy and found a tumor. I lay in intensive care for about a week. The doctors wanted to send me to Baptist Hospital because they could not do anything else for me. As a matter of fact, they were ready to cover me with the death blanket at any minute. They said, "If he lives overnight, it will be a miracle." When I went to Baptist Hospital, I was also put in Intensive Care. My weight started at 180 pounds, but the disease made me swell up to 260 pounds. My eyes, hands and fingernails were yellow, and I was swollen from above the waist on down. The pain was awful, and I had to be given Demerol every four hours.

One day I had a lot of friends and co-workers come to see me. They came in two at a time. I thought it was just a day for a lot of company, but the truth was that I only had three days to live. The doctor had said that if anybody wanted to see me, they had better come. Word was that I was dying, and it would be a miracle if I even left the hospital. My mother wanted to know from the doctor if she should tell me. He said, "Only if he asks." I was scared and knew what was happening, but I didn't want to be told that I was dying.

I had a real bad day, and death was actually taking place. My eyes rolled back in my head. I started sweating real bad, and my heart was beating extremely fast. I felt like my body was splitting in two and that at any minute I would be looking down at my own body. It scared me so bad that I jumped up in bed and yelled, "I don't want to die. I don't want to die. I don't want to die." The nurses got me calmed down, and I was o.k.

The doctors started chemotherapy treatments and let me leave the hospital once I started responding to the treatments. I know the doctors and the hospital were a big factor; but the most important thing that really made the difference were the prayers coming from four counties and God's decision to let me live.

For the next couple of years, I went through more chemo treatments. After that the doctors examined my liver and told me that the cancer was gone and that I was healthy as a horse. God had healed me. The cancer remained gone from my body for over eighteen years.

The cancer was gone until March of this year. My stomach hurt for three months, and I was losing weight fast. I lost forty pounds, and the lymph nodes on my neck swelled up. I thought that it was an ulcer at first, never dreaming that the cancer would be back after so long. I went back to Baptist for a yearly check-up, and they confirmed that the cancer had returned. My doctor looked very sad when he told me. They admitted me back into the hospital and scheduled another biopsy. The results came back, and my doctor was excited this time. He told me it was the same thing, and we were going to treat it the same way.

The CT scan showed a spot on my liver about as big as a softball and another on my spleen just about as big. After five treatments, it had shrunk to less than half the size it was. At first they wanted to do two more treatments and another CT scan. This past Thursday, I found out that after only one treatment the doctors want to go ahead and do another CT scan in a few more weeks. They seem to think that the cancer will be completely gone in a few months. I strongly believe that it will because as Psalm 23: 4 says,

> Yea, though I walk through the valley of the shadow of death, I will fear no evil, For You are with me; Your rod and Your staff, they comfort me.

I know that all this is possible because of the healing powers of Jesus Christ. He healed me twice, in 1982 and in 2000. It was also possible because of you the people here at Landmark Church of God praying for me. I would like to say thank you for that. Prayers are answered. When you pray for the people in this church bulletin, the prayers are heard and do work. I'm one of them.

I'd like to thank Eddie Wilson for coming to the hospital and praying over me, Pastor Hudson for his thoughts and prayers and Reverend Frank Black for his prayers and friendship and for allowing me to give this testimony. I would also like to thank Annette Moose who has had me in her thoughts and prayers and especially my sister Judy English and her husband Lynn for introducing me to the Landmark Church of God and for getting me here. You have a wonderful church here, and I am very impressed with the love that has been shown to me here; however, the real thanks goes to God.

Praise the Lord! Most people don't get a miracle in life, and I've gotten two. My testimony is just a small way for me to give back to God for all of the wonderful things that He has done for me. I am so glad to share what He has done for me with you. I would like for you to remember that miracles still happen. After all, I am living proof. Thank you for listening.

Pastor John Soroka

Praise ye the Lord. O give thanks unto the Lord; for He is good: for His mercy endureth forever. Who can utter the mighty acts of the Lord? Who can shew forth all His praise?—Psalm 106: 1-2

It is easy to praise the Lord when you're blessed and everything is going your way. Few of us have any trouble giving thanks when the sun is shinning and we're living on the mountain top; but when our faith is tried, and we face a situation that defies an explanation, it's then that our true faith in the Lord and our unfailing love for Christ is demonstrated.

A number of years ago, after my wife and I were married, and we were raising our family; I faced a situation that left me puzzled and my faith sorely tested. One evening as I was sitting in our living room, I suddenly was overcome with a horrible feeling that I was having a heart attack. Along with this feeling, there was an overwhelming presence of suffocation that made me feel I was about to die. I became short of breath, and my heart started beating rapidly. Along with perspiration, I had all the symptoms of a heart attack.

It seems that a presence of an evil spirit was descending upon me, and I felt so helpless. My family quickly gathered around, and we immediately called on the Lord for His help. After awhile, the symptoms subsided, and I was able to rest. Without knowing it, I was about to enter a new phase of my walk with God. I was hoping that this was an isolated incident, but it was only the beginning.

A few days later, the same scenario took place—the rapid heart beat, the sweating, and the feeling that I was going to die. Each time we prayed and asked the Lord to intervene, and each time the situation returned to normal. This went on for weeks which eventually turned into months. I was in continual prayer, but it seemed that the Lord was letting me experience this situation for an unexplainable reason. I was careful to examine my life and confess any sins that I may be guilty of. It seems I was going through a trial that God was using to develop my faith in Him.

These attacks would occur almost anywhere, in my home, at work or while I was driving the car. It even happened while I was in church. I had to quickly leave where I was at the time and just wait it out. Needless to say, it was very frightening and perplexing. I knew I wasn't crazy and losing my mind; but I suppose if I had been examined by the medical profession, I might have been locked up. I didn't know it at the time, but our Lord was fully in charge of everything from the beginning.

This all came to an end one night when I was awakened from sleep with this sensation of dying, and a feeling of evil overcame me once again. I went into the living room and began to pace the floor as I did many times before. I kept praying and talking to the Lord when I felt God speaking to my heart to start praising Him and forget about the symptoms. It was such a wonderful feeling that I experienced, and I immediately began to lift my voice in praise and adoration to Jesus who was with me in that room. It was then that this oppression that had plagued me for months began to leave, and I was delivered then and there.

I also felt the Lord prompt me to rebuke the devil. The scriptures admonish us "to resist the devil, and he will flee from you," and that is just what I did. I reminded Satan that he was a liar and that he had no part in my life. It was at that moment that his hold over me was broken.

I have since learned that I was experiencing panic attacks. This is a malady that affects millions of people around the world. When I hear of others who have this problem, I am dismayed when I hear of the fortune being spent on doctors and medicine to combat this disorder. I know that God allowed me to go through this trouble to test my faith and teach me to trust in Him. But the real victory did not come until I learned the power that exists when you praise the name of our God.

Satan cannot remain when we lift our voice in praise and adoration to our Savior, Jesus Christ, who paid the price for our healing at Calvary. I have since talked to many who are going through this same problem, and I always relate my story of how God delivered me by just praising His name. It has been over twenty-five years since this first occurred, and God has given me the victory ever since. I now know that everything we experience as a Christian is to prepare us for a work God has for us down the road.

As II Corinthians l: 3,4 says:

> Blessed be God, even the Father of our Lord Jesus Christ, the Father of mercies, and the God of all comfort; Who comforteth us in all our tribulation, that we may be able to comfort them which are in any trouble, by the comfort wherewith we ourselves are comforted of God.

Karen and Bob Spalding

He brought out His people with joy, His chosen ones with gladness. —Psalm 105:3

Since the beginning of the church, men and women have portrayed Jesus Christ in various art forms and settings. It is rare, however, to see any canvas portraying Jesus laughing. The "Laughing Christ" hanging in Saint Mary's Episcopalian church in Ashe County, North Carolina is a beautiful exception to the standard portrayals of Christ. This painting by Bo Bartlett, a student of Ben Long, represents the artist's belief that Jesus had a sense of humor and knew how to enjoy life. (See the appendix for more details about this painting.)

Verses of scripture such as Psalm l05: 3 seem to indicate that God must have a sense of humor and a spirit of laughter. The Hebrew word for joy in this verse is *sason* which means cheerful, gladness, joy, mirth and rejoicing. Throughout the Word of God, His son, our Lord shared not only the sorrows of the people but also their joys in celebrations such as the wedding feast.

As a fairly new Christian, Karen had been diligently seeking the Lord especially through Bible study. She did not know a lot about the character of the Lord other than His incredible love. She had certainly never thought about Him having a sense of humor. That all changed one day while she and Bob were moving furniture in a warehouse.

Prior to this workday, God had been dealing with her about the need to live out the truths presented in the fifth chapter of Ephesians especially Ephesians 5: 22, "Wives, submit to your own husbands as to the Lord." Karen was very tired when she and Bob began to move a dresser from a flatbed trailer into a storage bay. She had been irritable all day just wanting the work to be over with so she could go home and rest.

As they began the work, Karen disagreed with the way Bob wanted to move the dresser. Just as she said to Bob, "I don't think it'll work," she thought about the verse in Ephesians 5:22, "Wives, submit to your own husbands as to the Lord," but decided to ignore it. Bob let her have her own way. Suddenly, the mirror on the dresser shattered. On the back of the mirror she noticed an old, weathered sign that was brown around the edges which read, "Do not attempt vast projects with half vast ideas." Karen could not believe what she was reading and just stood staring at the mirror. When Bob first read the sign and looked at the mirror, he acted as if he did not understand what had just happened. Then all of a sudden both Bob and Karen began to laugh uncontrollably. She began to think, "How much God must have loved me to go to this extreme to teach me this lesson from Ephesians 5:22. I realized that He had a sense of humor," she concluded.

What a testimony this is to God's faithfulness to teach His children so many lessons of life. He tells His people to "lean not unto (their) own understanding" (Proverbs 3:5b); yet when they do He is still able to bring them out with joy, gladness and humor and at the same time impart to them the wisdom they need.

Karen and Bob Spalding

And God is able to make all grace abound toward you: that ye, always having all sufficiency in all things, may abound to every good work.—II Corinthians 9: 8

God enabled our family to have the "sufficiency in all things," mentioned in II Corinthians 9:8 as He provided countless small and large spiritual, emotional and physical blessings for us. Although the ways God has made His grace abound toward us may seem small or unimportant to others, they caused us to grow in faith and created a desire in us to give back liberally to God. As I John 5:4 says, "....this is the victory that overcomes the world, even our faith."

Many times God provided clothes for me and the family. Once I prayed for a pair of shoes for one of our sons. I walked into a second-hand store and saw Buster Brown shoes with the label intact as if they'd never been worn. The shoes were polished like new and cost $5.00.

Most women like for their husbands to take them on shopping sprees. One night the Lord sent Bob shopping on the way home from work about 2:00 a.m. As he was driving home, there they were—brand new clothes lying all over the highway. Although he did not know my size and could not see the sizes of the dresses in the dark, he brought home six dresses and two suit jackets that fit me perfectly.

God also once provided me a summer wardrobe when I agreed to conduct a yard sale for a friend. Once I found a winter coat in Goodwill that I later saw in Belk for $159.00. I know that God owns the cattle on a thousand hills, but I also believe that He is a smart shopper. Those were all times when I felt that Psalm 104: 28b applied to me as it says, "Thou openest thine hand, and they are filled with good."

Learning to totally trust Him can be so much fun. One time when I traveled by train from Indiana home to Florida with our three sons, I sent our son Bobby to ask the conductor if $ 1.00 (all the money I had) would buy a carton of milk and a cup of soup. The conductor sent Bobby back with the soup, the milk and the one dollar bill. Psalm 89: 1 reads:

> I will sing of the mercies of the Lord forever: with my mouth will I make known thy faithfulness to all generations.

Not only did God provide the milk and soup, He had also created a permanent testimony for Bobby. He still remembers how we prayed and God faithfully responded.

It is really a delight when I recall all the times God provided vehicles for us in extraordinary ways. One time when we desperately needed a car, we saw an ad for a car on the church bulletin board. Much to our surprise, when we went to look at the car, the owner gave us the baby blue 1963 Valiant which we drove for three years with only minor repairs. There was something really amazing about that car.

The Scripture says that laughter is good medicine (Proverbs 17:22). Though it wasn't new or the best looking car, we have great memories of driving it. Everywhere we went, we were able to witness through a bumper sticker on the car which read, "DON'T LAUGH. IT'S PAID FOR." As people would laugh at the bumper sticker, Bob and I would respond, "Don't laugh. It's paid for just as our way to heaven is paid for through the work of Jesus Christ on the cross. Matthew 5: 14 reads:

> Ye are the light of the world. A city that is set on a hill cannot be hid.

It was obvious that our testimony could not be hid.

Another time Bob had admired our neighbor's antique Valiant and asked for the opportunity to buy it should the neighbor ever desire to sell it. It was in A1 condition with a brand new rebuilt engine. At Christmas when the neighbor died, his family told Bob that the man had told them to sell the car to Bob. We paid $250.00 for the car and drove it proudly for five years. I believe God delighted in giving Bob the desire of his heart just as He said he would do in Psalm 37: 4:

> Delight thyself also in the Lord; and He shall give thee the desires of thine heart.

Years later, Bob and I were trying to sell our car to pay the taxes on our home. When the car would not sell, the Lord directed us to give the car to a church whose members were willing to fix it for a needy family. Later, we had the joy of seeing this family driving this same car around town. God met our financial need in another way as we were obedient to do "things His way." Acts 20: 35 reads:

> I have shewed you all things, how that so labouring ye ought to support the weak, and to remember the words of the Lord Jesus, how He said, "It is more blessed to give than to receive."

When I recall God's tender mercies and love, I remember a time when I was a very new Christian housewife who desired for God to be my interior decorator. I wanted my home to be a blessing to others and especially my husband. My memories go back to a plush pink carpet provided free. I had wanted a feminine look in my front room to match my grandmother's elegant, antique furniture which had been newly recovered and given to us as a gift. One day a couple we had just met called and said, "We have been doing some redecorating in our home. As we were taking up the carpet from the formal living room, the Lord laid it on our hearts to give it to you." It was perfect.

Then there was the time we prayed and agreed not to go into debt to buy Bob a computer. We were excited when an upgraded computer arrived on Bob's birthday unexpectedly from my brother. Later another computer arrived from my other brother.

You might imagine the surprise on Bob's face when while working on a freight dock, he saw a crate arrive for us filled with a couch and love seat from my family for Christmas.

Another time, without telling anyone, Bob and I had prayed for funds for me to attend a ReSeven retreat. A friend called from out of town saying that God had laid it on his heart to send me $ 107 for a retreat—the exact amount I needed.

Several times God provided for us through people we had never met. One time after extensive knee surgery our son Karl needed a

$350.00 knee brace we could not afford. A Sunday School class in a different church heard about the need and took up an offering for $350.00. Nahum l: 7 tells us that:

> The Lord is good, a strong hold in the day of trouble; and He knoweth them that trust in Him.

Who would have believed that a man who was only an acquaintance would show up at our house with a bag full of rolled up pennies that came to $50.00. He had heard that Bob had lost his job leaving us in desperate financial need. This same man and his wife came back another time with a box of huge potatoes that lasted us for a month. We ate potatoes every way you could dream of fixing them. All we had were potatoes, but we had the best potatoes you could eat! I had told the children that God would provide. As we were learning to be totally dependent upon God, others were fulfilling Matthew 6: 11 in our lives: "Give us our daily bread." Through others we were also learning the truth of I Peter 3: 8:

> Finally, all of you be of one mind, having compassion for one another, love as brothers, be tenderhearted, be courteous.

God has provided traveling mercies for our family. One time when my van broke down in the middle of four lane traffic, I immediately began feeling great anxiety. Stalled in the middle of the road with three anxious children is no way to begin the day. The moment I recognized that I had to confess my need with my lips to God, a man arrived to help. His provision was just a whispered prayer away. Indeed, Psalm 94:9 is true when it says:

> He that planted the ear, shall He not hear? He that formed the eye, shall He not see? I want to smile when I say that I have learned to look for God in the day to day, seemingly, ordinary events of life.

God encouraged me to develop my artistic talents through a stranger who came to our door from a park across the street. The man was hungry. As Bob asked me to make him a sandwich, the Holy Spirit brought Hebrews l3:2 to my remembrance:

> Be not forgetful to entertain strangers: for thereby some have entertained angels unawares.

We decided to feed this fellow whose appearance was much like a hippie from the 60's. He stayed with us for a while. He never paid rent, but he saved our house from being destroyed by fire. When he left, he gave me a large roll of canvas and an entire set of oil paints as pay. He was an artist. This was when I discovered that God had given me this gift to paint. Three years later, this man wrote us and said that he had married a preacher's daughter. They had become missionaries to India.

One day God impressed me to give away a painting on which I had worked a very long time to a youth center for their new counseling room. The Lord created in me a desire to give it away. This would have been very difficult to do otherwise. I was surprised when my husband agreed but knew this was another way God was confirming His leading in my life. At the same time, He also gave me the Scripture in Ecclesiastes 11: 1:

> Cast thy bread upon the waters: for thou shalt find it after many days.

I was encouraged the day we presented the painting entitled "Fishers of Men" to the youth director. At that time I really had no idea what God intended to do later. Over the years, Bob would sometimes remark, "I really would have liked to keep that painting, Karen, but I'm glad you did what the Lord told you to do."

Well, three years later just before Bob and I moved to North Carolina, we received a call from the directors of the youth facility. They were closing the facility and wanted us to have the painting back so that it could remain in our family. I've often wondered how this painting which has been seen by relatively few people might be used one day to bless others. Now it has become a testimony in this book to God's creative and majestic power which He uses through His beloved children. Since that time God has reiterated His desire for me to use my artistic skills for Him. A number of times friends have unexpectantly given me money to buy paints and brushes to use this talent for the Lord.

There is a day in my mind and heart that will never be erased. It was a day when a lady came to our house carrying two bags of groceries. About twenty-nine years ago, two bags of groceries would feed our family for almost a week. Lucille was a precious lady of God who took the time to go the extra mile with me. This is the first time I remember someone I didn't know giving me something I really needed. She led me to put my trust in Jesus as my Savior, but she also shared her life with me. There were times when I felt in such debt to her. She would only remind me of the great debt Jesus paid, so I could know for certain I was going to heaven.

I didn't realize then that this single act of kindness began a journey for Bob and me where we would learn to recognize that God is able to supply all our needs. He is, indeed, Jehovah Jireh, our Provider. He has taught us that we can be content in all circumstances of life especially when His joy is our strength. We have learned that "little is much when God is in it." Bob and I could never repay the Lord for all the inexhaustible ways that He has answered our prayers and satisfied our needs.

Those who believe do serve a God who paid the debt they could not pay. He provided the greatest gift of all—eternal life— as He stretched out his hands on the cross and said, "It is finished" (John 19:30). In so doing, as Hebrews 12: 2 says, "He became the "author and finisher of our faith."

I have seen God provide groceries, clothes, transportation, art supplies, money, the desires of our hearts, household supplies, traveling mercies, and opportunities to use our gifts and bless others. I have seen God make all grace and sufficiency abound toward us enabling us to abound to good work as II Corinthians 9: 8 tells us.

Dee Stovall

My house shall be called a house of prayer for all nations.—Isaiah 56:7c

God's Blessings One Day at a Time

Every day is a blessing. Some days the blessing may be longer in revealing itself, but every day has a blessing in store. Prayer works. The Lord brought me to North Carolina, not by my choice, but because He chose to deliver me.

I was born into a comfortable family. I had every materialistic thing I could have ever wanted, every opportunity, every advantage; and I was miserable. Everything in my life came with a price, and love appeared to be measured by product. If we did this, or that, or whatever, then we would be rewarded. Feeling loved was supposed to be understood, and it was shown through what was given.

Although as an adult I understand that my parents loved me, as a child I became manipulative in order to get what I wanted. My childhood was riddled with, "I expect perfection out of you, and anything else is not acceptable." A lot of tragedy occurred, and the soul was just beaten down until it was just nothing. I functioned and played the game.

Church was a large part of our life, and yet I did not know that God was a God of love, not punishment. We were taught to fear God relentlessly, and yet be in awe of Him. Indeed, the blessing was that in this type of understanding God becomes a phenomenal thought, and really, I am glad that I was taught so strongly to revere the Lord.

Rebellion kicked in when I was in my teens, and only as an adult did I realize the blessing. God had chosen to cause me to be allergic to alcohol. As a result, although parties and bar scenes soon became the norm, I was protected by the hand of God. I danced the night away, went with whomever, wherever and however, choosing to live the world's way.

The world's way is sorrowful; that's a hard, bitter lesson. It hurts to see friends crushed by vehicles. It's sad to see them hauled off to jail. It's pitiful to see friends lying in hospital beds from drug overdoses and others riding the subway to abortion clinics. Trying to find happiness in this lifestyle wasn't the answer. God patiently waited for me to call on Him, and yet I neglected Him.

Church had been so ingrained in my mind that I never stopped attending. The sermons meant nothing, and the people just "didn't understand." Until one day. The sermon reminded me to pray, and pray I did that I would hear the voice of God. It wasn't a sincere prayer; it was more cynical than anything.

My life had become one of fear, honest fear for my life. The people I chose to be with were drug dealers, and many had alternative life styles. But, to God I said, "If you're truly God, then let me hear you." Shortly after that, I knew God intended to bring me to North Carolina and deliver me from my lifestyle. God clearly revealed this plan. But....It was several months before I ended up in North Carolina; and all that time, God protected me and set into place wonderful opportunities. God provided a job and a home before I even arrived.

Calvin and I met in a local church. He is a blessing—steady, constant, even-tempered and sincere. He encourages me in my life's calling without doubt or criticism. God blessed me with a wonderful and multi-talented husband. With the blessing of Calvin came Justin and Lindsey. They, too, are a blessing. Because of them, I know God has taught me a great deal.

With these blessings, though, came a great reason to pray. All of us have situations and circumstances which are difficult and seem insurmountable. God has sustained me through many frustrating circumstances and caused me to hold onto the scriptures. We are promised that nothing shall separate us from the love of Jesus Christ in our lives. God is teaching me to learn to love.

How did we get to Landmark? Through a person inviting us. Why did we come again? To hear the second part of a two-part sermon. That Sunday Jim Staples held Tabitha Martin up in his arms. It was her first Sunday in church. He just held her talking to the congregation about the needs of the Martin family. He spoke with such sincerity and kindness. I realized that there was something different about the family of God at Landmark.

Many, many people at Landmark have prayed for us. Some know us well, and some just know how to pray. God brought up a group of praying people. Your prayers have encouraged us. They've taught us to join in the family of God, to not give up but to stay and grow, learn and mostly to get down on our knees and pray. The family of God at Landmark showed us that they care without a price. God blessed us with a church family that unconditionally loved. We thank God for the people that are part of our life. God picks good friends.

God has a great sense of timing. When Calvin and I were putting in our fence, we needed a tool called a come-along. Well, we didn't have a come-along, and for just one project we really didn't want to own a come-along; so we prayed. Calvin was driving that week on I-77, and there was a come-along lying in the breakdown lane. There were no owners around, nothing in sight. It was a gift from God.

Another time, I was home alone; and like many people, the inconveniences of life always occur when the spouse is at work. Well, our pump had stopped, and I didn't know what to do; so I prayed. Yes, out in the middle of the front yard, and loudly, "God, we don't have any water, and Calvin's not going to be home until tomorrow afternoon."

Just then, I do mean immediately, a truck pulled into our driveway. I have no idea what the individual intended to stop for because to me he was an angel, so I acted like the individual was a divine miracle. Over I went to greet him and show him our pump without asking if he wanted to see it. With a pleasant smile, he lifted the heavy well house lid, primed the pump, returned to his vehicle. Off he went never to be seen again. God had given me water when I was thirsty.

Deliverance is another huge aspect of my testimony. The Lord has delivered me from many bad situations and sinful ways literally JUST IN TIME. Greatest of all, He delivered me from myself. The greatest gift of all is salvation. Without His saving grace, there would be no hope of eternal life; but concerning life on this earth, without His grace, hope, forgiveness, and love, the day-to-day challenge of life would be unbearable.

Many times I've cried and screamed at God, "WHY Lord, WHY?" Faithfully, He has brought me back to, "I love you, and you will learn to love others. You will learn to love the unlovable and to live a Christian lifestyle so that others will see Christ in you."

Ezekiel 34: 26a says, "There shall be showers of blessing." The Lord wants to bless His people; and through it all, He alone is King.

Betty Threatte

I beseech you therefore, brethren, by the mercies of God, that you present your bodies a living sacrifice, holy acceptable to God, which is your reasonable service. And do not be conformed to this world, but be transformed by the renewing of your mind, that you may prove what is that good and acceptable and perfect will of God. For I say, through the grace given to me, to everyone who is among you, not to think of himself more highly than he ought to think, but to think soberly, as God has dealt to each one a measure of faith.
—Romans 12: 1-3

I was married in 1945. That same year I was also sanctified and filled with the Holy Ghost. My husband, Benjamin, also found God at that time. Since then God has been my strength through many ups and downs. I would not want to walk any day without God. Romans 12: 1-3 expresses the way that I have tried to live my life. I have truly experienced God's grace in my life and in the lives of my husband and our eight beautiful children.

When my son Benjamin was four years old, he found some matches one day and began playing with them. The matches were lit, and he was burned with third degree burns over eighty percent of his body. I'll never forget the telephone call at work telling me that he had been burned. He was burned so badly that the Shriners took him to Ohio to have skin grafted.

We were members of the Fifth Street Church of God at that time, and everybody there was praying for Benjamin. The doctors didn't know if Benjamin would live or not, but I knew that he would live because God had given me the measure of faith I needed to see me through. God did bring Benjamin through. He saved his life. I got through the experience on my knees, the only way I know to get through life's challenges.

Benjamin still has many scars from the burns. Every one of those scars is beautiful to me because as Pastor Williams said, "Scars are evidence of God's healing power." Every time I see one of his scars, I see God's hand in his life.

In Romans 12: 1-3, God tells us to "not be conformed to this world, but (to) be transformed by the renewing of (our) mind." My husband walked away from God choosing instead to be conformed to this world. Several years ago he had heart surgery. When Benny had the heart attack, the doctors gave him a shot to break up a blood clot. As a result, he had a stroke.

The doctors didn't think he'd make it, but I had a measure of faith. I knew he'd make it. Benny's a determined man, and the Lord is my Rock and my best friend. God did bring him through, and Benny found God again. Now Benny relies on God himself.

I've told everyone in my family, "If you don't make your life right with God you're going to get a calling card from God. Don't wait until you get your calling card." Benny got his calling card. It's sad that sometimes as Romans 12: 1-3 admonishes us not to do, we think too highly of ourselves; and it takes a personal crisis to bring us to where we need to be with the Lord. God's grace and mercy has kept our marriage together now for fifty-seven years through many ups and downs.

I have stood on the Word and tried to walk the walk in front of my children, yet several of them have faced crises in their lives which led them to reconsider their relationship with the Lord. God spared the life of my daughter, Bonnie. She was in a car wreck and broke her neck. My son, Jerry has had several operations and recently found God. God has also saved my son, Michael. I keep telling my children that they're going to get their calling card from God. We must "think soberly, as God has dealt to each one (of us) a measure of faith (Romans 12: 1-3)."

My oldest son, Steve, was in Vietnam. He had joined the service when he was seventeen or eighteen. I was very young. I'll never forget the day that a military officer knocked on my door and told me that my son had been hit in Vietnam and badly hurt. They sent him to a hospital in Washington, D.C., where he stayed for a month. Today his body is still filled with shrapnel, but God brought him through because people prayed. God had dealt me a "measure of faith," and I never lost faith that God would save my son's life.

I am still praying for members of my family and reminding them not to wait to get right with God until God leaves His calling card. I'm grateful for His faithfulness. I don't know how people make it without God in their lives. I certainly would not want to walk even one day without Him. As the song, *Praise the Name of Jesus*, says:

He's my Rock,
He's my Fortress,
He's my Deliverer,
In Him will I trust.

He has been my Rock and my Fortress. He has drawn many in my family to a personal relationship with Him. He has delivered my loved ones from the ways of the world. He has delivered my husband and children from death. Through all of the twists and turns of life, He has been my strength.

Today it is my desire to live my life in such a way that I will "present (my body) a living sacrifice, holy acceptable to God, which is (my) reasonable service. (I desire to) not be conformed to this world, but (to) be transformed by the renewing of (my) mind, that (I) may prove what is that good and acceptable and perfect will of God...(and) not to think of (myself) more highly than (I) ought to think, but to think soberly, as God has dealt to (me) a measure of faith (Romans 12: 1-3).

Reverend Timothy Tin

Your eyes saw my unformed body. All the days ordained for me were written in Your book before one of them came to be. How precious to me are Your thoughts O God! How vast is the sum of them! Were I to count them, they would outnumber the grains of sand. When I awake, I am still with You.—Psalm 139: 16-18

The Journey of My Early Childhood

I began to attend various church activities with my mother when I was very little. I was converted and baptized at eight years old. Two years later, my mother brought me to Thailand to visit my father, and my father took us to Laos. We had a wonderful family life during that period of time.

One day my mother prayed to God that she would dedicate me to the Lord as a minister of the gospel if God would bless my father's business. After my mother's prayer, she decided to stay in Laos for a long time. Meanwhile, God sent a messenger to tell us that the Communists were coming to the city where we were living in the next few days. They asked us to escape the persecution of the new government. Before the Communist army marched into our city, we crossed the Mekong River to enter the border of Thailand by night. The next day we were told that the Communists had taken over the whole country of Laos. We thanked God for saving our lives instead of blessing my father's business.

I left my family when I was a teenager. My mother had taken me back to Taiwan because she was afraid of the Communists. Although we had been experiencing the grace of God in South Asia, I turned to a belief in science instead of the truth during my teenage years. I went to Hong Kong at the end of 1979 trying to obtain a United States visa to further my studies overseas. Unfortunately, the political situation between the United States and Taiwan had been changed into a broken relationship. My application was rejected. I was also not allowed to stay in Hong Kong. Therefore, I decided to reside in Macau for the meantime.

The first thing I did in Macau was to apply for residency. Then I looked for a school. I began to live alone as I did not have any friends or relatives over there. God's hand reached down to me when I felt lonely and frustrated. One day, I went to a gospel night after receiving a related flyer; however, I did not listen to the message, especially the part about receiving Christ.

In fact, I had hatred and doubts towards God. I did not want to dwell on religious issues. All I wanted was to know some friends. At the gospel night I met some Christians who always discussed religion with me; but each discussion turned into a debate, and they would simply give me some gospel booklets to read. Although I had experienced the miracle of salvation as a child, I still didn't believe God.

One night, I thought about Jesus' healing power when I could not go to sleep because of a nasal infection. I prayed to God to heal my illness. I thought that He should be able to heal me if He is the real God. I did not feel anything after my prayer, and I thought that Jesus was simply not real.

Several days later I met with a Christian friend. He was spraying some medicine in his nose, and I asked him about the medicine. I found out that he also had a nasal infection. I told him I had the same illness as he did, but he stared at me in surprise as he said that I did not look like one of those nasal infection patients. In that moment I realized that Jesus had answered my prayer though not immediately. He had cured me. I did not receive Christ then, however, as I still had doubts about God. Instead, I met Him in a movie theater!

I went to see the movie Ben-Hur one day which was the last day of its show. I watched every scene of the movie thinking of it quietly by myself in the theater. The background of the movie was in Jesus' time. The plot was so touching that it moved me to tears. I not only saw how God had led the life of the leading character, but I also saw the way God had guided me. I even felt God's presence in the theater.

He wanted so much to draw me closer to Him. I discovered that He was the director of my whole life. The theater ceased business right after I left that day; yet this very God has been with me until today! When I read the New Testament the night of June 20, 1980, I experienced God's abundant love once again. He was willing to forgive my sin and redeem my life on the cross, and He had risen from the dead and wanted to save me and change my life. I, therefore, repented and received Christ wholeheartedly.

Call to Ministry

Besides affirming that I was reborn after receiving Jesus Christ, my life was also changing. All people whom I know realized that I am a Christian because I had an urge to share this good news with them by giving my personal witness. I was actively involved in church serving God in various areas. I also studied the Bible and different spiritual books diligently. Stories of great spiritual leaders were my favorites. The sacrifices of these leaders shaped my perception of the future. Macau is a very small city, yet it was the first place where Christianity was brought to China. It was also the place where I was born in heaven when I met God in an amazing way.

My mother had dedicated me to God when I was ten years old. I had been saved at eight years of age and committed my life to God's service, yet God's calling seemed to be unclear to me. In a summer youth camp held in 1981, I was moved by the Holy Spirit to dedicate myself to God and live my life for Him.

Later in the summer of 1982, God led me amazingly to China. As I traveled to Gui Lin, I saw a tremendous number of Chinese (people of my own race) wandering like sheep without a shepherd. God's words came to my mind, "They are ripe for harvest, but there are too few workers. Whom can I send?" I answered God, "Lord, here I am. Send me." I decided to seriously study God's words with the purpose of equipping myself to preach the gospel in the future.

After praying for two months, God had prepared me to go to Macau Bible Institute; but I refused to go immediately because the teachers and facilities there were insufficient. Furthermore, I thought that the difficulties faced by ministers were too big for me and felt that I was not qualified to serve God.

These difficulties drove me away from God's calling. On the day when the entrance exam was held, I was reading Exodus, chapter four in the morning. The verses explained how Moses tried to find excuses to turn away from God's calling. Then God said to him,

> Who gave man his mouth? Who makes him deaf or mute? Who gives him sight or makes him blind? Is it not I, the Lord? Now go; I will help you speak and will teach you what to say (Exodus 4: 11-12).

I then realized the power of God who would be responsible for those He saved/called. This is further explained in Romans 8: 28:

> And we know that in all things God works for the good of those who love Him, who have been called according to His purpose.

God is the best teacher, for all those who submit to Him willingly will attain wisdom; so I would be a fool if I disobeyed God. This was how I decided to take up the challenges of bearing the cross, the way to victory.

Preparation for Ministry

Upon graduation from Macau Bible School, I was invited to take up teaching and administration work at the school. I was also responsible for ministering to the congregation of Macau Ping about church. In order to revive the church, I organized a gospel team with my classmates at Macau Bible Institute to share the Word of God on the streets and with the church's brothers and sisters. A lot of new Chinese immigrants came to Macau at that time. Quite a number of them had received Christ on the streets and later went to the church.

God gave me the opportunity to further my study in Hong Kong in 1987. I attained a Masters Degree in Divinity at the China Graduate School of Theology. In September 1990, I began to serve at the North Point Alliance Church specializing in evangelism and follow up work. I helped to establish a nurturing system and launched a 2-lead-2 evangelism movement.

The 2-lead-2 program is an evangelistic movement which mobilizes Christians two by two to share the gospel. Luke 10: 1 says,

> After these things the Lord appointed seventy others also, and sent them two by two before His face into every city and place where He Himself was about to go.

One day as I was reading this Scripture, the Lord showed me that the best way to equip the Christian to share the gospel is to send them two by two. Jesus sent the seventy-two disciples out, two by two, to prepare the way for Him.

I believe that we should use the model of our Lord to organize the people to preach the gospel. The goal of this movement is to have two Christians unite together through praying and sharing their testimony to lead two persons to know the Lord. As Ecclesiastes 4: 9-12 says,

> Two are better than one because they have a good reward for their labor, for if they fall, one will lift up his companion. But woe to him who is alone when he falls, for he has no one to help him up. Again, if two lie down together, they will keep warm; but how can one be warm alone? Though one may be overpowered by another, two can withstand him, and a three fold cord is not quickly broken.

By the grace of God and the dedicated efforts of all co-workers, over 600 people received Christ in 1992. As a result an additional Sunday service was extended.

Following the economical reform in China, a lot of Chinese and Taiwanese intellectuals and professionals began to attend church. Mandarin evangelism thus became a new direction of our ministry. Without delay, we formed a Mandarin (Putonghua) Evangelical Bible Study not only to convert them but also to equip them to preach the gospel in their home towns. Many Christians have contacts with business professionals, and our church is located in a business area; therefore, I began to launch business evangelism with several Christian businessmen. The Businessmen Gospel Fellowship of North Point Alliance was thus established.

In September 1994, God gave me the opportunity to establish a church in a suburban area (Shatin Fo Tan) in Hong Kong. The Conservative Baptist Jubilee Church was established through the faith of God.

Then in May 1996, by the grace of God, the Lord led my family to the United States through a great miracle. It has always been a dream of mine to come to the United States, but God had always shut the door. My visa application was first rejected by the United States Immigration Service in 1980. After I received the Lord at Macau, I tried to obtain a student visa in order to study theology in a seminary in 1985. Because I had insufficient documentation and financial support, my application was again rejected. I was very disappointed.

Ten years later I was married with a baby boy. One day my wife, Susanna and I were discussing our future. She, asked me,

"Do you think we should go to the U.S. to further our studies or to serve the Lord?"

I said, "Forget about it! I don't want to be rejected by the U.S. Immigration Office a third time."

My wife continued, "But you must have the courage to try again!"

I answered, "No, I don't think that God will let me fail that way."

My wife asked, "Then which way do you think God will lead us to go to the U.S.?

I told her, "I don't know! Unless God opens the door for us, I will never try to knock on that door again. If it is God's will for us to go to the U.S., He will bring us to the U.S. by a very unusual way. He will provide everything for us. He is the Jehovah Jireh, isn't He?"

Disappointed, my wife kept silence after these conversations because she knew that I was challenging God to perform another miracle for me. I didn't know that the words I had said would become a prophecy. I didn't notice that God was listening to our words.

Three days later on a rainy day, I went to my church by taxi. The taxi driver turned on the radio. There was an announcement just within seconds about a lottery with the U.S. Immigration Office.

Immediately, I was attracted by that news and remembered the conversation between my wife and me about God's way to bring us to the United States. The next day I went to the Immigration Office. An officer gave me a letter of instruction. I was amazed by this extremely small chance to immigrate to the U.S. by lottery.

My wife and I followed the instructions and wrote two letters. We stood before a post office box and prayed publicly to the Lord, "Dear Lord, if this is your way of bringing us to the U.S., then please pick one of these two letters; and we will know that it is your will for us to go to the U.S.!" We dropped the letters into the mailbox and waited for God's answer.

In the summer of 1995, we received a special letter from the U.S. Visa Center. I will never forget the first word in that letter, "Congratulations!" I hardly believed that it was real. We thanked God for His miracle that let us come to the United States. How wonderful He is! He is always answering our prayers! God's way is the best way. His plan is better than our plan. If we can learn how to wait upon Him, He will surely lead us into His wonderful place; for as Isaiah 55: 8-9 says,

> As the heavens are higher than the earth, so are My ways higher than your ways and My thoughts than your thoughts.

In September of that same year, I became one of the co-workers of the Chinese Evangelical Free Church. I have been serving as the sole pastor of the Faith Christian Church in Rosemead, Southern California, since 1999. May God greatly bless you as you read my testimony.

Note: During her trip to Israel from March 28 to April 9, 2001, Martha Dobson met Reverend Timothy Tin who pastors the Faith Christian Church in Rosemead, Southern California. He shared his testimony with her during the trip. She was so moved by the story of how God's hand in his life drew him from the time of his family's escape from Communist persecution in Laos to his ministry in the United States now, that she asked him to share his testimony. He was happy to share the above testimony with the readers of this book.

Ann Trent

If we confess our sins, He is faithful and just to forgive us our sins and to cleanse us from unrighteousness.—I John 1: 9

Like many of us, there was a time in Ann's life when she did not understand that God really did love her and that He had forgiven her. Once she understood that then she had to learn to forgive herself. The following testimony is her story.

"God has done so many wonderful things in my life. It was hard to choose which testimony to share; however, God laid the following one on my heart to share. It is rather simplistic; however, it may help someone else.

"I was saved as a child, but when I became a teenager, I left God. Several times I came back, but I always wandered off again. After hitting rock bottom and seeing my daughter Jessica nearly die at the hands of her father, I made a vow to God to serve Him. I promised God if the Department of Social Services (DSS) would not take my baby away, I would start back to church.

"Later that day, DSS did come and take her into protective custody. (She was nine weeks old.) I was devastated. It was two weeks before I could bring her home. I nearly did not go to church that week, but I remembered that it is better not to vow anything to God, than to vow and not stand by your vow.

"God was always with me and carried me through a very difficult time. He has blessed me over and over every day. However, I had so much guilt inside of me. I knew God's Word, but I didn't believe that I was forgiven.

"I was at my church revival. I do not recall the visiting preacher's name, but he had just come from Oklahoma City the very week after the bombing. One night he called us all down to the altar. I remember getting to the back of the group where I wouldn't be noticed. We all prayed; and afterwards the pastor came all the way to the back and told me that God wanted me to know that He did love me, and He did truly forgive me. He told me that I needed to forgive myself.

"At that moment, I felt God's love so deeply. I knew He was speaking to me through this pastor. Several days later, I received the Baptism of the Holy Ghost. I have put my trust in God. Even when things are going bad, I can look back and remember that day and know that God truly loves me and wants the best for me."

Indeed, as Ann confessed her sins and put her trust in God, she learned that He is truly, "faithful and just to forgive us;" to help us forgive ourselves and to direct us in the paths that are best for us.

Pat Warren

I can do all things through Christ who strengthens me.—Philippines 4: 13

From the time I was a little girl, I'd cry to go to church. Church was the most important part of my life. That's where my joy came from.

A time came when there was a pastoral change in our church. There wasn't anyone to do the many things that needed to be done. I worked with the young people so that there would be a program for my children. I got involved with the choir. I had studied piano and organ, so I substituted for the pianist and organist whenever I was asked. I could never say no.

When I came to Landmark Church of God, it was nice not to do anything for a while. Then I began to direct the youth choir, to work with Ladies' Ministries, to teach Sunday School and to work with the Evangelism Explosion program. I was also working full-time and taking care of my family.

In 1990, I began feeling bad. I had unexplained pain throughout my body. I just didn't feel good. In 1991, I got worse. I began to feel really depressed. My feelings weren't like the temporary, sad mood swings everyone experiences at times. One day I went into my Sunday School class to teach. The kids were not behaving. I just broke down.

I had already felt a release from God to give up the youth choir. I had promised God that I would never give up the youth choir without such a release from Him. Now I knew that I would have to give up my Sunday School class as well. Finally, I had to give up all of my church activities. I was out of church. Then I took a leave of absence from my job. People didn't seem to understand. I pray that others who may be going through a similar experience may be ministered to as I share my testimony and diary entries.

> March 1992. Dear Lord, I thank you for another day. I don't understand what's happening to me. Ever since I was a little girl, I have gone to church. I loved going to church. I've done a lot of things in church. But why did I do them? Was it because I really loved God, or was it because I needed to feel important? I need answers.

My doctor's first diagnosis was a chemical imbalance which he blamed on my hormones. His treatment didn't help. My mother had been through a similar experience. My doctor wrote in his notes that he believed I had suffered from this problem all of my life. I have always enjoyed time alone. I believe that this is hereditary. Yet I have wanted to please others as well.

> March 1992. I enjoy cooking and having people over. I've tried to make people feel welcome in our home. Why do I feel so lonely? This hasn't been a very good day for me.I haven't felt well today.

I told my doctor that I wanted to go to a Christian counselor. For a year and a half I went to a Christian counselor who helped me to see how much I had allowed my family to depend upon me. My momma and sister depended on me so much. I had so many family obligations. I could go for a month and never miss a day seeing my mom. I just couldn't say no to my family members.

I said in my diary that I had not been able to concentrate on the piano like I need to. I wanted so much to become a good pianist and to be able to help others—not only my family. I recognized that I had tried to do so much—to be Superwoman. Finally, I said:

> Dear Lord, I give Superwoman to you. Help me to become the person you want me to be, not who I want to be. I've tried

> so hard to be what others expected that I seem to have lost the motivation to do. Sometimes I feel like something has died inside me, but still deep in my heart, I still love you, Lord and want to do something. I know in time I will with your help. Help me, Lord, to overcome this that I'm going through. Forgive me of all the things I've done and said that are wrong. Thank you, Lord, for all you've done for me.

During these two years, so much happened. I went from being Superwoman, doing everything for everyone to the relinquishment of all my church activities and my job. I was experiencing pain throughout my body, depression, mood swings, a lot of crying, loneliness and feelings of guilt. Then my physical symptoms worsened. I began to have ulcers on my left leg. I had to take more leave from my work because my leg worsened. I couldn't work. Now with no job, I had no insurance and expensive medicine. I continued to have issues with my mom to deal with. I wrote in my diary:

> Oh, Lord, what am I going to do about my mother. You know I love her, but sometimes I feel she tries to put guilt on me. You know that I've tried to be there for her, but it never seems to be enough. Please let someone come into her life that will be a friend to her—someone who enjoys doing the kind of things that she likes to do. I don't know how to help her anymore. When I left to come home, she was crying. I can't stand to see her like that. The next week I continued to write, I talked to my Mom today. When she says something that sounds like she's telling me what to do, I feel a stressful pressure in my head. I know I have to deal with this. Another time, I wept to myself, I think about my Mom, and I feel like someone is trying to control me. It feels like I'm in some kind of grip, and someone is closing tight. I love my Mom, but I don't know how to make her understand how I feel. Dear Lord, please help me. I don't know what to do. I don't want to hurt my Mom.

I knew that through all of this I had to trust God. I never lost my desire for God. Sometimes I couldn't pray. I wrote in my diary on Sunday, March 29, 1992,

I went to church tonight for the first time in a month. It was hard at first, but I became more relaxed as the service progressed. Yet in April I wrote, I know that I need to get alone and read your Word, dear Lord, and to pray. I am having difficulty doing this. Please help me to develop good study and prayer habits. I know this is vital for my spiritual welfare. Dear Lord, I know that I will again work in church someday. Help me, Lord, to wait on you and allow you to do the work in me that You want to do.

I came to the place in my illness that I couldn't be in crowds. I slept a lot during this time. When I was having a bad day, I would just go to bed. I walked a lot. One Monday I penned, "Walking in the morning makes me feel good." One time I noted that I had "spent too much time alone. Yesterday my nerves were bad, but I made it through the day." Sometimes I tired out so easily. There were times that I just didn't know what I was feeling. There were times that I could do nothing. I was just so tired. I had no initiative to do anything.

Another day, Monday, April 6, 1992, I shared another battle with my diary:

Dear Father, this night I give my weight problem to you. I have struggled for too long with this problem. Please help me to have discipline in my life. Thank you for everything—good or bad because I know that I have learned and am still learning. Please help me to grow spiritually.

Almost a month later I screamed to myself, "I tried hard today to watch what I had to eat. I didn't exercise. Later I wrote:

I realize that I have been abusing myself. I've been making excuses for not going to church. I really don't have much to choose from to wear. I've gained so much weight. I'm ashamed and embarrassed about my appearance. I try to loose weight, but nothing works. I've lost control, and I don't know what to do. Dear Lord, I feel helpless.

April 1, 1993. I am tired of having this weight problem.It may be that I am hiding behind my weight problem. I want to overcome all the things that are hindering me. Dear Lord, I know I can do all things through You, but what can You do through me?

There were times that I didn't believe anyone cared about me. I felt so helpless.

> I want people to care about me. I have to be honest and say I don't feel like anyone really cares about me. I feel alone at times. I feel like there is anger bottled up inside me. I'm not exactly afraid. I don't believe I live in fear, but I feel like sometimes I'm going to explode. Dear Lord, I feel helpless.

One night during a revival service, an evangelist prayed for me. He didn't know what was wrong. Since then I've had to take no medicine. My doctor told me that I'd have to take it all my life. I've learned to stay away from stress and to work hard on what I can do. I have my limitations. It took a lot for me to recognize that we all have limitations. In my diary I documented this progress:

> April 4, 1993. Today I went to church for both services. It felt good to be in services twice today. The Lord has touched me this day. Lord, thank you for Your Word tonight. My desire is to serve you—to use my talents to the glory of God. I desire the anointing of God upon my life. Lord, what can You do through me?

> April 24, 1992. I really felt so much better today. This was a good day. I felt good.

> April 27, 1992. Yesterday, I went to church twice. It was the first time in over a month that I was able to go twice. Today has been a good day. I enjoyed helping with the yard work. It felt good to be outside. Being active today was good for me. It has been hard for me to pray, but dear Lord, with Your help, I will overcome.

> May 3, 1992. Yesterday, we arrived at the beach. Within 30 minutes Larry, Cindy and myself were out on the beach. It sure was relaxing. It was a good day. I enjoyed the day.
> May 10, 1992. As I reflect over the past week, I can say it was a good week. Larry and I had a real good time at the beach.

I have learned that I have to distance myself from my mom some. I thought I was doing what I was supposed to do when I did so much for her. Now I've learned that I can't solve all her problems. I no longer believe that I must go to see her every Saturday. I can go less often instead. As I wrote:

> I talked to Mom today and told her that I had to change the way I had been doing things. I do feel better in some ways. I know I have to make changes in my life.

God's worked in my relationship with my mother. She can't control my life anymore. God has done so much! Now I'll call and check on her. God has given me a boldness to be able to say, "No," or, "Mom, I don't want to hear that now." God helped me to deal with my anger and to forgive my mother. I no longer let people control me. God helped me with this. God rearranged my priorities. I didn't realize I'd spent so much time with Mom that I had taken time away from my own family.

I have often wondered why I had to go through all of this, but now I understand people who are going through depression. It breaks my heart to see people go through it. When Peter was in jail, the church prayed; and he was supernaturally released from jail. I believe that God often breaks our hearts so that we can really pray. Sometimes now God gives me the words to share with someone. I no longer have to take medicine. Once in a while if I'm in a stressful situation, I'll use the herb, St. John's Wort.

I've learned that going to a Christian counselor is nothing to be ashamed of. If a person has a heart problem he or she goes to a heart specialist. Depression is treatable. When someone is suffering from depression, he or she may also need to seek the help of a "heart" specialist—a Christian counselor.

Depression is a word that is often used to describe feelings. Everyone feels gloomy or fed up from time to time. Such feelings are a normal part of the emotional ups and downs of life. Depression, however, that is not short-lived and continues over an extended period of time is something else altogether. It is time to go to the Lord and ask Him what is going on. It is time to ask Him for direction. Depression is a warning sign that something in a person's life must change.

I could never say, "No," to people. I had many family obligations. I tried to be Superwoman—to be what everyone else expected me to be. Dealing with stress was difficult for me. I had to learn that, like everyone else, I had limitations. Eventually, I began to experience such symptoms of depression as poor concentration when I tried to read the Word, to pray or to practice the piano.

I experienced a loss of energy and interest in activities I had enjoyed. It was hard for me to be in crowds. My nerves were often bad. I tired out easily and often just didn't know what I was feeling. Often I had no initiative to do anything. I would make excuses not to go to church. I felt lonely. I had mood swings and cried a lot. When I didn't do everything I thought I should do, I'd feel guilty. I suffered from physical illnesses such as the ulcers on my left leg. I slept a lot. When I was having a bad day, I would go to bed. I battled a weight problem. I often felt helpless—that no one cared about me. I felt like there was anger bottled up inside of me, and that I was going to explode.

If you are experiencing similar symptoms that are not short-lived, I encourage you to seek help first from the Lord for His direction. I also encourage you to seek professional help so that you can learn to change what you can and need to change in your life and to deal with those things which you cannot change.

As I trusted God and leaned on Him with all of my heart, He strengthened me and directed my paths. He has done so much in my life. I love Him more than ever. He ministered to me through the Word and prayer and directed me to a Christian counselor and to a revival service. Both the counselor and the evangelist ministered to me. My family also became very protective of me. Now I am back in church singing and playing the organ. I enjoy my family and friends. I have changed things that I could change in my life and learned to handle the stress in my life and to accept my limitations.

I have learned that, indeed, as Philippians 4: 13 says, "I can do all things through Christ who strengthens me." Ben Triplet wrote a song that is one of my favorites and sums up my testimony. It is based on Proverbs 3:5-6:

> Trust in the Lord with all your heart, and lean not on your own understanding; in all your ways acknowledge Him, and He shall direct your paths.

What a precious, blessed hope we have in our Lord and Savior, Jesus Christ. What He's done for me, He can do for you!

Jeannie and Allen Weatherman

O Lord, be gracious to us; we have waited for You. Be their arm every morning, our salvation also in the time of trouble.
— Isaiah 33: 2

Who can understand the depth of emotion and grief one experiences when doctors say that a son or daughter may not make it or that they have no answers for a serious medical problem? Unless a person has himself been in this situation, he cannot possibly fathom such despair. Only one, our God, can understand. Psalm 147: 5 says,

> Great is our Lord, and mighty in power; His understanding is infinite.

Who can understand a mother and father's anguish when they do not know what to do next? Only, one, our God can understand.

> Have you not known? Have you not heard? The everlasting God, the Lord, the Creator of the ends of the earth, neither faints nor is weary. His understanding is unsearchable. —Isaiah 40: 28

Who can understand the destructive power of stress on the physical body when parents are so exhausted from tears, sleeplessness and worry that they wonder if they can put one foot in front of the other any longer? Only one, our God, can understand. In the book of Isaiah, Hezekiah said,

> The word of the Lord which you have spoken is good!....At least there will be peace and truth in my days.—Isaiah 39: 8

Allen and Jeanie came to understand the depth of such emotions over a period of years when both of their children were sick. In 1998, the Lord woke Jeannie up one night and kept her up until 2:30 a.m. telling her that it was time for her to share with others what He had done in her family's life. When she said, "I can't," He said, "You won't. I'll do it." And God did do it. He provided the anointing Jeannie needed to share her story.

When she shared her testimony at a Landmark Church of God Ladies' meeting, she did three things the Lord had instructed her to do: l) She put a chair for God beside her as she spoke; 2) She showed a picture that God had told her to ask Andy McLaughlin to draw; and 3) She invited her neighbor Beverly to the meeting.

Jeannie's story begins when their daughter, Donna, was in the fourth grade. "Donna cried constantly," Jeannie said. "She had lots of fear. Her thoughts controlled her. She didn't want us out of her sight. Allen and I, Beverly Flowers and my parents were the only ones who could control her.

"We took her to the doctor," Jeannie continued. "He told us that she was jealous of her brother. We didn't believe him. Allen and my mother would take her shopping so that she would have time with each of them alone. That didn't help. She became so afraid of germs that she couldn't seem to stop washing her hands. She was so smart in school, yet many times we would have to go get her because she could not stop crying. Often, Beverly would volunteer to go get Donna because Donna was comfortable talking with her. I can truthfully say that it was a living hell," Jeannie shared.

"When she was in junior high and senior high school, it was nothing to receive fifteen to twenty calls a day from Donna crying. We handled every day as we could, one day at a time. We didn't know what to do.

"One night Gayle Aiken invited me to a Women's Aglow meeting. At the end of the meeting, God gave one of the women a Word of Knowledge for me: 'You and your family are getting ready to go through a black tunnel.(The picture of the black tunnel is included at the beginning of this testimony.) If you will keep your eyes on the Lord, you'll come through.'"After the meeting Jeannie asked Gayle what this meant. She said, "My momma always said, 'Put it on the shelf. If it comes true, you know it was of the Lord. If it doesn't come true, you know it wasn't from the Lord.

"When Donna was in high school," Jeannie continued, "life was so difficult for me. As a child, when something broke, my daddy always fixed it. After I got married, Allen fixed everything. But

Daddy and Allen couldn't fix Donna. I was devastated. We couldn't go anywhere unless Beverly or my parents stayed with Donna.

"In high school the medical problems worsened. Donna started losing weight; and our son, Chris, who was now in the fourth grade began finding blood in his urine. At Duke Hospital, the doctors told us that they might have to put tubes in his kidney. I believed in God; but He was up there, and I was down here on Earth. If Daddy or Allen couldn't fix it, I didn't know what to do.

"About this time I began attending a Bible study that God had inspired Sandy Madison to begin after the death of her child. As I attended this Bible study, I heard that Jesus Christ is the same yesterday, today and forever (Hebrews 13:8). I learned that God still heals. I wanted a miracle, but I had to wait. I went to every healing meeting that came anywhere near. Allen and I stood on Isaiah 53:5: '...and by His stripes we are healed.' We learned that our Lord is our Father, not just a man sitting in heaven.

"At this same time while Donna was finishing college, Chris was in the hospital several times with kidney stones. Donna broke up with her boyfriend. Every new experience would give her such a difficult time. She couldn't drive. Allen took her to college. Thinking I was having a heart attack, the doctors put me in the hospital. Then they put Allen in the hospital. We were both suffering from stress. We had no idea until then what a powerful effect stress could have on the body. The Madisons helped us so much during this time.

"Later Donna married Mike, but the marriage didn't last. She called us fifteen times during her honeymoon. She just couldn't deal, and Mike couldn't deal. When she and Mike separated, Donna came home. Who's not sad when their marriage doesn't make it?

"Donna couldn't eat or function very well. One night she was so bad that Allen picked her up in his arms like a child (a twenty-two year old) and carried her to the hospital. I was so exhausted that I couldn't go. After two months in the hospital, the doctors still couldn't figure the problem out. Many times I tried to give her to the Lord, but I guess I kept taking her back. I don't know.

"Then one day a friend called saying that she had heard a doctor on Good Morning America describing a chemical imbalance that caused symptoms like those Donna had experienced for so many years. Allen called the television station to get the name of the doctor and hospital. The next day he must have called that doctor and hospital a thousand times. He would not return the call. Then Allen called our senator. Ten minutes later, the doctor returned the call saying that the medicine could only be found in England. Allen told the doctor that he would go to England, but the doctor suggested that we apply for Donna to be part of a research project in Raleigh.

"Everyone we knew was praying that Donna would be accepted for the project. God answered that prayer. I have a wonderful brother who lives in Mebane near Raleigh. He went with her to the hospital every day for almost a year. Half of the patients in the research project were taking sugar pills; the others were taking the new medicine. Those taking the medicine began to improve.

"During this time, Donna was Daddy's girl, not mine. She just wanted her Daddy. Chris saw a lot and cried a lot. I became so afraid that I'd lose Donna that I grabbed a hold of Chris. Anything that was done for Donna was done by her Daddy. He'd stay up all night if she wanted to talk. Meanwhile, Chris was still bothered with kidney stones."

"I know people at church could probably tell that something was wrong, but Allen and I didn't share our personal lives much. On April 23, 1986, George Conger came up to us at church and said that God had put us on his heart to pray for. I wrote in my Bible that night, 'I believe the answer is on the way.'

Then on September 7, 1986, we were at the altar praying when Walter Byrd came over and put his arms around us. We'd never shared any of our problems with him. God spoke through him to us: 'I know your need. Remain faithful. Continue to trust in Me and I will bring it to pass.' He was a man of God. When I got down, my friend Gayle would have me read this promise. That message encouraged me so much.

"Donna finished college and moved to Tennessee to be on her own. It was nothing to have a $200.00 phone bill because when she needed to talk, she'd call. Finally, she moved back to Charlotte. Chris graduated from high school and began to enjoy life forgetting to take his medicine. He went down. I had so much fear of losing him. Since Beverly lived near us, I'd often call her and ask her to go see if he was at home. I just needed to know he was safe. The Devil had me in one more fix afraid that I was going to lose him. When he was living at our house, I'd often go to his room fifty times in one night just to look at him.

"One night Chris asked me to fix pancakes for breakfast the next day. The next morning, while I was fixing pancakes, Allen tried unsuccessfully to get Chris up. When Allen realized that Chris was having a seizure and couldn't get up, he shouted for me to dial 911. While Chris went by ambulance to the hospital, Allen, Beverly and I went by car.

"When we arrived at the hospital, the doctors wouldn't let us see him. Just prior to this, I'd lost my Daddy. The doctors were calling Code Blue when Pastor Williams arrived. We had been praying for about ten or fifteen minutes when the doctor came in. He said, 'I've had a son who was sick. I want you to know that I'm doing all I can do, but there's a Man in there. Jesus' hands are on mine.' We'd never heard a doctor say anything like this. We were amazed.

"For three days and nights we slept on the floor in the waiting room. One time the doctors tried to take him off of life support, but he stopped breathing. Three days later the doctors decided to take the life support off again. Many of our friends gathered with us to pray.

"Our friend, Wiley Aiken, left Raleigh to be with us as soon as Doug Madison called him. Wiley called his wife, Gayle, to pray. Crying, Gayle called her mother and said, 'You've got to start praying.' Her mother responded, 'Say no more. The Lord woke me up in the middle of the night to pray. The burden was so heavy that I prayed until I got a release.' She had no idea what she was praying for. She just knew that her heart was deeply burdened for Chris.

"When Allen learned that God had burdened her to pray, he found more courage to fight. He knew that God was in control. When the doctor said that Chris might not make it, Allen was able to give Chris back to God; I could not. After Allen released Chris, he found an amazing peace. Chris was able to remain off the life support and breathe. Chris continued to struggle, but as time passed, he got better. He has not had those problems since.

"After Chris left home, he had a hard time getting started in life, but he turned his life around. Donna improved so much on the medicine she began taking. Then she met Michael. He's a God sent man! I've had to learn to trust the Lord and lean on Him first. Donna had been told that she couldn't have children, and, look at the beautiful granddaughter we have! God gave me a new son and another daughter. I couldn't have better!

"All that I can say is that prayer always works. We struggled with our children's illnesses for thirteen years. I had wanted immediate miracles, but it didn't work that way. I don't know why. One of the ladies I worked with was so understanding.

Sometimes I just needed to cry. She'd let me cry. If I needed to talk, she would listen. I didn't want to see other people laugh because I couldn't laugh. Sometimes I'd say to my friend, Beverly, that I just wanted life to stop. When I would say things like this, she would never put me down. She'd just listen.

"We're also grateful for friends like Ann and Bill Baynard and Betty and Don Edwards (He's with the Lord now) who helped us and prayed for us when we needed someone. It made all the difference in the world to have friends there to meet needs we had as the needs arose.

"God has done such a work in the lives of Donna and Chris. Now we have peace. I'd like to encourage you to just smile when you see other people. You don't know what they're going through. If the Lord lays someone on your heart to pray for, don't try to figure out what's going on. Just pray! Someone's life may be at stake!"

Allen and Jeannie did learn to wait on the Lord, and He was so gracious to them. He was their arm every morning and their salvation in the trouble. They found that when the depth of emotion and grief is beyond comprehension, the Lord is, indeed, mighty in power and infinite in understanding. When they didn't know where to turn next and when they were exhausted from tears, sleeplessness and worry; they learned that the Creator neither faints nor is weary. They know that the Word of the Lord is good! Isaiah 33 : 10, 15 ,16, 20-24 says in part:

> Now I will rise," says the Lord; "now I will be exalted; now I will lift Myself up....He who walks righteously and speaks uprightly, He will dwell on high; bread will be given him, His water will be sure...."The majestic Lord will be for us a place of broad rivers and streams, in which no galley with oars will sail, nor majestic ships pass by (For) the Lord is our Judge, The Lord is our

Lawgiver, The Lord is our King; He will save us; And the inhabitant will not say, "I am sick."

Now there is peace and truth in the days spoken of in Isaiah 39: 8. As the scripture in Isaiah talks about in Isaiah 33, God was exalted in the lives of Jeannie and Allen because they had walked righteously and spoken uprightly. God did provide for them. He was a place of streams—of living water, and now no one in their household says, "I am sick." They have learned to speak healing. Do they still have problems? Yes, because they live in this world. But now they have someone to look to. Praise the Lord!

Jackie and Kathleen White

And I say unto you, ask, and it shall be given unto you; seek, and ye shall find; knock, and it shall be opened unto you. —Luke 11: 9

Jackie and Kathleen "Shug" White have learned the truth of Luke 11: 9 as they have asked the Lord for salvation, healing, deliverance, protection and provision and found the doors opened unto them.

Jackie was raised in the church but did not ask the Lord for salvation until he was twenty-eight years old. When he did ask, however, God granted him the desire of his heart. With a grateful heart, Jackie could now echo the Psalmist's words:

This is the day which the Lord hath made;
we will rejoice and be glad in it.—Psalm 118: 24

After Jackie was saved people would often offer to introduce him to women he might date, but he refused to date anyone unless the Lord directed him to do so. He would say, "When the Lord is ready for me to have a wife, He'll show me." Jackie had always known that his wife would have black hair. Jackie's sister and her husband, Reverend Jerry Smith were living with with Jackie and his parents. Each time his brother-in-law, Reverend Jerry Smith would offer to introduce him to someone, Jackie would ask her hair color. Finally, one day Reverend Smith came home and said, "I've found you a girl with black hair who can sing so pretty. Jackie said, "Tell me more."

He called Kathleen and took her to church on their first date. Six months later they were married. Jackie asked the Lord for the wife He had for him. When Jackie waited upon the Lord's direction, God brought the love of his life to him. Once more Jackie and Kathleen rejoiced in the day the Lord had made.

When Jackie and Kathleen spoke of difficult times they had faced, Jackie said, "Some people give up on the Lord when there are difficulties. These times always drew me closer to the Lord." For example, Jackie used to take six to eight arthritis pain pills per day to be able to work at Pilch. At twenty-one years of age, he suffered from two slipped discs which led to osteoarthritis as he got older. He suffered so badly that at times Kathleen and their son, Keith would have to put on his socks and shoes. He took so many pills that he began to have severe stomach problems. Finally, Dr. Stegall told him that he would have to go on disability and that he would never be better without a miracle. For several years, he was not able to work at all.

The medication made Jackie very nervous. One day he decided to quit taking the medicine since his back hurt all of the time anyway. He said to Kathleen, "I'm going to church to see what the Lord will do." Jackie said that he believes that, "If you'll wait on the Lord and let Him know you're dependent on Him with faith, He'll do something because He has promised to." One Sunday morning at Landmark Church of God, he asked the pastor and others to pray with him as he prayed, asking in faith for a miracle.

A few days later, Jackie noticed that he could no longer find the large sore spot on his back that had burned like fire every time he bent down. God had healed his back! As Jackie asked and continued to seek God gave him his miracle. Without that healing, he would be unable to do the work he does everyday now, even for half a day. Again, Jackie and Kathleen were glad for the opportunity to rejoice and praise the Lord.

Prior to his healing, God had provided in advance for their finances by promoting Jackie unexpectedly to hatchery foreman. His manager said to him, "Everything you do, you do right. I'm going to make you my right hand man." As Jackie explained it, "I no longer had to punch a time clock. I was on salary.

"When I had to tell them about the disability, my manager said, 'Shut the door. I want to talk to you. You've been one of the best workers we've ever had. You have shown respect for the company. You've done everything you've known to do. We hate to lose you, so you're going to stay on salary until you receive your disability.'

"I stayed on disability for about six months. This was the favor of God. In fact, one day I went to get my check, and my manger told me that he would deposit my checks for me. He paid me in full for over six months, and I didn't even have to go get the checks.
"Jackie and Kathleen asked for God to meet their financial needs, and He did so "exceedingly, abundantly, above all (they could) ask or think (Ephesians 3:20).

Another time while brushing his teeth, Keith found a hole large enough for a Q tip in one of his teeth. He was only three years old and had never had a filling in the tooth. Keith said to his parents, "Ya'll pray for my tooth, and Jesus will heal me." Even as a child, he believed in the power of prayer. Jackie and Kathleen did pray asking the Lord for a miracle.

That day Kathleen made a ten o'clock appointment with the dentist for the next day. When Keith ate breakfast that day, he opened his mouth to find that the hole was gone. His tooth was completely normal. When Kathleen called the dentist to explain why they would no longer need the appointment, the secretary just stammered and hung up the phone. They praised the Lord one more time for the day He had made.

A number of years ago one evening about 11: 00 p.m., Jackie and Kathleen's home received about $ 3,000 in damage from an electrical storm. Keith had a CB radio that had been grounded. Lightning hit the window where the wire to the radio ran and burst the window. Normally, Keith would have been stretched out across the bed in his room. Had he not been in the other room, he would have been killed. There was so much voltage that a ball of fire blew out of the receptacle and traveled the length of the bar in the kitchen where they were sitting. Just as the fire got to the end of the bar, it disappeared before it harmed them. It was a miracle that all three of them remained alive.

In Keith's room, the force was so powerful that the pattern of the drapes were splashed onto the windows and the walls. It looked as if someone had painted the walls. Jackie turned on the attic fan to take out the smoke. The electrician said that if there had been one spark from the fan, they would have all been engulfed. God honored Jackie and Kathleen's faith and protected them. Once again, they were rejoicing and praising the Lord.

Jackie and Kathleen asked the Lord for protection again during an altar service at the State Street Church of God in Greensboro, North Carolina. The power of God fell so very strong on one lady. The Holy Spirit told her to lay hands on a lady who had suffered from headaches for years. Immediately, the power went through the lady, and her headaches left. The demon spirit who had afflicted her, however, went into the lady who had prayed. As Jackie said, "She was fixing to leave when her head started to hurt. I told her she couldn't leave like that. I went to the pastor and evangelist and explained the problem., We prayed and rebuked the demonic spirit. I saw it leave. It looked like a ball of hair. I saw a similar evil spirit several years later at the Troutman Church of God."

"Pastor Russell Tedder was the pastor. He saw the ball of hair coming straight at him. It landed on his throat and tried to choke him to death. Everyone saw him grab his throat. People realized that there was a problem and began to pray. The evil spirit left. Later, Kathleen was praying with someone at the altar when she began choking and couldn't breathe. When Jack and others began to pray, the evil spirit left unable to hinder her from praying for someone who really needed help. Under her breath, Kathleen was saying, 'God help!'" Jackie and Kathleen asked for help, and God gave them the desire of their hearts. They were rejoicing and praising the Lord.

Jackie recalled one time when God woke him up to pray for protection for his nephew, Mike Mason who was in Vietnam. Kathleen remembers him groaning in the spirit so deeply that she became frightened and woke him up. All he was able to say was,

"Mike—in danger." Jackie said, "We were praying for all we were worth. It was daytime there while we were praying.

Later, we asked him what was happening. He said that his best buddy was blown up next to him while they were walking in fields with mines. Mike didn't get a scratch. Just before Mike had left for Vietnam, there had been a service at the parsonage where the Holy Spirit had given me a message and interpretation in tongues: 'Michael is coming back.' Annette Moose's mother, Pat received the same message that night. God did bring him back. "When they asked for protection for their nephew, God granted their request. They praised the Lord.

Throughout their lives, as Jackie and Kathleen have walked in faith; they have seen God open doors for them giving them the desires of their hearts for family and friends. When they asked, God saved them and brought them together in marriage. He has healed their bodies, delivered them from evil spirits, protected them from the storms, and provided for them financially. Indeed, they are able to welcome every day as one made by the Lord for which they are glad and do rejoice.

Coy Whitson

I can do all things through Christ which strengtheneth me. —Philippians 4: 13

In the 1960's I coached a girls' basketball team. When we won a game, the girls would hug me. One time my wife, Nanette, was standing near by and cleared her throat. I reached over and tapped her on the shoulder three times. When she asked me what that was for, I said, "I love you." We used this secret code throughout our marriage. Anytime we would tap the other on the shoulder— one, two, three times—we would understand that the other was saying, "I love you."

Six months after Nanette's death at 9: 00 a.m., I was traveling on highway 40 out of Hickory on my way to the North Carolina mountains. I had the van on cruise and was on the right side of the road. I was playing a cassette tape she had made for me. I was feeling blue and was talking out loud. I said, "Honey, I love you and wish you were here."

I looked up at the sky, and it was blue. I kept looking, and a yellow moon appeared. I was astonished; but as I continued to look, a second one appeared. Then a third one appeared in the same position. It was in the same position as our secret code when we wrote it down.

The circles of light stayed there for about ten seconds and then passed into the car on the driver's side and out in the same way. I didn't feel afraid. I believe that it was God's way of letting me know that Nanette is o.k. and that everything is going to be o.k. God sent a special star for the Wise Men to follow. He sent a cloud by night for the Jewish people in the wilderness. I believe that He continues to use signs and wonders today to comfort His people just as He did for me.

I don't know who was driving the car while I was doing all of the looking, but I believe that God sent an angel and a sign I could relate to to help my grieving. Nanette's favorite Scripture was, "I can do all things through Christ which strengtheneth me (Philippians 4: 13)."

She taught that scripture to all of our grandchildren. When they had problems, she'd wrap her arms around them and quote this verse. Those words sustained our family through her illness and death—through all of the difficult times. The tragedy certainly brought our family closer together.

I thank God for the sign He sent just for me. I know it was from Him because I was filled with the peace that passes all understanding. I know that, "I can do all things through Christ which strengtheneth me" (Philippians 4: 13).

Daisy Wike

Now this is the confidence that we have in Him, that if we ask anything according to His will, He hears us. And if we know that He hears us, whatever we ask, we know that we have the petitions that we have asked of Him.—I John 5: 14-15

On October 11, 2000, my husband walked out on me. I was devastated, to say the least. I felt as if a rug had been pulled out from under me. I called him and begged him to come back, but it didn't do any good. I cried, and I prayed, and I cried; but for me there was no piece of mind.

I called a Sunday School teacher, and he and his wife both prayed with me. That night I went to church. I thought that the more people I had praying the better it would be. God would just have to fix things between us.

I have two sisters, but I couldn't call them. I had been through a divorce once before, and I didn't really want to hear what they would have to say. I went to work the next day, but I cried all day. On Friday, it was the same scenario. I cried all day. On Sunday, I attended a church where we had been members before moving to Statesville. It's a big church, but I felt I had a lot of friends there. The Sunday School class prayed for me and for my husband. At the altar call I went up to the front of the church where the pastor anointed me with oil while the whole church prayed for us.

On Monday, I went to work. I had not heard from my husband, so I did a lot of crying and praying. I really didn't want to go on living. I started praying for God to either take my life or give me a reason to go on. I don't know how I managed to get through the week. Only one person called me that week, and she was from the small church we had been attending here in Statesville. I did receive a card on Wednesday from a lady named Helen at the church who said I could call anytime. I didn't know her though, so I didn't call.

On Saturday, I hit bottom. I sat down and wrote out a suicide note. I had it all planned. I had enough pills in the house to do the job. When I got through with the note, I was feeling kind of numb. I happened to think about the card the elderly lady had sent me. I guess it was my last cry for help. I didn't think I had much to lose, so I called her and told her how I was feeling. She said I needed to talk with a friend she had met while she was in the hospital. She said that she had been where I was. She, too, had tried to commit suicide, but God had pulled her through.

When I got off the phone, I didn't feel much better; however, this lady's friend Clara called me within a few minutes. Clara had asked Helen for my name and phone number. She told me that her name was Clara and began praying for me. It was as if the Lord were talking through her to me. Then she started singing to me. It was a real blessing. She wasn't praying and singing for my marriage or for my husband. It was just for me. When we finally hung up, it was about 3: 00 p.m. I went outside and started to feed my dogs. I was feeling much better then. That evening, however, a man came by the house looking for my husband, and I had to tell him what had happened. I started crying. When he started to leave, he stopped and gave me the telephone number of a lady named Pansy who had helped him and his wife when they were having some problems. I called her, but she wasn't home. I left her a message, and she called me back a little later.

Together, Pansy and Clara picked me up and stood me back on my feet. They helped me to get through Christmas and New Years. I saw my husband a few times. Even though it upset me each time I saw him, I found that I still felt like I was walking close to God. God had put these two ladies in my life when I needed them the most. I am sure that He had them waiting for me. He already had things worked out. I had reached out to these ladies asking for help; and as I John 5: 14 says,

> Now this is the confidence that we have in Him, that if we ask anything according to His will, He hears us.

He did hear me. I didn't get my husband back, but He gave me my reason to go on; and He did it in such a way that I know it had to be God. It was amazing to me that these two ladies who helped me had the same names as my sisters (Clara and Pansy) whom I didn't feel I could ask for help.

As I began to put the pieces of my life back together, I started doing things around the house. I had a small front porch but no way to get in my back door. I had some lumber, but no one seemed to have time to help me. I decided to build myself a deck. My daddy was a carpenter; my father in heaven was a carpenter and I had worked in furniture most of my life.

I got a couple of books from Lowes and made my plans. The Monday after Easter, a girlfriend came over to help me get started. She didn't come back. Each time I worked on the deck, I began my work with prayer for God to help me. I asked for wisdom and strength to do the job. I was very devoted to my work and used all my spare time working on my deck. I continually felt that I had someone looking over my shoulder. Every once in a while someone would give me ideas that I had not planned on but that I needed to do. I felt very close to God and enjoyed every minute of the work.

One Saturday about the middle of April, God told me I needed to hurry and get the deck done because something was going to happen. He didn't say what or when, but I felt so strongly about it that I told Pansy about it at church the next day. I had been praying for God to use me for His power and glory. I didn't know it, but He was getting ready to take me up on my prayer.

On Wednesday, May 2, I got off work and started home. I looked at my gas gauge. I had about one-fourth of a tank full of gas. I always try to fill up the tank when it gets that low, but for some reason I decided not to fill it up. Usually when I get off work, I'm in a hurry; but this time I took time to stop for tea and to wash my car. I'm sure now that I was in God's will all the time. I was about three miles from home on a country road. It was a beautiful day. I was listening to Joy F.M. on the radio and enjoying the drive.

Suddenly I looked ahead of me and saw a truck in my lane going ahead of me and two small cars coming in my direction. When I first saw them, I thought one was towing the other because they were so close together. The truck passed them, and the car in the back with two boys in it pulled out to pass the other car with two girls in it. The girl driving must have put her foot to the floor on the accelerator because both cars seemed to be coming at me with everything they had. I noticed a gravel road going into some chicken houses and told the Lord that it looked like a good time to get out of the road.

As I was getting out of the road, I saw the boys' car break loose. I remember saying, "God, he is losing it." About that time, he went sideways into the girls' car. I was out of the road at this time but still moving. When he hit the girls' car, the force of the accident threw the boys' car into my direction again. I know that I was giving my car gas, but it seemed that I couldn't move. I remember saying out loud, "God, he's going to hit me," and God said, "Turn your head and close your eyes." I did. A shower of glass came over me. I remember the sound and felt him hit me; but when I opened my eyes, it was all over. He had knocked me twenty-six feet sideways and had hit me on the side of the car with my gas tank. If I had filled the tank, there would have been gas everywhere.

I looked down and remember saying, "Thank you, Lord," because I wasn't in any pain. I had three scratches on my left arm, bruises on my left hand and arm. The inside of both wrists were bruised from the air bag. I got out of my car and used my cell phone to call 911. I could hear the girls screaming about 300 feet up the road. They had hit a culvert and flipped upside down. The boys had done a 360 degree turn after hitting me. They had clipped a power pole and gone into a field about 300 feet.

When I looked at my 96 Saturn car, I knew it was totaled. I know how Peter must have felt when he was walking on the water to meet Jesus. When he took his eyes off of the Lord, he started to go under. As I walked around my car looking at the damage, I started thinking about the car; and my knees buckled. As I started to sit down on the ground, a young lady named Monti pulled off the road and stopped her car. I had never seen her before. She asked if I were all right and invited me to sit in her car. As she had stopped to pick up her baby, she had heard but not seen the wreck. I could think of no one for her to call for me. She called her family for help.

Her mother-in-law came to pick up the baby. Her husband, Roy, stayed with my car until people came to pick it up. She followed the paramedics into the hospital, waited on me and took me home. She helped me unload my stuff and prayed with me before she left.

I felt that God had put an angel in my life that day to take care of me.

The next day the highway patrolman told me that if my car had not been where it was when the boys hit me, the boys would have probably been killed. They would have most likely hit a nearby power pole head-on going eighty miles per hour. I asked God why the boys couldn't have missed the girls' car. He reminded me that my little angel was driving behind me. If they were going eighty miles per hour when they met me, they would have likely been going much faster when they met her. She might not have had the option of getting out of the way. As it was, the paramedics took all five of us to the hospital. All of us were released. I had to have therapy for a few weeks for a neck problem but am fine now.

A little wiser, I lost my car; but God gave me a testimony I will never forget. When I recovered from my injuries, I finished my 48 x 8 foot deck. It may not be perfect, but it suits me and the Lord just fine. I John 5: 15 says that whatever we ask according to His will, we will have. I know now that if I need something and will just ask the Lord for help, He will always come through for me.

Nearer My God to Thee

Nearer, my God, to Thee, nearer, my God, to Thee!
E'en though it be a cross that raiseth me;
Still all my song shall be, nearer, my God, to Thee,
Nearer, my God, to Thee, nearer, to Thee!

Though like the wanderer, the sun gone down,
Darkness be over me, my rest a stone;
Yet in my dreams I'd be nearer, my God to Thee,
Nearer, my God, to Thee, nearer, to Thee!

There let the way appear, steps unto heaven;
All that Thou sendest me in mercy given;
Angels to beckon me nearer, my God to Thee,
Nearer, my God, to Thee, nearer, to Thee!

Then, with my waking thoughts bright with Thy praise,
Out of my stony griefs Bethel I'll raise; ,
So by my woes to be nearer, my God to Thee,
Nearer, my God, to Thee, nearer, to Thee!

Or if on joyful wing cleaving the sky,
Sun, moon, and stars forgot, Upward I fly,
Still all my song shall be, nearer, my God to thee,
Nearer, my God, to Thee, nearer, to Thee!

—Sarah P. Adams, 1841

Betty Jean Williams

Therefore submit to God. Resist the devil, and he will flee from you. —James 4:7

On July 27, 1999, Betty Jean Williams, the sister of Reverend Franklin D. Black, had surgery in Huntsville, Alabama to remove the right kidney and half of the left kidney which were cancerous. She became very ill and was not expected to live. During this time, she had a wondrous spiritual experience where she experienced the truth of James 4:7. Her story is a testimony to God's mighty supernatural intervention in the lives of his children when they pray one for another. The following is her story as she shared it with her brother by telephone.

"Betty Jean, that certainly was a marvelous experience. Part of it was terrible, but the latter part brought joy and thanksgiving and praise to God. I've heard your testimony two or three times, and it seems to get better every time I hear it, so let me hear it again today. Tell me what happened to you.

"I felt rather proud of myself. But let me tell you, this last trip, it took all of the arrogance away. I no longer feel too proud of myself because I know today, I am not in control. It took this to really open my eyes. Beginning on Thursday, December 23, 1999, I spent nineteen days in intensive care at Cape Canaveral Hospital in Florida. I was there for Christmas with my granddaughter, Dawn Anderson, who has Chron's disease. Only bits and pieces of that two weeks do I remember. I do not remember any of my family being here. I felt that I had been dumped and left which is a horrible feeling. I was not a prayer person at this time.

"They tell me I was hallucinating. I don't care what they call it, but I have never seen evil as evil as I saw during that two weeks. There was a being that stood up against the wall, never taking his eyes off of me, just staring with his black, beady eyes. I was in absolute, total fear and remember trying to tell my daughter to listen—that they were whispering. She kept saying, 'Mother, there's no one there.' I said, 'You're not listening. Listen.' I couldn't make anybody understand or believe. I began singing, *Nearer My God To Thee*.

"I've been told I talked to Frank. I don't really remember it, but it was as if he knew. No one else understood. No one understood, but he did. He told me that the devil will look for you at your weakest path and that he would pray and they would leave. I believed that. I believed it in all my heart."

It was at this time that Pastor Black stated to Betty Jean that she was about to take a great step—a step into the presence of God Almighty. He told her that when he rebuked the devil in the name of Jesus, he would flee. He did pray, "In the name of Jesus, I rebuke you, Satan, and cast you out of Betty Jean's presence."

"I am told that I calmed down after Frank told me this. My blood pressure and heart rate was just soaring. My family had been called and told that it was just a matter of time. I believe, had I continued that would have been true. But I am told that after talking to Frank, I calmed down. I cannot quote any of this in days or time. I don't know."

"But I do know that once this evil was gone, I was standing—I really don't know how to describe it. There were four beings on each corner, and I'm in the middle. They were white, totally white, but more like pillars of salt—no human shape. Like I said, I don't really know how to describe it, but I'm in the middle and look like them. The four are around me. I remember asking my daughter,' God in three persons, but who is number four?'They were not understanding what I was asking—Who is number four because I had four people around me.

"One more time Frank was called. His words were,'Those are your guardian angels.' I am here to tell you that that was the most blessed healing I have ever in my life had. I felt so safe, so serene and so secure. If anyone had ever told me that you could feel that good, I wouldn't have believed it. I felt so good that I didn't want to leave that place. I wanted to stay. When I found that I had to leave,and I wasn't able to stay, all I kept thinking was,'I am ready to go back when You are ready for me. Save my place, dear God, save my place.' I guess that just about sums it up.

"I do know before I came here they say I was depressed. Over the past few years, I've done a lot of crying. When I came through this, one of the things I told my daughter was,'I no longer feel the need for tears.' And no one will know what a good feeling that was! It was as if everything had been lifted. I went through that two weeks, the most horrible and still the most blessed. If it took that evil to give me the blessing, then so be it, so be it.

"I feel that, Frank, you and your church are the ones to be given credit for the fact that I am here today. Alone I would not have made it. All these years that you have talked to me, I have listened. Only now do I understand. Thank you."

"Betty Jean, thank you very much."

"Frank, I've always enjoyed spirituals. O.K? Would you believe—that is all I play? Now I don't even want any other music. I just can't believe that the turn around was so much. I just can't get enough. They're beautiful."

"It's spiritual food for you," Pastor Black said. "It's strengthening and very helpful."

"You were the only one who understood. You were the only one," Betty Jean continued.

"Is there anything else we can do for you?"

"Frank, there's nothing else. I have been given everything."

"Really, you feel closer to God than you've ever felt?"

"Absolutely. After my kidney operation, I felt pretty proud. This time around has left me with humility. It got my attention. I'll grant you that. I know now what power is. It's for sure I don't have it."

"You have reached the position with God that when you come against Satan anytime, Jesus Christ has all authority over him. You have the same touch with God that I have. You can rebuke Satan. He'll have to flee from you. That's the Word."

"Frank, all I do is lie here day after day and say, Please,God, save that spot for me. I felt so serene. I don't want to loose this spot. It is mine."

"You felt one step away from heaven, didn't you? I'll relate what I said to you. I said, 'Betty Jean, you are about to take one of the greatest steps that you've ever taken in your life. You're going to step into the presence of God Almighty, and the glory of Him will surround you. Just remember, it's just one more step. The Lord has promised never to forsake or leave you. It's like testimonies we've heard of people coming close to death. There was a tunnel with a light at the end. Where they were, they didn't want to come back; but God wasn't through with them."

"He's left me very humble. I don't think anyone will ever see that cocky side of me again."

"I would that Louise and I were there and able to put our arms around you and tell you we love you."

"Frank, I feel it."

"Betty Jean. we love you. We'll be in contact. God bless you."

When Betty Jean called Pastor Black, he KNEW that if we submit our lives to God, we CAN resist the devil. He rebuked Satan in the name of Jesus; and as the devil has to do, he fled. The demonic beings left Betty Jean's presence. Psalm 91: 9-12 says:

> Because you have made the Lord, who is my refuge, even the Most High, your dwelling place, no evil shall befall you, nor shall any plague come near your dwelling. For He shall give His angels charge over you to keep you in all your ways. In their hands they shall bear you up lest you dash your foot against a stone.

Betty Jean and Pastor Black had made the Lord their refuge. She believed that when he prayed God would answer. God did give His angels charge over her, preventing any evil from befalling her.

After Betty Jean had shared her testimony, she and Pastor reminisced about all the times they had witnessed God's faithfulness. He shared with her that people from his church were willing to pay his airfare and to help in any way to enable him to travel to be with her. He was unable to go since his wife, Louise, had been sick; yet God was faithful to provide what he needed.

Pastor Black shared a time when they were young during the Depression. "In Williston, South Carolina there were just no jobs," he said. "It was a hard place to get a job to really make a living. Dad was talented, and mom was talented. When he couldn't be working on watches or radios he'd get a job painting or something. On this particular day we were going to school; and it was either you or Mildred who did not have any paper, and you had to have paper to write on. Mother pressed dad. It was the first time I had ever seen her press Dad. He took out his last coin in his pocket and gave you for your paper. That was his last dime."

Betty Jean responded, "How much more can you give?"

"He was a proud man. Whenever they were giving out food during the depression, Dad wouldn't take it to begin with. Our home got so desperate that the next time they came around he took it for his family. There were many times that we would not have had meat on our table except that he went hunting."

"Mamma did quite well with her limited income. In the midst of all this harshness," Betty Jean continued, "we had a hobo knock at our back door. Mother was making breakfast. She made him a plate of grits, and I don't know whether it was rabbit or squirrel. She had fried it and simmered it in the gravy. She put the gravy over grits and handed it to that hobo. What little we had, it was also shared."

Psalm 119: 90 says, "Your faithfulness endures to all generations." God honored the faithfulness of Betty Jean and Pastor Black's parents to Him by being faithful to them in their time of financial need. As adults, God honored Betty Jean's praises to Him as she sang, *Nearer My God To Thee.*

He was faithful to His Word in James 4:7 as Pastor Black prayed and He rebuked the devourer. The demonic beings fled, and God's angelic beings surrounded her as Psalm 91: 9-12 describes. Her depression lifted, replacing her tears with a new and deeper joy and peace than she had ever known. The doctors believe that they got all of the cancer, but the best news of all is the assurance Betty Jean has of her place in heaven as she turns seventy years old on August 22.

Dick Williams

...My grace is sufficient for you, for my strength is made perfect in weakness...." —II Corinthians 12:9

I was blessed to have been raised in a God fearing and loving country home. I had heard about God's grace at church and in my home; however, I did not understand it until later in my life when I truly experienced its sufficiency during some most difficult times.

My mother had been a school teacher. She was so loving and expressed love to me in many ways. My Dad, however, was quieter and less expressive. He never said, "I love you," or hugged me; yet, there was no question in my mind that he loved me. I was raised Methodist and was very blessed with several dear ladies in the church who instilled the Word of God in me at a young age. My Dad never smoked or drank. I never grew up hearing and seeing so many of the things young people confront today. I went to a Christian college where the strong values my parents had taught me stuck.

In the army, however, I was introduced to other values. I worked in criminal investigation and saw it all. I really give a lot of credit to our chaplain, a Catholic, Italian priest who helped me so much. During his Bible study, he would tell it like it was. I had a guilt complex and gave up the looser life. I think the chaplain just turned loose the conviction of the Holy Spirit. Most of my friends were Catholic. After I completed my military service, I returned to college.

After college, I built a successful business. Unfortunately, I also returned to some of my sinful ways and allowed Satan to rob me of my joy. I thought I was living right. Actually, I was just being religious. I had been baptized at the age of twelve and thought that I had accepted Jesus. In reality, I had a very shallow understanding of what it means to have accepted Jesus as Lord and Savior especially compared to the understanding I have today.

Later, I married my wife Sherry and moved to Florida. The Lord blessed us with a generous income. I didn't tithe, go to church or thank God. Suddenly, as quickly as the income had come, it was taken away. What a psychological shock! We had to sell all of our goods to get enough money to come home.

One day a couple who was looking at the boat we had for sale invited us to church. This was our first experience with Pentecostal worship. The pastor helped us a lot. I thank God that the Holy Spirit continued to tug at me because one night I answered the altar call and asked Jesus into my life anew. I asked Him to forgive my sins and was truly born again. Things that I thought I enjoyed had been taken away, but now I found that those things no longer appealed to me. It was such a relief to know that God had forgiven me. I can't describe the peace and joy I felt. What a loving God He is!

In our neighborhood, we used to party every Saturday night and go out to eat. We stopped going out. Instead, we went to church on Saturday night and Sunday. We lost our home and everything we had. We went from putting all of our emphasis on the things of the world to feeling that we hadn't lost anything. It was all His to start with anyway.

He took it away, I believe, because we weren't good stewards with it. The loss of income was sometimes difficult when I couldn't do all the things I'd previously done for my children. My loss of income was often embarrassing for my children. It was not an easy time; however, He never let me down. I started another business, and God truly blessed me. His grace was sufficient.

Until our Pentecostal experience, I didn't know much about the Holy Spirit, but I began to grow in my understanding. In the past, my job was first. I lived wherever I lived because of my job. We were buying a lifestyle. I never asked God what I should do. I did everything on my own. Now I found that it was more important to first find a church where I felt I could worship freely.

God continues to bless me financially and spiritually. One night for example, my daughter Elizabeth and I were talking. I asked her, "Do you know for sure that if you died tonight, you would go to heaven?" Through the help of the Holy Spirit, I was able to lead her to the Lord. Indeed, God's grace was sufficient.

One Sunday at the altar, I had said to God from my heart, "Use me. I want to make myself available. I want to serve you." I never imagined how He might use me. During my quiet time, God began to deal with me about going into the harvest by teaching Sunday School at the Fifth Street shelter. I had had some experience witnessing, yet I argued with God. For several weeks I wrestled with what I believed He was asking me to do. One night Pastor Tracy came to me at the altar at church. I shared what God had laid on my heart. He said, "Let's pray." He began to prophesy to me, and I was slain in the Spirit. God confirmed through Tracy what He wanted me to do. Satan has attacked this ministry in many ways, but God has always been faithful.

Sherry and I had a difficult time starting our latest business, yet we made a commitment to tithe. I remember that we had nothing to tithe. I had $ 100 that I had planned to tithe. At the last minute I didn't give it because I remembered a bill that I had to pay. The next morning, I gave it away by mistake thinking I had given a one dollar bill. No one gave me any change or said anything to me. I didn't feel that I could tithe; consequently, our finances went from bad to worse. We learned an important lesson about the necessity of tithing.

Satan has attacked the Fifth Street ministry, my family and my finances; yet, in all things he is defeated. Since the day at the altar when I committed my life again to the Lord, I have never gone back to my old lifestyle or lost my trust in Him. He's blessed me so much.

Once when I prayed at the altar, He immediately took away my addiction to cigarettes. II Corinthians 12:9 says, "...My grace is sufficient for you, for my strength is made perfect in weakness...." Indeed, His grace has been sufficient for me during the most difficult times in my life—my broken marriage, my business losses and my discouragement in ministry. He has been and is my strength. His grace will also be sufficient for you no matter what you face. He will be you strength if you will ask Him.

I'll Always Find

I'm thinking of where I am right now.
I'm thinking of where I want to go.
I'm thinking of what I want to be.
Oh, how I need to grow.

Searching for the answers,
The questions never cease;
But in my heart that's so deep and true,
You somehow bring me peace.

My love for You I know is true,
In faith and prayer, I'll show to you.
Please be patient; please be kind.
Your love for me I'll always find.

—Elizabeth Williams

Elizabeth Williams

Therefore, having been justified by faith, we have peace with God through our Lord Jesus Christ, through whom also we have access by faith into this grace in which we stand, and rejoice in hope of the glory of God. And not only that but we also glory in tribulations, knowing that tribulation produces perseverance; and perseverance, character; and character, hope. Now hope does not disappoint, because the love of God has been poured out in our hearts by the Holy Spirit who was given to us. For when we were still without strength, in due time Christ died for the ungodly.
—Romans 5: 1-6

I don't remember when I was saved. I've just always known Jesus. Although I grew up Presbyterian, I came to the Landmark Church of God in 1997. I'm grateful for the love and peace of God that had been poured into my heart by the Holy Spirit. There have been times of discouragement and tribulation in my life that have produced perseverance and hope for me.

For many years, I had been disenchanted with the church world. From the time I was twelve years old, I had only attended church a couple of times until I came to Landmark. When I was in the seventh grade, I loved the church. When my pastor was charged with child pornography, however, my world blew apart.

At the same time, my parents divorced and my grandfather passed away. This combination led to getting involved with a bad group of friends and with smoking pot and drinking. Unfortunately, this was not just a "phase" I was going through. These bad habits lasted until 1999, but God began working on me in 1995. This was the most difficult year of my life.

In February 1995, my mother became very sick. She was diagnosed with cirrhosis of the liver due to taking too many Extra-Strength Tylenol. She had previously had three back surgeries; and along with her full-time job, she worked two part-time jobs to help raise three children. This took a tremendous toll on her body, and the Tylenol was the only thing that allowed her to keep up. She was put on a transplant list. For seven months we spent time in and out of the emergency room and doctors' offices.

Finally, God decided she had been through enough. During her seventh month on the transplant list, cancer took over her liver, spine and lungs in a matter of two weeks. The doctors did a lung biopsy. After surgery, they told us she would never make it off life support and that we needed to decide what to do. My brother, my sister and I knew she had a living will; so four days later we sat with her as they unplugged the ventilator. I thought my heart was going to break in two. It took exactly six hours for her to leave this world and move Home. Vince Gill's song, *Go Rest High on the Mountain* had just come out. I thought of the words, "Go rest high on the mountain. Hear the angels sing." All I could do was whisper in her ear, "Mom, go sing with the angels." I thank God for a short time of preparation; some people aren't given that chance. Thank you, God!

The morning of her burial, it was drizzling outside. Her favorite song was, *Amazing Grace*, and she loved the bagpipes; so after the preacher spoke at the cemetery, we had a student play *Amazing Grace* on the bagpipes. It was amazing. The sun came out and shone down on us as though the Lord was giving us confirmation that she was with Him. When we got into our cars, it got dark; and the rain began to pour down. God definitely had His arms wrapped around us comforting our grieving hearts.

Mom passed away four days after my sister was supposed to be married. About two months before she died, my sister postponed the wedding. Five months later, she walked down the aisle, and one month after the wedding, God blessed her with becoming pregnant.

He gave us a beautiful gift of life to replace the one we had lost. God has also given us such comfort, and I praise Him for this! He allowed me twenty-seven years with the most wonderful mother I could have ever asked for!

As mentioned before, I was smoking pot at this time, but under so much conviction. I always thought of God when I was "high." In September 1997, I came to a revival at Landmark. Boy, what a shock this was coming from a Presbyterian church! But, God used this opportunity. The evangelist called me up from the crowd, laid hands on me and prayed. I went home and got "high." Crying out for answers, for peace and for help making the right decisions, I wrote the poem, *I'll Always Find*:

I'm thinking of where I am right now.
I'm thinking of where I want to go.
I'm thinking of what I want to be.
Oh, how I need to grow.

Searching for the answers,
The questions never cease;
But in my heart that's so deep and true,
You somehow bring me peace.

My love for You I know is true,
In faith and prayer, I'll show to You.
Please be patient; please be kind.
Your love for me I'll always find.

It's amazing to me how God is always wooing us back, no matter how far we go.

Between 1997 and 1999, I would pop into Landmark once in a while. In 1998, I was bartending and met a man ten years older whom I began dating. I even brought him to church with me on occasion. I loved this man; I would have walked on hot coals for him, but surprise! God had other plans for me. On September 13, 1999, I went down to the altar in the Sunday night service. I kept feeling as if God were trying to prepare me for something. I even wondered if "my time were almost up." Well, it didn't matter. I fell on my knees and just began sobbing, begging for forgiveness. I felt so unworthy and just wanted to get right with my Father.

The following Thursday night I learned what God had been trying to prepare me for. The man I loved with all my heart broke up with me. I went outside and cried and prayed for God to fill me with peace. I instantly felt it flowing through my body. Immediately, I stopped crying. I couldn't have continued if I had wanted to. All I could do was smile and say, "Thank you, Father!" Had he not broken up with me, I would not be where I am today. I've been at Landmark every Sunday since.

On October 10, 1999, exactly four years since I had lost my mom, I was baptized in water. I gave up smoking pot and cigarettes; however, cigarettes sneaked back into my life three months later on New Year's Eve while I was housesitting. After my plans failed, I was disappointed and feeling alone; yet, I was smart enough to watch the Inspirational Channel and to praise God by myself. Since then I have had a few weak moments and smoked cigarettes, but I always receive strength and put them down again. It's amazing to me what an awesome God we serve! Even when we mess up, He still loves us and as the Potter, He molds us and shapes us. Thank goodness I serve a God who never gives up on me. II Corinthians 4:3-4 says:

> But even if our Gospel is veiled,
> It is veiled to those who are perishing,
> Whose minds the god of this age
> Has blinded, who do not believe,
> Lest the light of the Gospel of the glory
> Of Christ who is the image of God
> Should shine on them.

I'm glad the veil has been removed from my eyes. I was one of the ungodly for whom Jesus died. I am no longer blinded; I believe and know in whom I believe. The light of the Gospel of the glory of Christ has shone on me. God has taken bad situations in my life and turned them to good.

I was in a bad work partnership at the same time my boyfriend and I broke up. My partner spent money that was supposed to be put on bills. This left me stuck owing a lot of money. I lost my car and my boyfriend and had to move home. When I did, my father took me upstairs one night and prayed with me. My life began to change even more. I am blessed with a wonderfully loving, giving family; and I thank God for them.

My Hope has not disappointed me. I needed to earn more money and had to leave my job. I had met a very spiritual sister there and hated to leave, but I just wasn't making it. Thank you God for my sister! I applied to a company where I would make much more money. I contacted them for several weeks, but someone was always out or in a meeting. I prayed, "Okay, Lord. Put me where I need to be;" but I really needed this money. Well, God had other plans for me. I applied at Piedmont Healthcare for a position I had had several years ago as a medical assistant. I wasn't sure about the medical field, but God was. I was hired the same day I applied.

I have more self-esteem now than I've had in a long time. He has blessed me with so many patients that needed to meet me as much as I needed to meet them. It has given me the opportunity to witness and share my love. I have so much love inside of me that is just waiting to be poured out. I trust the Lord to provide for me in all areas of my life. When He sees fit, He will send me a godly man with whom I can share my heart and life and have a relationship with God.

I also want to thank God for His presence in my life, waking hours and sleeping hours. I have been privileged enough to spend time with Him in dreams. His Word is true when It says, "I am with you always." I also want to thank Him for my brothers and sisters in Christ. Through them He has taught me and blessed my soul!

I love the Lord, and I love my church. As I worship and read, I continue to learn so much and to grow in my walk with God. I "have peace with God through our Lord Jesus Christ...and rejoice in hope of the glory of God." Tribulation has worked to teach me perseverance, character and hope. This Hope has not disappointed me because the love of God has been poured out into my heart by the Holy Spirit. "I'm thinking of where I am right now. I'm thinking of where I want to go. I'm thinking of what I want to be." I am growing. As I continue to search for answers, He continues to bring me peace. As the veil was removed from my eyes, He continued to be patient and kind with me. In faith and prayer, I know that His "love for me I'll always find."

If you do not know my Savior and if you do not have the peace in your heart that I have found, may I encourage you to read John 3:16 and to pray the prayer in the last chapter of this book. I know that you will find His love for you and that you will never be the same again. I praise you, Lord Almighty! Hallelujah! Glory be to You!

I Have a Hope

My heart was so torn and burdened with care,
Trouble and sorrow were heavy to bear;
But I called on the Lord, and in my despair,
He came unto me and lifted me up and answered my prayer.

Though sorrow may come to darken my way,
I have an Anchor, a Hope and a Stay.
So I'm praising the Lord. I'm glad I can say,
That Jesus delights to answer the prayers of those who obey.

To all those who weep, the Lord draweth nigh.
He, too, is weeping. He hears your heart cry;
Oh, but in Jesus Christ, the soul never dies!
For He is the Resurrection of Life; My mother shall rise!

I have a Hope that is steadfast and sure.
I have an Anchor that will endure;
Yes, my Anchor holds beyond the grave,
For Jesus, our Lord, the great Resurrection is mighty to save.

Irma B. Williams

Because I live, ye shall live also.—John 14: 19

Dr. Edward L. and Irma B. Williams pastored the Landmark Church of God in Statesville, North Carolina from 1992 to 1998. The following is Irma's testimony to the origin of her song, *I Have a Hope.*

I Have a Hope

I was living in North Dakota when I received the heartbreaking telephone call, "Irma, Mother is dead." That was the voice of my brother sobbing. Our beloved mother was no longer breathing.

My thoughts were jumbled: What Happened?

"Yes, I will be there tomorrow," I cried.

Flying Republic from Minot, North Dakota, to Orlando, Florida, gave me time to think. I remembered how Mother had talked with me on many occasions of death and dying, and I also remembered how she had grieved for her own dear mother long after her death." Mother's gone," I cried; yet, I felt comforted. What a paradox. I definitely felt the prayers of the people of God. I knew someone was praying for me. The unseen power and love of God through the wonderful Holy Spirit was sustaining me.

I arrived in Florida comforted by the thought that Mother was at rest and peace. Later, as I stood by the casket looking at her body, the Word of God came into my mind and soul and being: "Behold, I shew you a mystery; we shall not all sleep, but we shall all be changed" (I Corinthians 15: 51).

I touched her hair and patted her. Then I associated the word house with her body—this earthly house of clay. This thought comforted me: Her body was the house in which she lived. I perceived that Mother—my real mother was not here; this body was just the house in which she lived down here. One day she would have a new body. She had simply moved to another home; and, the move was glorious.

As I pondered and meditated, hope came: "Because I live, ye shall live also" (John 14: 19). What comforting words. Then I felt joy. Mother is alive. She is with Jesus. I will see her again.

Another Bible verse came to my mind, "To be absent from the body...(is) to be present with the Lord" (II Corinthians 5:8). Oh, how thankful I felt that I had committed to memory these Bible truths.

The next morning I awoke with the following words resounding in my heart: I have a hope. These words even had a melody. My heart was singing, "I have a hope; it is steadfast and sure."

I began to sing aloud. "I have a hope; it is steadfast and sure..." The song was being born, and I continued the flow. "I have an anchor that will endure. Yes, my anchor holds beyond the grave...."

Here I was rejoicing in my spirit at such a time as this.

I continued to ponder the meaning of the words, Hope, Resurrection, and Jesus. These terms became synonymous to me. I thought, "Did not Jesus Himself say, 'I am the resurrection, and the life: he that believeth in me, though he were dead, yet shall he live" (John 11: 25).

What consolation. The Word of God kept on comforting me through the power of the Holy Spirit: He has "begotten us again unto a lively Hope..."(I Peter 1:3). Even though I was grieving, I felt thankful and blessed that Mother had taught me well the Word of God. I believed that I would have the hope of being with her again.

Within a few days, I returned home and wrote the words to verses one and two of the song, *I Have a Hope*.The words are:

Verse 1- My heart was so torn and burdened with care,
Trouble and sorrow were heavy to bear;
But I called on the Lord, and in my despair,
He came unto me and lifted me up and answered my prayer.

Verse 2- Though sorrow may come to darken my way,
I have an Anchor, a Hope and a Stay.
So I'm praising the Lord. I'm glad I can say,
That Jesus delights to answer the prayers of those who obey.

Several months later, our family was headed toward Florida for a visit. I felt very sad in my heart; I did not want to return so soon because the memories were too fresh and painful. As I prayed about my circumstances, the Lord made Himself very real to me, and His presence seemed to open my understanding in a greater measure. Then the profound truth came alive to me: in Jesus Christ, the soul never dies.

Not long after this experience, the third verse began to formulate in my mind:

Verse 3- To all those who weep, the Lord draweth nigh.
He, too, is weeping.He hears your heart cry;

(Did not He weep with Martha and Mary at the tomb of Lazarus? Yes, and it was with loud groanings. Jesus cares.)

Oh, but in Jesus Christ, the soul never dies!
For He is the Resurrection of Life;
My mother shall rise!

Chorus- I have a Hope that is steadfast and sure.
I have an Anchor that will endure;
Yes, my Anchor holds beyond the grave,
For Jesus, our Lord, the great Resurrection is mighty to save.

I still have a hope.

The song, *I Have a Hope* , has been published by Tennessee Music and Printing Company in Beautiful Gospel. This testimony was published by Adult Student LRL (Life Related Learning), Lesson Eight, Our Living Lord (Easter) in the Spring Quarter 1987 and is used with the permission of the author, Irma M.B. Williams.

Irma B. Williams

Delight thyself also in the Lord; and He shall give thee the desires of thine heart. Commit thy way unto the Lord; trust also in Him; and He shall bring it to pass. —Psalm 37: 4-5

A Healing Miracle

Even though I was still very drowsy from the medication, I knew I was going to be fine. Vaguely, I could hear the nurse saying, "Mrs. Williams, your baby is here...You have a boy—9 pounds and 14 ounces."

This is a true story about Friday, July 4, 1958. While the United States was celebrating its one hundred and eighty-second birthday, Michael Edward was born to the Reverend Edward L. and Irma B. Williams in Fort Worth,Texas.

Later as a nurse was rolling me down the corridor in a wheelchair from the recovery room to my hospital room, we went by the nursery. Behind the glass window another nurse held my baby up for me to see. He looked as chubby and cute as a cherub. However, Michael was definitely having problems. He was placed in an incubator and could not be brought to me.

On Saturday evening my husband came to my room with Dr. Touzel, the pediatrician. Both of them stood at the foot of my bed. The doctor gave me the shocking report: "Mrs. Williams, your son is going to die. Half of his heart is enlarged. There are so many noises inside that his heart count cannot be determined. If he stays out of the incubator for even ten minutes, he turns a dusky blue color all over...." I could not let myself accept the full impact of those words: Your son is going to die!

During the hours that followed, Psalm 37 took on fresh meaning for me. Verses 4 and 5 became especially meaningful to me:

> Delight thyself also in the Lord; and he shall give thee the desires of thine heart. Commit thy way unto the Lord; trust also in him; and he shall bring it to pass.

At this time, my husband was pastoring the Northside Church of God in Fort Worth, Texas. Later this same congregation moved to another location and was named the Diamond Oaks Church of God.

When the congregation received the distressing news, they met on Sunday night after church and began to pray for Michael. Many other people united in prayer for the healing of our child. Since it was the week of the Fourth of July, the Alabama and the Georgia camp meetings were in progress. The people attending those meetings prayed with us. Also, our friends and relatives in Tennessee and Florida were praying with us.

While I prayed to the Lord and read His Word, I reasoned in my mind: Was not my confidence in God? Did not the Bible say Jesus Christ is the same yesterday, and today and forever" (Hebrews 13:8)? Did not our Declaration of Faith teach that "divine healing is provided for all in the Atonement?" Had not Jesus Christ Himself promised, "And whatsoever ye shall ask in my name, that will I do, that the Father may be glorified in the Son. If ye shall ask anything in my name, I will do it" (John 14: 13-14)?

These precious truths inspired me to believe God's promise to heal those who put their trust in Him. Perhaps the Lord would be gracious and heal my baby. I prayed! I pondered! My husband and I agreed that we must pray for God's will to be done in our lives, and I became willing to give my baby back to the Father. Then, I felt the divine presence of the Holy Spirit's comforting power.

Something wonderful happened that Sunday night on the sixth of July. The Lord reached down from Heaven and healed our baby boy! Early Monday morning I heard a nurse walking hurriedly down the corridor of the hospital. In her arms she was holding a crying baby, and she turned in at my door. The baby was Michael!! The nurse said, "He could wait no longer. This baby is hungry, and he wants to eat!"

For the first time I reached out and touched my baby. I held him in my arms. He did not have to be put back into the incubator. When it came time for me to leave the hospital, Michael went home with me.

At his regular six week's check-up, Dr. Touzel remarked, "Mrs. Williams, I term this miraculous."

Michael has developed normally in every way. All through high school he played the trumpet in the band, and everyone knows that playing an instrument in a marching band is vigorous exercise.

On the Fourth, as our nation celebrated its 200th birthday, Michael celebrated his own eighteenth birthday.

In its bicentennial issue, a local newspaper in Cleveland, Tennessee, *The Morning Sun*, ran a front-page story featuring Michael's celebration of his history-making birthday. The editor inquired, "Michael, what would you ask for if you could be granted a birthday wish?"

"I would ask for our nation to be drawn closer to the Lord," Michael said. "We've drifted so far away, and I just think we should get closer to Him. I have just returned from our church youth camp near Chattanooga, and the Lord was really close to us there."

Later Michael married Rhonda Elain Brewer. They have two children, Kristina and Shaun, and three grandchildren, Michael Skyler, Haley Elaine and Christopher Alexander.

Just recently Michael and Rhonda attended their son's graduation in Fort Leonard Wood, Missouri. Michael himself served in the United States Army. Shaun was so healthy and physically fit that he could be attached to the 10th Special Forces Group (Airborne) Division. He actually enjoyed jumping out of planes and helicopters.

How great our God is to help us and heal us in time of trouble. To God be all the glory and honor and praise!

Patricia Wise

Bless the Lord, O my soul, and forget not His benefits: who forgives all your iniquities, who heals all your diseases, who redeems your life from destruction, who crowns you with loving kindness and tender mercies. . . .—Psalm 103: 2-4

At age twenty-eight, I was saved and filled with the Holy Ghost. From the beginning, I had an anointing on my life to pray, witness and testify.

After twenty-six years of marriage and five children, my husband left. I then had to go to work. I was heartbroken and couldn't sleep. I was on the verge of a nervous breakdown. I ended up in a doctor's office pouring my heart out to him. He told me we had to get my nerves under control. He put me on tranquilizers that felt so good and helped me sleep. I had suffered from insomnia all of my adult life; but now I had a job to hold down. I struggled to survive from day to day.

God healed my broken heart and later gave me a husband who loved me. I kept taking the sleeping pills and didn't realize I was getting addicted. At the time I didn't realize what addiction was, and for ten years I tried to get off the pills by going to anti-depressants. This took me deeper, and Satan came into my mind.

I could no longer feel God and was tormented in my mind. The devil then tried to tell me God had left me. I would wake up in the night to a cold sweat. That is when drugs caused a demonic activity. I kept hearing this voice, believing it and telling myself God had left me. I had left His presence and could no longer find Him. I began to think of suicide like Saul when the Spirit of God had lifted off him. I was dead inside and just a shell.

In February of 1987, on a cold Sunday morning, I grabbed the keys of my car and took off to a lake. My husband and I had ridden out there on a Saturday. He said that a school teacher had run her car off into this lake. I thought, "This is the way to do it." I ran my car off into the lake from the road. I was unaware that I had left my window open. As the car submerged into the water, I got out of the window. My jacket and shoes came off as I rose to the top of the water. I could swim very little, so I laid on my back on the water. I realized I didn't want to die. I began to float and got to shore.

I was in trouble with the law, and they wanted my husband to commit me. He refused, but I had to be put in a hospital for thirty days. The children borrowed the money, and they flew me out to City of Faith in Tulsa. I was then tormented more than ever. I was there with the people of God. God did not see fit to heal me there. I was in hell just saved from the flames.

I would look in the mirror, and my eyes that were once filled with the love of Jesus Christ were now filled with darkness. I saw Jesus weep through an Oral Robert's student. God said to me, "Pat, I suffered for you so you wouldn't have to go through this. I was in a pit of snakes all around me and no way to get out. I would feel in my spirit like my life was being squeezed out of me.

When I returned home from getting no relief, a woman neighbor would visit me. She would lay her anointed hands on me, and I would get temporary relief. God only knew the hell that I was going through. God spoke to my husband while I was in the hospital that He was healing me. That word came to pass on March 14, 1988. I awoke that morning knowing that something had happened.

I walked into my kitchen and picked up my Bible. I had not prayed or read a word yet it was all over. As I went into the living room, the Holy Ghost fell on me. I walked up and down my hall thanking and praising Him and speaking in tongues. I was totally healed in spirit, soul, mind and body. I am now on no medicine of any kind. I have depended on God for sleep, and He has always come through. I praise Him for His love, grace and mercy.

No power on earth could have delivered me. As Psalm 103 says, it was God who forgave my iniquities, who healed my disease, who redeemed my life from destruction and who has crowned me with loving kindness and tender mercies. I have received a miracle and praise His holy name. I want to serve, praise and obey Him. He is my life and everything in my life is in Him. I am complete, and Christ is all I need. He is more than enough. I thank you Lord.

Alysia Yount

But it is good for me to draw near to God; I have put my trust in the Lord God, that I may declare all Your works. —Psalm 73: 1

I've grown up in a Christian home, and I've always believed in God; but as I got older I began to drift away from Him. I started trying the things of this world. Praise the Lord, I never tried drugs. For many years I was hanging with the wrong crowd. I was in bondage and thought things were fine.

I eventually got married to a man who was not a Christian. I thought I could change him. We were married for a short time and moved to Alabama. While living in Alabama, I started to become severely depressed. One day I got up and started crying out to the Lord to take me home to heaven or to allow me a way to get out of this situation. He gave me an outlet, and I struggled with depression for a year after that.

In March of 1997, I visited Lee University and fell in love with it. I got an application but decided I was too old and didn't send it in. The next year, I went back to visit Lee; and this time, I decided to send in the application. I was at a desperate point trying to figure out what the Lord wanted for me. I was going on faith by sending in the application because I didn't have excellent grades in high school, and I had never taken the ACT or SAT tests which you need to attend a university.

I did have a little advantage because I had taken some classes at Mitchell Community College which I learned would keep me from having to take the ACT or SAT. I wasn't sure, however, I had enough credits at Mitchell to get me accepted at Lee. In the mean time, I was trying to get my life straightened out. I was having a hard time changing because I had not given up all of my so-called friends. Finally, I received an acceptance letter from Lee and began packing to leave for school.

I was very nervous because I was twenty-four years old and was going away to college for the first time, and I didn't know a single person there. I got there, and it felt like home. I was blessed with a wonderful roommate who will also be my roommate next year. I auditioned and was accepted into the Campus Choir. I did, for some reason, have a hard time fitting in with the people in the choir. I was very lonely and had to depend solely on the Lord. Even though I was having a hard time, I still loved it there at Lee. Every day I was drawing closer to the Lord. I was learning the truth of Psalm 73: 1 that, "...it is good for me to draw near to God...."

By watching the people in the choir, I learned how and was free to worship the Lord. I became closer to the Lord than I ever thought possible. I couldn't get enough of Him. The next semester, the Lord blessed me by allowing me to become the Recording Secretary for the choir. This position helped me to become close with some of the people in the choir. At the end of my second semester, I was nominated and voted to be the Vice President for next year.

I was baptized in the Holy Spirit shortly after my second semester started. I've seen the Lord do some awesome miracles; for example, a choir member's mom was healed of terminal cancer while our musicians played over her at the Maryland Winterfest.

I am so thankful that, despite my many faults and failures, the Lord still loves me and wants to bless me. I still have hard times and sometimes when life gets stressful, I want to turn back; but my feet are planted on the Rock. Indeed, "...it is good for me to draw near to God. I have put my trust in the Lord God that I may declare all (His) works" (Psalm 73: 1). I will follow Him completely with all my heart, body, mind and soul.

Brenda Hardiman Yount

And my God shall supply all your need according to His riches and glory. —Philippians 4: 19

On April 13, at the age of thirteen, I accepted Jesus as my Savior. I can still remember the feeling I had that day, such peace and joy.

Through the years there were trials but nothing compared to when my Mother died. I was thirty, and my daughter Alysia was ten weeks old. For the first time in my life, I was not in control of the situation. My Mother was my world. She had always been there for me, and now she was gone. I can remember being in so much grief. While riding to the funeral in the funeral car, there was so much heaviness on me that I could not move. I knew I could not get out of the car when we got to the church; and for the second time in my life, I cried out to God for help. At that moment, I made Jesus Lord of my life. When we arrived at the church, I felt as light as a feather. I honestly don't think my feet were hitting the concrete walkway. I did not see angels, but I know in my heart they were there lifting me up. This was the first supernatural experience I had ever had.

We buried Mother on Wednesday; and the following Sunday, our Baptist choir sang, "Because He Lives I Can Face Tomorrow." It was like no one else was there except me, and I know God had them to sing this song to me. I realized then how music can minister to people and how this is a calling in itself to proclaim God's Word through song. The following Wednesday night, I joined the choir. That was twenty-five years ago. I still do not take it lightly that God has chosen me to minister to others through song.

Five months after the death of my Mother, I was baptized in the Holy Ghost. I will never forget it; it was during a hellish thunderstorm in the middle of a cow pasture in Front Royal, Virginia. Some Christian sisters and myself were attending a big Christian retreat. We had been allowed to meet in this huge pasture since there were so many of us. This storm came up, and a lot of people started to leave. Our speaker told us to stay right where we were—that Satan was mad. He said for us to start praising and worshipping the Lord. We did; and all of a sudden, it quit thundering and lightning, and a DOUBLE rainbow came out. I had never seen one until then, nor have I since.

I would like to add one thing in case there is someone reading this that has not made Jesus their Lord and Savior. DO IT NOW! There is no way that I could make it in today's world without Him. Christ Jesus supplies all of my needs according to His riches in Glory.

Chris Yount

Beyond Belief

For God so loved the world that He gave His only beloved Son that whoever believes in Him should not perish but have everlasting life.—John 3: 16

For God so loved the world that He gave His only begotten Son...

My life has always been influenced by Christianity. While growing up, my family spent a few years testing the waters of different denominations before deciding on the Church of God. Regardless of where, every Sunday and most Wednesdays, I spent in church. "No church is perfect," they would say, "but this is where we believe God wants us."

And I agreed. Landmark Church of God is where, at the ripe young age of six-and-a-half, I was saved and baptized. I did not think that I was some great sinner in need of repentance, for I was far too young for that. No, it was the love that got me. It takes a lot to let your only Son die for a bunch of seemingly ungrateful strangers. I wanted that man's death that I had been hearing about, Jesus's death, to be worthwhile. I wanted to make it count, at least in my life.

....that whoever believes in Him....

By the tenth grade, I was proudly marked as a goody-goody Christian. Every time I was allowed to go to church, I was there. I loved it. It was my life. If only I could have driven, I would have been there every time the doors were open. Every night was capped by prayer and reading the Bible. By staying in Him, God has helped me to avoid the holes that many of my friends have fallen into. God had a purpose for my life; I could feel it, and I wanted it.

...should not perish....

Some people were wondering if I still went to church with them. They rarely saw me anymore. But I was nineteen years old; I had better things to do. Those better things included many of the things I vowed I would never do. Since the spring of my sophomore year in high school, my life had been slowly progressing downhill. Becoming popular was one of the things that happened to me. I strived and compromised to gain status. By the winter after graduation everyone knew who I was, but no one knew what I believed in. The funny thing is, neither did I. Only it was not funny—it was sad.

Winterfest, a youth revival that occurred every year, was something that I looked forward to and enjoyed every year. I had made plans to attend this year; but two weeks before we were to leave, I changed my mind. I did not want to go. I was planning on going to the beach with some friends instead, but my youth leaders would not hear of it. I was going regardless.

...but have everlasting life.

Life is a simple word whose meaning has always been so infinitely complex. I had never really understood why, until my life was changed. My life was complex because I made it so by not listening to Christ. It was infinite because Jesus' blood made it so. Now it is just infinite, no longer complex because I gave it back to God. That's where it was to begin with and where it should have been all along.

A fire was sparked within me, and it grew. It consumed everything in me—all the pain and sin, problems and worries. It has become so intense that sometimes I have to just let go and dance because if I stand in one place my feet will burn. Anyone that gets close to me can feel the heat. The problems that once broke and crumbled me are now simply logs thrown on the fire to make it burn brighter and hotter. The shots Satan takes at me are consumed before they ever reach their target. It is the fire that I want to spread to everyone I come in contact with, the one that burns forever. It is the fire of Jesus Christ. He started it in my life; and it burns as a sign to the world that Satan is defeated, and Jesus has won.

Gene Yount

Now unto Him that is able to do exceedingly, abundantly above all that we ask or think, according to the power that worketh in us, unto Him be glory.—Ephesians 3:20

As a young person growing up in the Presbyterian Church, Gene had no idea of the force of God's power that he would one day encounter. He was sprinkled when he was baptized and followed the traditional teachings of the church, but never experienced the power of God.

He joined the Army when he was seventeen years old and began smoking, drinking, using drugs and involving himself in the filth of the world. In Gene's words, "I took all Satan offered for twenty-two years. I thought I was somebody." It would be twenty-two more years before he would come to understand that, indeed, God, "is able to do exceedingly, abundantly above all that we ask or think" (Ephesians 3:20).

Just before his fortieth birthday, he came down with severe hepatitis. The doctor said, "Go home. I can do nothing."

"For eight weeks," Gene said, "I got high to kill the pain and cried 'cause it didn't help."

"Then one Sunday morning," he continued, "I accidentally turned on T.V. to Jimmy Swaggart. I sat down, got high and saw Janet Pascal and John Starnes singing about Jesus. Something I never felt before came over me. I even watched Jimmy Swaggart but was turned off. Too loud. Too far out! I turned off the T.V.

"Next Sunday a.m. I fell out of bed, still very sick. I got high and anxious to see Janet and John again, sat down. I heard them sing, and *it* came on me again! This time ten times stronger. I could hardly swallow, and I began to shake.

"After the song," Gene said, "I struggled to my feet and began to cross the room to turn Jimmy off; but half-way there, he said, 'You can run as far as you want, but you'll never out-run God.'

"Just then," Gene said, "I froze. Somebody (the Holy Ghost) put His hand on my head, and I felt 2,000 volts of Holy Ghost power. It shook me hard. It burned away twenty-two years of sin and filth. I laughed and cried all at the same time. I shook and laughed and cried, but I could not move. I don't have any idea what else Jimmy said; but when he gave the altar call, I came to, fell on my knees, placed my hand on the T.V. and said The Sinner's Prayer.

"Then miracles began to happen day in, day out. HEALING! DELIVERANCE! VICTORY! I could write a book. And here today, sixteen years later, it is just as real, only more so. THE GREATEST EVENT IN MY LIFE! "

Indeed, God has done "Exceedingly, abundantly above all that" Gene could have asked or dreamed of. Whether Gene is opening his Sunday School class with prayer or sharing what God has done in his life, he knows that the power of God that worketh in him is real. He's experienced all 2,000 volts of it and knows that the God he serves is an awesome God!

Donna Zawisza

Being confident of this very thing, that He who has begun a good work in you will complete it until that day of Jesus Christ. —Philippians 1: 1

Philippians 1: 1 is a life scripture for me. God has taken me from childhood when I had no real understanding of being born again to today when I have a personal relationship with Jesus Christ. Every day of my life, I see evidence that God is working to complete the good work He has begun in me.

When I was seven years old, I was in the second grade and longed to have Jesus with all my heart. I was attending a Catholic school which I had been attending since kindergarten. At that time in the Catholic church, children were not allowed to receive communion until third grade after a year of special classes. This meant that by church law communion must wait. Even though I had no understanding of being "born again," I just knew that I yearned for Jesus to come to me.

I was always "visiting" Jesus after school by stopping in at the church which was next to the school. One day after school, a friend and I went into the church to "visit" with Jesus. I told her of my deep desire for Jesus. She then told me that while attending a different Catholic Church one Sunday, she had gone to Communion. No one had stopped her because they didn't know that she was only in the second grade. That day I knelt by the communion rail and poured out my heart to Jesus and told Him how much I wanted Him. I asked Him to come to me. I know He heard my prayer and came into my heart and saved me.

When I was thirty-one years old, I recommitted my life to Jesus. Looking back, I realize that it was at that communion rail when I was just seven years old that my walk with Him began. I started to see and to understood that even though I hadn't always been faithful to Him, He had *always* been faithful to me. He continues to be faithful to me. As Philippians 1: 1 says, I am confident that "He who has begun a good work in (me) will complete it until that day of Jesus Christ."

The doctrine of transubstantiation in the Catholic church teaches that communion physically becomes the blood and body of Jesus. This false teaching left me believing that if I couldn't take communion, I couldn't have Jesus; but when I knelt down and prayed for Him to come to me, He cut through all the false teachings and came to me. This was the beginning of my struggles with this teaching and many others as I made my way to the truth.

The Catholic church also teaches that a person cannot receive the Holy Spirit until confirmation and that a person is saved with the act of baptism. The church sees baptism as the parent's way of passing on the faith and guaranteeing admittance into heaven for their children. This is taken from examples in the early church of the whole household coming to Jesus at once. I know now that the Holy Spirit came to live in my heart that day when I was seven.

Fortunately for me, my family prayed directly to Jesus, not to Mary, as many Catholics do. I often went with my aunt in the middle of the week to church for prayer; and during those times, I would quietly play and listen to the prayers all around me. Church was always a place where I felt at home; and because of these prayer times, God never seemed distant or forbidding. Even though I was experiencing rejection in so many other areas of my life, I always knew that I was totally accepted by the Lord and that the acceptance was unconditional. I always knew that God loved me exactly as I was, and I always felt completely happy and safe in church.

As a child, the Catholic nuns were often frustrated with me because I asked so many questions they couldn't answer. Just as the nuns were frustrated with me, I was frustrated with them when they insisted that I must pray and ask Mary to talk to Jesus for me. They said that I couldn't pray to Jesus directly because I wasn't holy enough and that Mary being the mother of Jesus would talk with Him for me. This teaching comes out of the story of the Wedding feast when the servants went to her instead of Jesus. The concept of having to go to Mary as an intermediary angered me because Jesus was my friend, and I talked to Him all the time. The crowning of Mary as queen of heaven each May because she was Jesus' mother didn't sit well with me because she was still only a person like me. Only Jesus, God's Son wears a crown.

When I was in the fourth grade, I prayed and believed to receive the Baptism of Fire and the Holy Spirit when I received my Confirmation. I received and began having many awesome experiences. Even at that age, the gift of prophecy began to manifest in my life. I went to the nuns with my experiences for help and understanding; however they told me that only saints, special people who were holy, pure and set aside as special vessels could experience these things. I was making too much of the power because I was an unworthy vessel. They would say, "Donna, you don't want to be a saint. Life will be difficult." I felt that I was being pushed away from the Lord again. I got very angry.

I was already suffering rejection in so many areas of my life. In my neighborhood, I wasn't the right nationality because I was Polish and Italian, and I was living in a Bohemian, Slovak neighborhood. Now those whom I should have been able to trust to teach me the truths of the Lord with unconditional love were rejecting me because I wouldn't compromise. I was rejected in the church because I wouldn't compromise. I believed that if Jesus said that He'd do something, He would do it. The nuns rejected me because I was sold out in my faith. I believed that at my confirmation I had become a soldier of Christ. Instead of nurturing and teaching, I was receiving rejection. This caused me to become angry and resentful. I felt that they were telling me that I couldn't have a personal relationship with Jesus.

My father was gone nine months out of the year. I was rejected in my neighborhood because of my father's Italian nationality. My mother was not accepted because she was Polish and had married an Italian. I needed a father desperately, so I tried to get close to God and to the Lord; but the nuns kept road blocking me. As a child, I felt they had the power to tell me that I couldn't have the fullness of God. My mother had a record called "Jesus Loves Me." I would listen to that song over and over for hours. It was the only time at home that I felt totally loved.

I believe that I asked the questions I asked because God was leading me. Yes, the nuns and priests were wrong, but I believed that they had the authority and were right. I had no one else to turn to for the truth. I had so much rejection from my peers and from my church because of my faith that I began to search elsewhere for answers.

I sought refuge in the occult with the zodiac, fortune tellers, Tarot cards and so much more. I didn't realize the danger or the depths into which I was descending. I even got into mind control because I needed to be able to control others and protect myself from loss, rejection and loneliness. I thought that if I could control situations I would be safe. I didn't realize how close I was to the edge of the precipice and to the point of no return. I was unable to comprehend this until later when I recommitted my life to Jesus. I thought that if I were master of my own destiny I would be okay.

I didn't understand that I was doing something wrong because I had never been taught otherwise. I didn't understand that I was grasping the power of darkness to replace the light. I was lonely and didn't feel loved. I sought power over my life. Today, I **beg** any parent who is reading this testimony to teach his/her children the dangers of the occult. Even a **one time encounter with a Ouija board is dangerous. It opens the door to darkness.**

When I was twelve years old, a friend had gone to Hawaii and brought back some amulets for the goddess of love. In innocence as a child, I wore that amulet not realizing that I was opening myself to the demonic world. I began to harden my heart to God and to open it to the enemy. **The occult is not playtime.** I handled the things of darkness in my innocence. I was controlled and abused by Satan. I didn't even realize it. I thought I was in control. As I wore the amulet of a false religion, I was bowing before a false god. In my desire to have love, I walked into places and dealt with things that weren't good. I was always seeking to control my life, so I wouldn't be a victim.

In 1965, I married Ron in the Catholic church. I thought that if I were a good enough Catholic, I would be able to turn my life around. Although Ron was a Catholic, he didn't want to go to church; so I didn't go either. We had years of marital difficulty when, without a church, we had no spiritual food. I was not able to get pregnant. Instead of working through this pain with my family, I started to go deeper into darkness.

By this time, I knew it was wrong; but I was afraid to let go. I was afraid I'd lose control of everything. The pressure of not being able to have a child and family who would not tolerate adoption led Ron and me to divorce. Three months after our divorce was final, we remarried. We had never stopped loving each other. We just had difficulty living together.

We determined to put aside anything that would interfere with our marriage. We put in for adoption. Our new son was so much of my world, the most precious gift in my life, a gift from God. Somewhere inside of me, I knew I was not able to be the mother my son needed without help, help from God. I truly wanted to be the best mother I could be. For a time my fears were quieted, and I let go of the occult; but after a time, the fears returned; and I had one foot in the Catholic church and one foot in the occult. The place that Jesus had once filled was now empty.

When we first adopted Tom at two weeks of age, we were living in a three-family house. I know now that the Lord placed a born again, spirit-filled couple there. They continued to challenge me. They caused me to start to examine what I believed in. I went to the library to search Catholic law and theology. I began to search the Bible.

I continued with the occult until Tom was seven and started his first communion classes. Matthew 7:9-10 says, "Or what man is there among you who, if his son asks for bread, will give him a stone? Or if he asks for a fish, will he give him a serpent?" I remembered my pain with Communion classes and was determined that my son would know what he believed and why. Isaiah 11: 6 says:

> The wolf also shall dwell with the lamb.The leopard shall lie down with the young goat.The calf and the young lion and the fatling together; and a little child shall lead them.

In my case, God used my son to lead me. I began going to church in spite of arguments with Ron. Every time I picked up the Bible, I had an argument with Ron.

I began to teach Tommy and to read the Scriptures anyway. Then the Lord placed a woman in my path (Dorothy Provost) with whom I could share Jesus just like when I was seven years old. These times with her fed my soul. I'd leave her house after sharing and know that something was different. Isaiah 55: 11 says:

> So shall My word be that goes forth from My mouth: It shall not return to me void, but it shall accomplish what I please, and it shall prosper in the thing for which I sent it.

When I was with Dorothy, the conversation always turned to Jesus. I began sharing my childhood. I shared my beliefs now that I had examined them. I began to separate theology and the law from a Scripture-based faith. In the end, I knew what I believed and wouldn't accept anything that was not based on Scripture.

After we had been friends and had been sharing Jesus for several months, one day she told me that she had a word for me from the Lord. She said, "This is nothing personal, but you need to be either hot or cold because if you're lukewarm, He'll spew you out of His mouth" (Revelation 3: 16). Then she left my home. It was as if I had been hit with a brick. I couldn't breathe or move for a few minutes. Dorothy knew nothing about my life of compromise, but I knew exactly what these words meant.

I called our priest and asked where those words were in the Bible. He told me they were from Revelation. He told me not to let this upset me because it wasn't literal and I was a good Catholic and had nothing to be concerned about. I knew in my heart of hearts that he was wrong. I opened my Bible to Revelation and read until I found those words in Revelation 3: 16. I didn't understand it then, but I was under the conviction of God; and I knew something had to change!

I had been trying to find a way out of the darkness while still dabbling in my pig pen. After Dorothy had spoken those words, I started praying Lord's prayer every night before bed and asking the Lord for help, and I put down the things of darkness.

Things in my life got worse. I was working full-time because Ron's company was on strike. Our finances were devastated. My marriage was in bad shape again. All I could see was a brutal second divorce looming on the horizon and my son being destroyed. Somewhere inside me, I knew I couldn't go through divorce again. I couldn't see our son destroyed, but I didn't know how to stop it. I'd have been willing to die to stop another divorce. That was in December of 1977.

During all of this, the words from Revelation kept coming back to me, No Compromise. I was to the point where I couldn't put two thoughts together. I couldn't decide what outfit to wear. All I could see was darkness. Then one night I came home from work and was preparing to go up to bed for the night; and I walked into the dining room where I had a statue of Jesus. I had started to light a candle as a sign of prayer; and as I looked at the statue, I couldn't see the face of Jesus. I remembered being taught that when this happens, He has turned away from you. I was broken. I fell on my knees and begged Him to take all of the destruction, all of the vomit and all of the sin from my heart. I begged His forgiveness and gave up my own way. I said, "I don't care how you have to do it even if it means my death, just don't let us get divorced and destroy our son."

That night I surrendered everything to Him and recommitted my life to Him. I got up off that floor; and for the first time in ages, I had peace. I didn't understand how I could have such peace when nothing had changed between Ron and me. Every time I went to church and read the Bible, the problems continued. Then the Lord showed me that I had to tell my husband that things had to change. I was terrified to confront Ron, thinking that that would finish us, but I obeyed the Lord.

I told Ron that I wouldn't divorce him, but that I would raise our son alone rather than have an earthly father pull him away from the heavenly Father. I told him I was sorry for everything I had done to bring us to this point and asked for his forgiveness. He asked what I wanted him to say, and told him it was his decision. When Ron didn't respond to that, I said, "Goodnight," and went up to bed still not knowing if anything was any different. Ron was silent the rest of the week. God honored my honesty.

Ron realized that he had to change. He began going to church with me. As Romans 8: 28 says:

> And we know that all things work together for good to those who love God, to those who are the called according to His purpose.

Indeed, God does work all things to good. I was rebaptized in the Holy Spirit. It is now 2003. That was 1977. I'm not who I was then. It is because of God's grace that I am who and what I am. As I Corinthians 15: 10 says:

> But by the grace of God I am what I am, and His grace toward me was not in vain; but I labored more abundantly than they all, yet not I, but the grace of God which was with me.

Between 1977 and 2002, a lot of inner healing for brokenness that was caused by sin has happened. I have required much deliverance in order to cleanse my temple because I so naively opened the door to darkness in my search for acceptance. God healed, restored and recreated our marriage, making it His marriage covenant. God used me on a mission trip to Poland. During that trip we sang a song that says:

> The Word of God is an itty, bitty seed scattered all around, and it never returns void.

That is what happened to me. When my friend, Dorothy Provost, said, "Hot or cold," I was shaken. The roots of the seed will crack open even the hardest stone and bring forth life. It did in my life. I'm proof of this truth. I didn't learn the Scriptures as I grew up. The hymns in our church were in Latin, yet God continued to draw me back to Him.

On that Poland trip, we handed out Bibles in one of the colleges. I gave a Bible to a person who took it, read maybe a verse, put it down. I watched another person pick it up and read a few verses before putting it down. Then a third person picked it up and took it. I know that in each of those lives a little seed was sown. There is awesome power in the Word of God. Those little seeds will bear fruit. God is faithful to His word. I believe that those seeds have grown in the lives of those people, as His Word has in mine.

Ron Zawisza

As you therefore have received Christ Jesus the Lord, so walk in Him, rooted and built up in Him and established in the faith, as you have been taught, abounding in it with thanksgiving. Beware lest anyone cheat you through philosophy and empty deceit, according to the tradition of men, according to the basic principles of the world, and not according to Christ. For in Him dwells all the fullness of the Godhead bodily;

and you are complete in Him, who is the head of all principality and power.
—Colossians 2: 6-10

I want to share about my life before and after the Word of the Lord came to life for me. It wasn't until after a Charismatic renewal retreat that I sat down and started to read the Bible. Before that, I knew the Bible was there, but I wasn't interested. Now I know, the Word of God can give me peace, health, joy, guidance and direction in my life.

John l: l-5 says,

> In the beginning was the Word, and the Word was with God, and the Word was God. He was in the beginning with God. All things were made through Him, and without Him nothing was made that was made. In Him was life, and the life was the light of men. And the light shines in the darkness, and the darkness did not comprehend it.

The first time I read John l: l-5, I didn't know who John was talking about. Now I know John was talking about my best friend, Jesus.

I am married, and my wife's name is Donna. We have a son named Tom and two daughters Morena and Gloria. At the time I first shared this testimony, we were living in Twinsburg, Ohio. and belonged to the Catholic parish there. I was born and grew up in Cleveland, Ohio where I went to Our Lady of Lourdes Catholic School until the eighth grade. While I was going to school there, I was an altar boy and sang in the choir. I knew all the prayers in Latin. I had been baptized, received my Communion and been confirmed. I didn't know why I was supposed to do these things; but I thought I had to do them to be a good Catholic, so I did them.

Toward the end of the eighth grade we moved to Maple Heights, Ohio, where I finished the eighth grade at Lourdes by taking a bus from Maple Heights. In the ninth grade, I went to Maple Heights High School and attended Catechism class at St. Monica. All through my growing up years, I didn't know the Bible was not supposed to be read by anyone except priests, bishops and popes. My father and mother didn't read the Bible either, but I do remember a Bible in the house.

The Bible was the big white book sitting on the table with the Infant Jesus statue sitting on top of it. There was also a lit candle and a silver dollar which my mother kept under the Bible. I never saw anyone pick up the Bible and read it. I used to pick it up, though to dust under it. That's how I knew about the silver dollar. I asked my mother why the silver dollar was there. She told me we would never be poor as long as the dollar was there.

After I graduated from high school in 1961, I started working in a gas station. I worked all kinds of hours, even Sundays. On Sundays I had to open the gas station at 9: 00 a.m., so I thought I had a reason for missing church. I did go to Catholic mass once in awhile, however.

After I quit the gas station, I started working at a garage with no work on Sundays. Now I could go to church every Sunday. Instead, I'd pick up my girlfriend who is now my wife and take her for coffee and doughnuts. This went on until April 1965, when we were married.

After we were married, we moved back to Cleveland, Ohio. We didn't join a church or go to Mass except on Easter and Christmas. In 1966, I was laid off from Republic Steel where I'd been working as a mechanic. On my last day, I packed up my tools, put them in the trunk of my car and left. That very night the trunk was broken into, and all the tools of my trade were stolen—$1,400 and seven years of work. I had to start all over, and we couldn't afford to replace the tools.

Since I had lost all my tools, I decided to change trades from mechanic to machinist. It meant starting all over again at the bottom. My salary went from $250 a week to $70 a week. Our finances were destroyed. By this time, we weren't even going to church on Easter or Christmas.

Things between my wife and me started getting bad. During this time we'd been trying to have a child. We were going for tests. Every month our hopes were crushed. Finally, the doctors told us we couldn't have children. We started to talk about adoption; but when I mentioned it to my parents they were totally against it. I listened to them, but that only caused worse problems. I didn't realize that I hadn't broken the ties with my parents because I didn't see any reason to. In fact, I was refusing to do that. Now I know that according to Genesis 2: 24 and Matthew 19: 4-5 that when a man leaves his father and mother and clings to his wife, the two of them become one.

Our marriage was falling apart. We were barely talking; and when we did, we argued. The pressure was tearing us apart. By 1967, I had an ulcer which meant constant medical bills on top of everything else. By this time, our parents were telling us about more than just adoption. Things got worse.

I thought I had no one to turn to. If I'd only realized that Jesus was there all the time just waiting for me to turn to Him, things would have been better; but I was completely blind about turning to God. I had been taught to fear God. How could I go to Him for help after the way I'd been living?

In October of 1968, my wife and I decided to separate from each other. We were still in love, but the pressures of this world were too much for us to stay together. We thought some time apart would help us rethink our values so that perhaps we could get back together.

The First Commandment says, "I am the Lord thy God....You shall have no other gods before Me" (Exodus 20: 2-3). I see now that all my life to that point, money and possessions had been my god. I was now financially crippled; and because of that, I had no choice but to move back to live with my parents. After I'd been there a short while, they told me I either had to file for divorce or move out. I filed for divorce. Because of my love of money and possessions, I'd given up my freedom to live my life as I chose.

In March 1969, the divorce was final. In May of the same year we were remarried by the state. We decided when we got back together that we would do everything we knew how not to repeat the past. We chose to move to Twinsburg, Ohio. for two reasons: 1) We'd always liked this town, and 2) it would put some distance between us and our families.

We moved into an old farm house on Chamberlin Road. This time we joined the Catholic parish of Saints Cosmas and Damian. That December we put in for adoption. We had decided that our desire to share our love with a child was right; and if anyone in the family felt otherwise, then we would break the ties. My wife and I were now going to church every Sunday. By this time, the Mass had been changed to English, and I didn't like it.

In July of the following year, 1970, we brought our son home. We named him Thomas Ronald. He was only two weeks old when I held him in my arms for the first time. My son!!!! I was now a father. Wow!!! What a feeling it was to hold my own son. A new life, a precious gift from God that He had given to my wife and me. It was a miracle. We had almost lost hope. Between all the years of waiting and being told we couldn't have a child, we finally had a son. On top of that we had been divorced. I see now that only God could have made this happen. Tommy was and is truly a gift from God.

At that time, we had Tom baptized. I continued going to church with my wife and son for about six more months. Then I was back to Easter and Christmas. My wife didn't give up going to Mass this time. She took our son and went.

Things were going pretty well between us, I thought. We argued once in a while about money and the way I spent it. You see, I still hadn't stopped making money and possessions my god. I was still putting these things before my family and the One True God. By March of 1976, I had two cars, a trailer and a condominium, I had a six day-a-week job and a side job in order to pay for these things. The world had convinced me this was the way to live. I had no time left for my family or God. In April of that same year, the bottom started falling out of my life for the second time.

In Matthew 7: 24-27, Jesus told the story of the two men who built their homes. One built it on the solid foundation of rock which is the Word of God. The other one built his home on the foundation of sand—the values of this world. I see now that I had built my life on sand. I was still trying to build my life on my own power and desires. When those things started failing, I had nothing to hold on to.

That April was the beginning of a four and one-half month strike with no benefits but food stamps. My wife had to go to work to pay for all our possessions. My pride and ego were being destroyed. I was now unable to even support my family. I was angry, angry with myself and what I felt was the unfairness of it all. I didn't know any other way to deal with disappointment. Life in our home became very tense. By the time the strike was over, our marriage was heading for a bitter end. I'd driven my wife to the point of leaving again, this time with our son.

Finally, it started to hit me. Something was seriously wrong with my values. If I didn't start making some real changes in my life, I was going to lose my wife and son for good. This was the beginning of a long road to the Truth, the beginning of my search to find the real reason for living.

I started back to Mass every Sunday. I still wasn't getting anything out of it, but I kept going. At Easter time of 1977, I decided I'd go to confession. It had been twelve years since I had gone. Then I began receiving the Blessed Sacrament (Communion). I still didn't care for the Mass until one Sunday I started listening to the Gospel. It was Luke 12: 13-21(Good News Bible). Someone in the crowd said to Jesus, "Teacher tell my brother to give me my share of the inheritance." Jesus replied, "Friend, who has set Me up as your judge or arbitrator?" Then Jesus told the crowd, "Avoid greed in all its forms. A man may be wealthy, but his possessions do not guarantee him life." Jesus then told them a parable in these words:

> There was a rich man who had a good harvest. And he thought within himself, saying, "What shall I do?" he asked himself. I have no place to store my harvest. I know!" he said. " I will pull down my grain bins and build larger ones. All my grains and goods will go there. Then I will say to myself, "You have blessings in reserve for years to come. Relax! Eat heartily, drink well. Enjoy yourself." But God said to him, "You fool! This very night your life shall be required of you. To whom will then whose will all this piled up wealth of your go? That is the way it works with the man who grows rich for himself instead of growing rich in the sight of God " (Luke 12: 16- 21) Good News Bible.

That Gospel and the Father's teaching hit me right in the guts.

Finally, the Mass started having meaning for me. When I started reading along with the person doing the readings, I saw and heard that God was talking to me, telling me something. But where were they getting the readings from? I didn't know. I asked my wife.

God had used her to get me back to church so that He could talk to me from His Word, so I figured she might know. She told me the readings came from the Bible. I couldn't believe all these readings came from the big white book I remembered sitting on my mother's table collecting dust. We had a Bible at home, but I still wasn't interested enough to pick it up and read it for myself. I was just curious about where the Sunday readings came from. I was being very stubborn with the Word of God. At one time I used to gripe about the Mass being in English. Now I see that it was just another way to avoid hearing God speak to me through His Word.

In May of that year my wife attended a Charismatic Renewal Retreat. She came home with twinkles in her eyes. She was flying high on Jesus. Over the next three years, I saw my wife coming alive more and more to the Word of God. I didn't know what to think.

Still I managed to keep too busy with worldly things to read God's Word myself. Then that November the Men's Renewal Retreat was being given again. Only this time, I found myself going instead of hearing about it. Wow! The Word of God came alive to ME!!! I was transformed from a pay-as-you-go Catholic to a Christian Catholic who is alive to God's Word and has found Jesus as MY Savior. Through God's Word, I started seeing a new way of living. I'd found the TRUTH!!!

As my wife and I began to open our hearts to the teaching of the Holy Spirit, He began to open our eyes to teachings of the Catholic church which did not seem to match Scripture. We began visiting an Episcopalian church while still attending the Catholic church. Eventually, we broke with the Catholic church and began attending a non-denominational church. When we moved to Statesville, North Carolina, we prayed about which church to attend. God led us to Landmark Church of God where we are currently members. God has been so good to us.

He has blessed us with eight grandchildren. We also raised two daughters which we adopted from El Salvador. He has continued to teach us and to draw us closer to Him.

In John 3: 5, Jesus tells Nicodemus, and He is speaking to all of us today, that, "Unless one is born of water and the Spirit, he cannot enter the kingdom of God." Today, I can truly say I am born again.

Today, I try to read my Father's Word every day, and my life has really changed since I've started living by His Word through the Scriptures. I have found peace of mind and soul. I may get upset at times, but that inner peace of the Holy Spirit never stops. Life is easier now because I know I don't have to do it alone. Jesus is always there to help me. One of my biggest problems now is going to work and hearing the men around me using my God's name in vain through anger or just plain habit. I used to do that myself. Now, it just tears me up inside to hear my Father's name used that way.

It's really hard not to fall back into this old way of living at times. Everything in this world tries to pull you down. That's why I spend as much time as I can everyday reading the Bible and talking with God. I know, too, that if I listen for Him to guide me, He will.

In John 14: 6, Jesus says, " I am the Way, the Truth and the Life. No one comes to the Father except through Me," and it's true. Through His Word, I've learned that materialism is a killer and how I should be handling the money God has given me. I still make mistakes, but now I have the Word to show me the mistakes and to teach me to correct them.

Shortly after the retreat, I was talking with a friend and sharing with him some of the things I'd learned from the Bible. He said something to me then which has stuck in my mind ever since. He said, "It's in the Bible, anything you want or need to know." He was talking about the answers to all of life's problems and situations. He was right. The more I read the Bible, the more I see that he was right.

I thank Jesus everyday for patiently drawing me back to Him through His Word. The following are some scriptures which have ministered to me. I pray that they may minister to you:

When you feel lonely and left out: Luke 6
When you're not sure what your value is and where you stand:
Genesis 1 and Romans 4:5.
When you wonder what God thinks of you: Romans 1-3
When you want to get right with God: John 3
When you feel guilty: I John 1, 2 and Psalm 51.
When you're tired: Psalm 23.

When you're hurting: Hebrews 12.
When you need courage: James 1, Hebrews 13 and Ephesians 6
When you're hassled: Isaiah 26 and Philippians 4.
When you need a little common sense: Book of Proverbs
When you think about injustice: Hosea, Amos and Micah.
When you feel defeated: Acts 1-8
When you feel happy: Psalms 95-101.
When you're afraid: Psalms 27, 91, 121 and 139.
When you need to make a decision: Proverbs 3 and James 1
When you want to find out what true love is: I Corinthians 13.
When you wonder who Jesus really was: John 6-10.
When you're trying to figure out the church: I Corinthians12 and Ephesians.
When you think about death: I Corinthians 15 and II Corinthians 5.
When you wonder about the world's future: Matthew 24, I Timothy 4 and Revelation.
When you've been offended: I Corinthians 6
When you wonder about government: Romans 13
When you find it hard to believe: Hebrews 11 and Genesis 12-24.
When you're trying to figure out what's right and wrong: Matthew 5-7 and Colossians 2.
When you said something you shouldn't have said: James 3
When you're sick: Mark 1-3 and James 5.
When you feel like copping out: Jonah
When you wonder about God's power: Exodus 1-15 and Isaiah 40.
When you can't figure out the reason for suffering: Job
When you wonder what following Jesus is all about: John 13-16.
When you're struggling to do right and can't quite make it: Romans 7-8.

Conclusion

And they overcame him by the blood of the Lamb and by the word of their testimony. —Revelation 12: 11

In this book many people have shared their testimonies of how they became overcomers through the blood of the Lamb and the word of their testimony mentioned in Revelation 12: 11. The following testimony could be anyone's testimony. See if you see yourself in it and if you have received all that God desires for your life.

Oh God! I hurt. Don't even reach out to me. I have a lot of "baggage" in my life that's too heavy for me to carry. O.K., so fix my problems and carry my parcels of pain, but please, don't require my time. I admit that there are times when the road I am walking becomes shapeless, a quicksand of fear! I can hardly function. I'm depressed. My nights are so, so empty. I've shut out my family and friends and closed the door on anyone who has hurt me. My body hurts, and I'm scared. The doctors say this is serious. I need some help!

What do you mean? God loved me with an everlasting love? He offers me heaven as a free gift? But I don't deserve it. And you say that I can do nothing to earn it. That's hard to believe. I'm not just a miscellaneous thought in God's "infinite" mind? You tell me that the greatest person who ever lived, who made the greatest offer that should never be refused, loves me and has answers to my dilemmas?

But I've made so many mistakes. I mean, I've really messed up big time. Sin, you say? Yes, I have sinned. You said His standard is perfection. There's no way I can attain that. I know you said He loves me, but you also said He's just and won't clear the guilty. I guess it's just hopeless for me.

You say that there's one named Jesus who experienced the hell I thought I endured? You say that He shed His blood at a place called Calvary for me? I've never shed one drop of blood for my sins. Surely, I haven't experienced the ravage of sin, pain and suffering like you say Jesus did. Really, He was God's Son, and He loved me that much?

He was made sin for me? What does this mean? He didn't deserve the scourging, the crown of thorns, the nail pierced wrists and side, the flesh torn from His back, his bones exposed or the vinegar rubbed into His bleeding raw flesh. Should God's beloved Son be despised and forsaken of men, spate on, mocked, smitten of His Father, like a lamb led to the slaughter?

What! You say, my wickedness grieved Him? Oh, God! You envisioned my face before you as you sweat great drops of blood, tormented in that last time of prayer before the Father? You saw me, as a sheep gone astray, turned to my own way with the cross before you, and you endured the pain to provide me with a better way? Then you overcame Satan, sin, sickness, and death when you rose from the grave on the third day? You did this for me that I might live?

Yes, now it makes sense to me that I must give up what I have been trusting in. I know that there can't be any other way. You said there's a mansion in heaven for me. You said that I can have life on earth as God lived it. I'm glad that I can have someone to help me carry my load, and that I can live without fear, depression, emptiness or sickness. How do I do this? Faith? What's that? I understand things I can see and touch or understand with my mind, but trust in Jesus Christ alone as my Savior? Make Him Lord of my life? I want to know for sure that I'll go to heaven. Even though I don't understand it all, I just know that I've found the answer.

I do want to accept this forgiveness today. I do believe that Jesus is my resurrected and Living Lord! I do want to know for certain that I'll go to heaven when I die. I do want to have compassion for others and to love those who hurt me. I do want to have the joy you mention. I'm eager to make up for lost time, but it's all so new to me. I do want Jesus to take the reigns of my life. I want to be a "shining light" in this world's darkness, but I don't know how. I don't know what to do. Can you help me?

If this is truly your desire, you have just made the greatest decision of your life—one that will fill you with peace and joy like you've never known and one that will change you and change your life. I invite you now to pray the following prayer sincerely from your heart.

"Lord Jesus Christ, I know I am a sinner and do not deserve eternal life. But I believe you died and rose from the grave to purchase a place in heaven for me. Lord Jesus, come into my life; take control of my life; forgive my sins and save me. I repent of my sins and now place my trust in You for my salvation. I accept the free gift of eternal life."

If you prayed this prayer, welcome to the family of God! Would you please let the Pastor of Landmark Church of God know of your decision by telephone at 704-873-9701, in writing at 2200 East Broad

Street, Statesville, North Carolina 28625 or by e-mail at www. pastor@landmarkcog.com. Thank you.

May God richly bless you exceedingly, abundantly beyond all you could ask or think.

APPENDIX

G.T. Bustin's Ministry

G.T. Bustin was a pioneer missionary to Central New Guinea. Coleen and Paul Kennedy knew Reverend Bustin and his family well. Reverend Bustin was the first missionary to this area where many head hunters lived. As he went to witness to these savages about Jesus, the Lord told him what to do and how to do it.

Until her death, his daughter Lenita Bustin also spent her life as a missionary living among these people and loving them. She had a Bible College for the young people. In fact, today one of the savages who was born again and attended her college, serves in the government of New Guinea as a true Christian leader.

Reverend Bustin also pioneered missionary work in Haiti and in the Bahamas. When God led him to go to Indonesia to check out the revival that took place in 1965, he obeyed and later wrote a book about the revival.

Laughing Christ

The *Laughing Christ* was painted for the Parish of the Holy Communion in Ashe County, North Carolina, during the summer of 1975 by Bo Bartlett who was assisting Ben Long in the preparation of the fresco of John the Baptist. Bo Bartlett was the model for John the Baptist.

"Bo has stated that he had always wanted to do a painting of Christ laughing because he thought of the Lord as a happy, joyous laughing person." In 1975, he was inspired by the miraculous healing of Father William Stuart, a good friend of the Parish of the Holy Communion.

One Sunday morning in January of 1975, Father Stuart did not come to conduct services at his Melbourne Beach, Florida, church. He had had a serious brain stem stroke. Doctors could give little encouragement for his recovery. Prayer vigils were set up near and far. Father Stuart suffered intensely for three days. Then something extraordinary began to happen. Within a two-hour period, his vital signs went back to normal.

He thought that the Lord was standing back of him at the head of his bed laughing uproariously like a man who has just caught that big bass. The Lord was not laughing at him, but with him as the healing was taking place. The following Sunday, the doctors dismissed him. Father Stuart walked from the hospital with his family to the car. The doctor said, "Give God the glory." Because Bo Bartlett was sensitive to this miraculous healing, he painted the *Laughing Christ.*

—This description of the *Laughing Christ* was taken from the marker below the painting.

Scriptural Index

All scripture references are from the New King James version of the Bible unless otherwise indicated.

Genesis

Therefore a man shall leave his father and mother and be joined to his wife, and they shall become one flesh. —Genesis 2: 24

For all the land which you see I give to you and your descendants forever. And I will make your descendants as the dust of the earth: so that if a man could number the dust of the earth, then your descendants also could be numbered. Arise walk in the land through its length and its width, for I give it to you. —Genesis 13: 15-17

Exodus

Who gave man his mouth? Who makes him deaf or mute? Who gives him sight or makes him blind? Is it not I, the Lord? Now go; I will help you speak and will teach you what to say. —Exodus 4: 11-12

But lift up your rod and stretch out your hand over the sea and divide it. and the children of Israel shall go on dry ground through the midst of the sea.—Exodus 14: 16

Then Moses stretched out his hand over the sea; and the Lord caused the sea to go back by a strong east wind all that night, and made the sea into dry land, and the waters were divided. —Exodus 14:21

And said, "If you diligently heed the voice of the Lord your God and do what is right in His sight, give ear to His commandments and keep all His statues, I will put none of these diseases on you which I have brought on the Egyptians. For I am the Lord who heals you.—Exodus 15: 26

I am the Lord your God, who brought you out of the land of Egypt, out of the house of bondage.You shall have no other gods before you.—Exodus 20: 2-3

Honor thy father and thy mother that thy days may be long upon the land that the Lord thy God is giving you. —Exodus 20:12

There shall be showers of blessing.—Exodus 34: 26a

Deuteronomy

And it shall come to pass, if thou shall hearken diligently unto the voice of the Lord thy God, to observe and to do all his commandments which I command thee this day that the Lord thy God will set thee on high above all nations on the earth: and all these blessings shall come on thee and overtake thee, if thou shall hearken unto the voice of the Lord thy God. —Deuteronomy 28: 1-2

...the great trials which your eyes have seen, the signs, and those great wonders.—Deuteronomy 29: 3

As thy days, so shall thy strength be.—Deuteronomy 33: 25

The eternal God is your refuge, and underneath are the everlasting arms; He will thrust out the enemy from before you, and will say, "Destroy!"—Deuteronomy 33: 27

Joshua

Every place the sole of your foot will tread upon I have given you, as I said to Moses.—Joshua 1: 3

Nehemiah

For this day is holy to our Lord. Do not sorrow, for the joy of the Lord is your strength.—Nehemiah 8: 10b

Job

Do you still hold fast to your integrity? Curse God, and die.
—Job 2: 9

For I know that my Redeemer lives, and He shall stand at last on the earth: And after my skin is destroyed, this I know, that in my flesh I shall see God whom I shall see for myself and not another.—Job 19: 25-27

Psalms

Ask of Me, and I will give you the nations for your inheritance, and the ends of the earth for your possession.—Psalm 2: 8

And those who know Your name will put their trust in You. For You, Lord, have not forsaken those who seek You....Have mercy on me, O Lord! Consider my trouble from those who hate me. You who lift me up from the gates of death. —Psalm 9: 10, 13

Let everything that has breath praise the Lord.—Psalm 10: 6

Such a man will not be overthrown by evil circumstances. God's constant care of him will make a deep impression on all who see it...for he is settled in his mind that God will take care of him. —Psalm 11: 6 (TLB)

The Lord is my rock, and my fortress and my deliverer; My God, my strength, to whom I will trust: My shield and the horn of my salvation, my stronghold.—Psalm 18: 2

For He has not despised nor abhorred the affliction of the afflicted; nor has He hidden His face from Him; but when He cried to Him, He heard.—Psalm 22: 24

The Lord is my Shepherd; I shall not want.—Psalm 23: 1

Yea, though I walk through the valley of the shadow of death, I will fear no evil, for you are with me; Your rod and Your staff, they comfort me.—Psalm 23: 4

For in the time of trouble He shall hide me in His pavilion: In the secret place of his tabernacle He shall hide me. He shall set me high upon a rock.—Psalm 27: 5

Weeping may endure for a night, but joy comes in the morning. —Psalm 30: 5

The angel of the Lord encamps all around those who fear Him, and delivers them.—Psalm 34: 7

Delight thyself also in the Lord; and He shall give thee the desires of thine heart. Commit thy way unto the Lord; trust also in Him; and He shall bring it to pass.—Psalm 37: 4-5

The steps of a good man are ordered by the Lord, and He delights in his way.—Psalm 37: 23

I waited patiently for the Lord, and He inclined to me. And heard my cry.—Psalm 40: 1

God is our refuge and strength, a very present help in trouble. —Psalm 46: 1

Be still and know that I am God.—Psalm 46: 10

Create in me a clean heart, O God, and renew a steadfast spirit within me. Do not cast me away from Your presence and do not take Your Holy Spirit from me.—Psalm 51: 10-11

Evening and morning and at noon I will pray, and cry aloud, and He shall hear my voice.—Psalm 55: 17

Cast your burden on the Lord, and He shall sustain you; He shall never permit the righteous to be moved.—Psalm 55:22

My heart is fixed, oh God. My heart is fixed: I am willing and give praise. Psalm 56: 7—(TLB)

But it is good for me to draw near to God; I have put my trust in the Lord God, that I may declare all Your works.—Psalm 73: 1

I will sing of the mercies of the Lord forever; with my mouth will I make known thy faithfulness to all generations.—Psalm 89: 1

Because you have made the Lord, who is my refuge, even the most High, your dwelling place, no evil shall befall you, nor shall any plague come near your dwelling. For He shall give His angels charge over you in all your ways. In their hands they shall bear you up, lest you dash your foot against a stone.—Psalm 91: 9-12

He that planted the ear, shall he not hear? He that formed the eye, shall he not see? I want to smile when I say that I have learned to look for God in the day to day, seemingly, ordinary events of life. —Psalm 94: 9

Bless the Lord, O my soul, and forget not all his benefits: who forgives all your iniquities, who heals all your diseases, who redeems your life from destruction, who crowns you with loving kindness and tender mercies.—Psalm 103: 2-4

Thou openest thine hand, and they are filled with good.
—Psalm 104: 28b (KJV)

He brought out His people with joy, His chosen ones with gladness.
—Psalm 105: 3

Praise ye the Lord. O give thanks unto the Lord; for He is good: for His mercy endureth forever. Who can utter the mighty acts of the Lord? Who can shew forth all His praise?—Psalm 106: 1-2

Oh, give thanks to the Lord, for He is good! For His mercy endures forever. Let the redeemed of the Lord say so, whom He has redeemed from the hand of the enemy.—Psalm 107: 1-2

Such a man will not be overthrown by evil circumstances. God's constant care of him will make a deep impression on all who see it....for he is settled in his mind that God will take care of him.
—Psalm 112: 6 (TLB)

It is better to trust in the Lord than to put confidence in man.
—Psalm II8: 8

This is the day which the Lord hath made; we will rejoice and be glad in it.—Psalm 118: 24

Forever, O Lord, Your word is settled in heaven.Your faithfulness endures to all generations.—Psalm 119: 89-90

You are my hiding place and my shield; I hope in Your Word
.—Psalm 119: 114

I will lift up my eyes to the hills—From whence comes my help? My help comes from the Lord, who made heaven and earth. —Psalm 121: 1-2

Those who sow in tears shall reap in joy. He who continually goes forth weeping, bearing seed for sowing, shall doubtless come again with rejoicing, bringing his sheaves with him. —Psalm 126: 5-6

The Lord will perfect that which concerneth me: thy mercy, O Lord, endureth forever; forsake not the works of thine own hands. —Psalm 138: 8

O Lord, You have searched me and known me. You know my sitting up and my my rising up; You understand my thought afar off. You comprehend my path and my lying down. When I awake, I am still with you. For there is not a word on my tongue. Oh, that you would slay the wicked, O God! But behold, O Lord, You know it altogether. You have hedged me behind and before and laid Your hand upon me. Such knowledge is too wonderful for me. It is high. I cannot attain it. Where can I go from Your everlasting Spirit? Or where can I flee from Your presence? If I ascend into heaven, You are there; if I make my bed in hell, behold, You are there. Even there Your hand shall lead me; and Your right hand shall hold me. If I say, "Surely the darkness shall fall on me; "Even the night shall be light about me; Indeed, the darkness shall not hide from You. But the night shines as the day; The darkness and the light are both alike to You. For You formed my inward parts; You covered me in my mother's womb....Your eyes saw my unformed body. All the days ordained for me were written in Your book before one of them came to be. How precious to me are Your thoughts O God. How vast is the sum of them. Were I to count them, they would outnumber the grains of sand. When I awake, I am still with You. Search me, O God, and know my heart; Try me and know my anxieties; and see if there is any wicked way in me. And lead me in the way everlasting.—Psalm 139: 1-8, 10-12, 16-19, 23-24

I remember the days of old; I meditate on all Your works. I muse on the work of Your hands. I spread out my hands to You; My soul longs for You like a thirsty land. Selah. Answer me speedily, O Lord; My spirit fails! Do not hide Your face from them lest I be like those who go down into the pit. —Psalm 142: 5-7

Great is the Lord, and greatly to be praised.—Psalm 145: 3a

He will fulfill the desire of those who fear Him; He also will hear their cry and save them. The Lord preserves all who love Him, but all the wicked He will destroy.—Psalm 145: 19-20

Great is our Lord, and mighty in power; His understanding is infinite.—Psalm 147: 5

Let everything that has breath praise the Lord.—Psalm 150:6

Proverbs

Let love and faithfulness never leave you; bind them around your neck, write them on the tablet of your heart.—Proverbs 3: 3 (*NIV*)

Trust in the Lord with all of thine heart; and lean not unto thine own understanding. In all thy ways acknowledge Him, and He will direct thy path.—Proverbs 3: 5-6

A present is a precious stone in the eyes of its possessor; wherever he turns, he prospers.—Proverbs 17: 8

A merry heart does good, like medicine, but a broken spirit dries the bones—Proverbs 17: 22

Train up a child in the way he should go and when he is old, he will not depart from it.—Proverbs 22: 6

Ecclesiastes

Cast thy bread upon the waters: for thou shalt find it after many days.—Ecclesiastes 11: 1

To everything there is a season, a time for every purpose under heaven.—Ecclesiastes 3: 1

Two are better than one because they have a good reward for their labor, for if they fall, one will lift up his companion. But woe to him who is alone when he falls, for he has no one to help him up. Again, if two like down together, they will keep warm; but how can one be warm alone? Though one may be overpowered by another, two can withstand him, and a threefold cord is not quickly broken.—Ecclesiastes 4: 9-12

Isaiah

Here I am. Send me.—Isaiah 6:8

The wolf also shall dwell with the lamb. The leopard shall lie down with the young goat. The calf and the young lion and the fatling together; and a little child shall lead them.—Isaiah 11: 6

The eyes of those who see will not be dim.—Isaiah 32: 3

O Lord, be gracious to us; we have waited for You. Be their arm every morning, our salvation also in the time of trouble. —Isaiah 33: 2

Wisdom and knowledge will be the stability of your times.
—Isaiah 33: 6

"Now I will rise," says the Lord; "Now I will be exalted, Now I will lift Myself up. "He who walks righteously and speaks uprightly, he who despises the gain of oppressions, who gestures with his hands, refusing bribes, who stops his ears from hearing of bloodshed, and shuts his eyes from seeing evil: he will dwell on high; his place of defense will be the fortress of rocks; bread will be given him. His water will be sure. Look upon Zion, the city of our appointed feasts; your eyes will see Jerusalem, a quiet home, a tabernacle that will not be taken down; not one of its stakes will ever be removed, nor will any of its cords be broken. But there the majestic Lord will be for us a place of broad rivers and streams in which no galley with oars will sail, nor majestic ships pass by for the Lord is our Judge. The Lord is our Lawgiver. The Lord is our King; He will save us. Your tackle is loosed. They could not strengthen their mast. They could not spread the sail. Then the prey of great plunder is divided; the lame take the prey. And the inhabitant will not say, "I am sick." The people who dwell in it will be forgiven their iniquity. —Isaiah 33: 10, 15, 16, 20-24

O Lord, I am oppressed; undertake for me! What shall I say? He has both spoken to me, and he Himself has done it. I shall walk carefully all my years in bitterness of my soul. O Lord by these things is the life of my spirit; so You will restore me and make me live. Indeed it was for my own peace that I had great bitterness; but You have delivered my soul from the pit of corruption. For You have cast all my sins behind my back. —Isaiah 38: 14-17

So Hezekiah said to Isaiah, "The word of the Lord which you have spoken is good!" For he said, "At least there will be peace and truth in my days."—Isaiah 39: 8

Have you not known? Have you not heard? The everlasting god, the Lord, The Creator of the ends of the earth, neither faints nor is weary. His understanding is unsearchable—Isaiah 40: 28

But those who wait on the Lord shall renew their strength; they shall mount up with wings like eagles. They shall run and not be weary. They shall walk and not faint.—Isaiah 40:31

When thou passest through the water, I will be with thee; and through the rivers, they shall not overflow thee; when thou walkest through the fire, thou shalt not be burned; neither shall the flame kindle upon thee.—Isaiah 43: 2

Behold, I will do a new thing; now it shall spring forth; shall ye not know it? I will even make a way in the wilderness and rivers in the desert.—Isaiah 43: 19

Why, when I came, was there no man? Why, when I called, was there none to answer? Is My hand shortened at all that it cannot redeem? Or have I no power to deliver? Indeed with My rebuke I dry up the sea. I make the rivers a wilderness; Their fish stink because there is no water, and die of thirst—Isaiah 50: 2

But He was wounded for our transgressions, He was bruised for our iniquities; the chastisement for our peace was upon Him, and by His stripes we are healed.—Isaiah 53: 5

For thou shalt forget the shame of thy youth and shalt not remember the reproach of thy widowhood any more. For thy Maker is thine husband; the Lord of hosts is His name....For the Lord hath called thee as a woman forsaken and grieved in spirit and a wife of youth when thou wast refused, saith thy God. —Isaiah 54: 4b-6

"No weapon formed against you shall prosper, and every tongue which rises against you in judgment you shall condemn. This is the heritage of the servant of the Lord, and their righteousness is from Me," says the Lord. —Isaiah 54:17

As the heavens are higher than the earth, so are My ways higher than your ways and My thoughts than your thoughts. —Isaiah 55: 8-9

So shall My word be that goes forth from My mouth; It shall not return to Me void, but it shall accomplish what I please, and it shall prosper in the thing for which I sent it.—Isaiah 55: 11

My house shall be called a house of prayer for all nations.
—Isaiah 56: 7c

Is this not the fast that I have chosen: to loose the bonds of wickedness, to undo the heavy burdens to let the oppressed go free, and that you break every yoke? Is it not to share your bread with the hungry, and that you bring to your house the poor who are cast out: when you see the naked that you cover him, and not hide yourself from your own flesh?—Isaiah 58: 6-7

Behold the Lord's hand is not shortened that it cannot save; nor His ear heavy, that it cannot hear.—Isaiah 59: 1

Jeremiah

Before I formed you in the womb, I knew you. Before you were born, I set you apart. I appointed you as a prophet to the nations.—Jeremiah 1: 5

For I know the plans I have for you declares the Lord, plans to prosper you and not to harm you, plans to give you hope and a future.—Jeremiah 29: 11

Call to Me, and I will answer you and show you great and mighty things, which you do not know.—Jeremiah 33: 3

Lamentations

Through the Lord's mercies we are not consumed because His compassions fail not.They are new every morning; great is Your faithfulness. The Lord is good to those who wait for Him, to the soul who seeks Him.—Lamentations 3: 22-23, 25

Ezekiel

I will make them and the places all around My hill a blessing; and I will cause showers to come down in their season; there shall be showers of blessing.—Ezekiel 34: 26

Daniel

Our God whom we serve is able to deliver us.—Daniel 3: 7

Nahum

The Lord is good, a stronghold in the day of trouble; and He knoweth them that trust in Him.—Nahum 1: 7

Malachi

Bring all the tithes and offerings. You are cursed with a curse, for you have robbed Me, even this whole nation.—Malachi 3: 10

Matthew

But while he thought about these things, behold an angel of the Lord appeared to him in a dream, saying, "Joseph, son of David, do not be afraid to take to you Mary your wife, for that which is conceived in her is of the Holy Spirit.—Matthew 1: 20.

You are the light of the world. A city that is set on a hill cannot be hidden.—Matthew 5: 14

Give us this day our daily bread.—Matthew 6: 11

For if you forgive others for their transgressions, your heavenly Father will also forgive you. But if you do not forgive others, then your Father will not forgive your transgressions. —Matthew 6: 14, 15

But seek ye first the kingdom of God, and his righteousness; and all these things shall be added unto you.—Matthew 6: 33

For in the way you judge, you will be judged; and by your standard of measure, it will be measured to you.—Matthew 7:2

Ask and it will be given to you; seek, and you will find; knock, and it will be opened to you.—Matthew 7: 7

Or what man is there among you who, if his son asks for bread, will give him a stone? or if he asks for a fish, will he give him a serpent? —Matthew 7: 9-10

Therefore whoever hears these sayings of Mine and does them, I will liken him to a wise man who built his house on the rock: and the rain descended, the floods came, and the winds blew and beat on that house, and it did not fall, for it was founded on the rock. But everyone who hears these sayings of Mine, and does not do them will be like a foolish mn who built his house on the sand. —Matthew 7: 24-26

And whoever gives one of these little ones only a cup of cold water in the name of a disciple, assuredly, I say to you, he shall by no means loose his reward.—Matthew 10: 42

And blessed is he who is not offended because of Me. —Matthew 11: 6

Come to Me, all you who labor and are heavy laden, and I will give you rest. —Matthew 11: 28

And He answered and said to them, "Have you not read that He who made them at the beginning made them male and female, and said, 'For this reason a man shall leave his father and mother and be joined to his wife, and the two shall become one flesh?" —Matthew 19: 4-5

Suffer little children, and forbid them not, to come unto me: for of such is the kingdom of heaven.—Matthew 19: 14

—saying to them, "Go into the village opposite you, and immediately you will find a donkey tied and a colt with her. Loose them and bring them to me.—Matthew 21: 2

For I was hungry and you gave me food; I was thirsty and you gave me drink; I was a stranger and you took me in. —Matthew 25: 35

Mark

Therefore I say to you, whatever things you ask when you pray; believe that you receive them, and you will have them. —Mark 11: 24

Luke

And as ye would that men should do to you, do ye also to them likewise.—Luke 6: 31

Give and it will be given to you: A good measure, pressed down, shaken together and running over will be poured into your lap. For with the same measure you use, it will be measured back to you.—Luke 6: 38 (*NIV*)

After these things the Lord appointed seventy others also, and sent them two by two before His face into every city and place where He Himself was about to go.—Luke 10: 1

The seventy-two returned with joy and said, "Lord even the demons submit to us in Your name."—Luke 10: 17 (*NIV*)

And I say unto you, ask, and it shall be given unto you; seek, and ye shall find; knock, and it shall be opened unto you.—Luke 11: 9

Then one from the crowd said to Him, "Teacher, tell my brother to divide the inheritance with me." But He said to him, "Man who made Me a judge or an arbitrator over you?" And He said to them, "Take heed and beware of covetousness, for one's life does not consist in the things he possesses." Then He spoke a parable to them saying: "The ground of a certain rich man yielded plentifully. And he thought within himself saying; 'What—shall I do, since I have no room to store my crops?' So He said, 'I will do this. I will pull down my barns and build greater and there I will store all my crops and my goods. And I will say to my soul, Soul you have many goods laid up for many years; take your ease, eat drink and be merry. But God said to him, 'Fool! This night your soul will be required of you. Then whose will these things be which you have provided? So is he who lays us treasure for himself, and is not rich toward God?—Luke 12: 13-21

John

In the beginning was the Word, and the Word was with God, and the Word was God. He was in the beginning with God. All things were made through Him, and without Him, nothing was made that was made. In Him was life, and life was the light of men. And the light shines in the darkness, and the darkness did not comprehend it.—John 1: 1-5
And one is born of water and the Spirit, he cannot enter the kingdom of God.—John 3: 5

For God so loved the world that He gave His only begotten son that whoever believes in Him should not perish but have everlasting life.—John 3: 16

All that the Father gives me will come to me, and the one who comes to me I will by no means cast out. —John 6: 37

Most assuredly I say unto you, he who believes in Me has everlasting life.—John 6: 47

I am the resurrection, and the life: he that believeth in me, though he were dead, yet shall live.—John 11: 25

In my father's house are many mansions; if it were not so, I would have told you. I go to prepare a place for you. —John 14: 2

I am the way, the truth and the life: No man cometh unto the Father, but by me.—John 14: 6

And whatsoever ye shall ask in my name, that will I do, that the Father may be glorified in the Son if ye shall ask anything in my name, I will do it.—John 14: 13-14
Because I live, ye shall live also.—John 14: 19

But the Helper, the Holy Spirit, whom the Father will send in My name, He will teach you all things, and bring to your remembrance all things that I said to you. Peace I leave with you; My peace I give to you; not as the world gives do I give to you. Let not your heart be troubled, neither let it be afraid. —John 14: 26-27

However, when He, the Spirit of Truth, has come He will guide you into all truth, for He will not speak on His own authority, but whatever He hears He will speak, and He will tell you things to come.—John 16: 13

So when Jesus had received the sour wine, He said, "It is finished." And bowing His head, He gave up His spirit.
—John 19: 30

Acts

But you shall receive power when the Holy Spirit has come upon you, and you shall be witnesses to Me in Jerusalem and in all Judea and Samaria and to the end of the earth.—Acts 1: 8

And when they had entered, they went up into the upper room where they were staying: Peter, James, John and Andrew; Philip and Thomas; Bartholomew and Matthew; James the son of Alphaeus and Simon the Zealot; and Judas the son of James. These all continued with one accord in prayer and supplication, with the women and Mary the mother of Jesus, and with His brothers. And to those days Peter stood up in the midst of the disciples (altogether the number of names was about a hundred and twenty) and said ....Acts 1: 13-15

I have shewed you all things, how that so labouring ye ought to support the weak, and to remember the words of the Lord Jesus, how he said, "It is more blessed to give than to receive. —Acts 20: 35

Romans

For I am not ashamed of the gospel of Christ, for it is the power of God to salvation for everyone who believes, for the Jew first and also for the Greek.—Romans 1: 16

For in the righteousness of God is revealed from faith to faith as it is written. "The just shall live by faith."—Romans 1: 17

Therefore, having been justified by faith, we have peace with God through our Lord Jesus Christ, through whom also we have access by faith into this grace in which we stand, and rejoice in hope of the glory of God. And not only that but we also glory in tribulations, knowing that tribulation produces perseverance; and perseverance, character; and character, hope. Now hope does not disappoint, because the love of God has been poured out in our hearts by the Holy Spirit who was given to us. For when we were still without strength, in due time Christ died for the ungodly.—Romans 5: 1-6

There is, therefore, no condemnation to those who are in Christ Jesus, who do not walk according to the flesh, but according to the Spirit for the law of the Spirit of life in Christ Jesus has made me free from the law of sin and death.—Romans 8: 1-2

And we know that all things work together for good to those who love God, to those who are called according to His purpose.
—Romans 8:28

For I am persuaded that neither death nor life, nor angels nor principalities nor powers, nor things present nor things to come, nor height nor depth, nor any other created thing, shall be able to separate us from the love of God which is in Christ Jesus our Lord.
—Romans 8: 38-39

Faith comes by hearing and hearing by the Word of God."
—Romans 10: 17

I beseech you therefore, brethren, by the mercies of God, that you present your bodies a living sacrifice, holy acceptable to God, which is your reasonable service. And do not be conformed to this world, but be transformed by the renewing of your mind, that you may prove what is that good and acceptable and perfect will of God. For I say, through the grace given to me, to everyone who is among you, not

to think of himself more highly than he ought to think, but to think soberly, as God has dealt to each one a measure of faith.
—Romans 12: 1-3

Love thy neighbor as thyself.—Romans 13: 9b

I Corinthians

But if the unbelieving husband leaves you, let him depart. A brother or sister is not under bondage in such cases; but God hath called us to peace.—I Corinthians 7: 15.

For he who speaks in a tongue does not speak to men but to God, for no one understands him; however, in the spirit he speaks mysteries.—I Corinthians 14: 2

He who speaks in a tongue edifies himself, but he who prophesies edifies the church.—I Corinthians 14: 4

But by the grace of God I am what I am, and His grace toward me was not in vain; but I labored more abundantly than they all, yet not I, but the grace of God which was with me. —I Corinthians 15: 10

Behold I shew you a mystery; we shall not all sleep, but we shall all be changed.—I Corinthians 15: 51

O death where is thy sting? O grave where is thy victory?
—I Corinthians 15: 55

II Corinthians

Blessed be God, even the Father of our Lord Jesus Christ, the Father of mercies, and the God of all comfort, Who comforteth us in all our tribulation, that we may be able to comfort them which are in any trouble, by the comfort wherewith we ourselves are comforted by God. —II Corinthians 1: 3,4

For all the promises of God in Him are Yes, and in Him Amen, to the glory of God through us.—II Corinthians 1: 20

But we all with unveiled face, beholding as in a mirror the glory of the Lord, are being transformed into the same image from glory to glory, just as by the Spirit of the Lord.—II Corinthians 3: 18

But even if our Gospel is veiled, it is veiled to those who are perishing. Whose minds the god of this age has blinded, who do not believe, lest the light of the Gospel of the glory of Christ who is the image of God should shine on them.—II Corinthians 4: 3-4

We are hard pressed on every side, yet not crushed; we are perplexed but not in despair; persecuted, but not forsaken, struck down, but not destroyed.—II Corinthians 4: 8-9

We are confident, yes well pleased rather to be absent from the body is to be present with the Lord.—II Corinthians 5: 8

If anyone is in Christ, he is a new creation; old things have passed away; behold, all things have become new.—II Corinthians 5: 17

And God is able to make all grace abound toward you; that ye, always having all sufficiency in all things, may abound to every good work.—II Corinthians 9: 8

For though we walk in the flesh, we do not war according to the flesh. For the weapons of our warfare are not carnal but mighty in God for pulling down strongholds, casting down arguments and every high thing that exalts itself against the knowledge of God, bringing every thought into captivity to the obedience of Christ. —II Corinthians 10: 3-5

And He said to me, "My grace is sufficient for you, for My strength is made perfect in weakness.—II Corinthians 12: 9

Galatians

But the fruit of the Spirit is love, joy, peace, longsuffering, kindness, goodness, faithfulness, gentleness, self-control. Against such there is no law.—Galatians 5: 22-23

And those who are Christ's have crucified the flesh with its passions and desires.—Galatians 5:24

Ephesians

In Him you also trusted, after you heard the word of truth, the gospel of your salvation in whom also, having believed, you were sealed with the Holy Spirit of promise.—Ephesians 1: 13

Now to Him who is able to do exceedingly abundantly above all that we ask or think, according to the power that works in us, to him be glory in the church by Christ Jesus to all generations, forever and ever. Amen.—Ephesians 3: 20-21

Wives, submit to your own husbands as to the Lord.—Ephesians 5: 22

I struggle not against flesh and blood, but against rulers, against the powers, against the world forces of wickedness in the heavenly places.—Ephesians 6:12

Stand therefore, having girded your waist with truth, having put on the breastplate of righteousness, and having shod your feet with the preparation of the gospel of peace above all, taking the shield of faith with which you will be able to quench all the fiery darts of the wicked one. And take the helmet of salvation, and the sword of the spirit, which is the word of God.—Ephesians 6: 14-17

Philippians

Being confident of this very thing, that He who has begun a good work in you will complete it until that day of Jesus Christ.
—Philippians 1: 1

Being confident of this very thing that the One who has begun a good work in you will complete it until the day of Jesus Christ. —Philippians 1: 6

Be anxious for nothing, but in everything by prayer and supplication with thanksgiving, let your requests be made known to God; and the peace of God which surpasses all understanding will guard your hearts and minds through Christ Jesus.—Philippians 3: 6-7

Be anxious for nothing,but in everything by prayer and supplication, with thanksgiving, let your requests be made known to God. And the peace of God will guard your hearts and minds through Christ Jesus. Finally, brethren, whatsoever things are true, whatsoever things are honest, whatsoever things are just, whatsoever things are pure, whatsoever things are lovely, whatsoever things are of good report; if there be any virtue, and if there be any praise, think on these things.—Philippians 4: 6-8

I can do all things through Christ who strengthens me. —Philippians 4: 13

But my God shall supply all your needs according to His riches in glory by Christ Jesus.—Philippians 4: 19

Colossians

...that their hearts may be encouraged, being knit together in love, and attaining to all riches of the full assurance of understanding, in the knowledge of the mystery of God, both of the Father and of Christ.—Colossians 2: 2

I Thessalonians

He who calls you is faithful who also will do it.—I Thessalonians 5: 24

II Thessalonians

But the Lord is faithful, who will establish you and guard you from the evil one.—II Thessalonians 3: 3

II Timothy

For God has not given us a spirit of fear, but of power and of love and of a sound mind.—II Timothy 1: 7

I know whom I have believed and am persuaded that He is able to keep what I have committed to Him until that day.—II Timothy 1: 12

Titus

In the hope of eternal life which God who cannot lie promised before time began.—Titus 1:2

Hebrews

Looking unto Jesus, the author and finisher of our faith, who for the joy that was set before Him, endured the cross, despising the shame, and has set down at the right hand of the throne of God. —Hebrews 12: 2

Be not forgetful to entertain strangers; for thereby some have entertained angels unawares.—Hebrews 13: 2

Jesus Christ is the same yesterday, today and forever.—Hebrews 13: 8

James

My brethren count it all joy when you fall into various trials. —James 1: 2

If any of you lacks wisdom, let him ask of God, who gives to all liberally and without reproach and it will be given to him; but let him ask in faith with no doubting.—James 1: 5-6

Therefore submit to God. Resist the devil and he will flee from you. —James 4: 7

Therefore to him who knows to do good and does not do it, to him it is sin.—James 4: 17

Is any sick among you? Let him call for the elders of the church, and let them pray over him, appointing him with oil in the name of the Lord: and the prayer of faith shall save the sick, and the Lord shall raise him up; and if he have committed sins, they shall be forgiven him.—James 5: 14

Confess your trespasses to one another, and pray for one another that you may be healed. The effective, fervent prayer of the righteous man availeth much—James 5: 16

I Peter

Blessed be that God and Father of our Lord Jesus Christ who according to His abundant mercy has begotten us again to a living hope through the resurrection of Jesus Christ from the dead.
—I Peter l: 3-4

Who Himself bore our sins in His own body on the tree, that we, having died to sins, might live for righteousness, by whose stripes you were healed.—I Peter 2: 24

Finally, be ye all of one mind, having compassion for one another; love as brothers, be tenderhearted, be courteous.—I Peter 3: 8

II Peter

As His divine power has given to us all things that pertain to life and godliness, through the knowledge of Him who called us by glory and virtue, by which have been given to us exceedingly great and precious promises, that through these you may be partakers of the divine nature, having escaped the corruption that is in the world through lust.—II Peter 1: 3-4

I John

If we confess our sins, He is faithful and just to forgive us our sins, and to cleanse us from all unrighteousness.—I John l: 9

You are of God, little children, and have overcome them because He who is in you is greater than he that is in the world. —I John 4: 4

Beloved, let us love one another for love is of God, and everyone who loves is born of God and knows God. He who does not love, does not know God, for God is love.—I John 4: 7-8

Whoever believes that Jesus Christ is the Christ is born of God, and everyone who loves Him who begot also loves him. who is begotten of Him. By this we know that we love the children of God, when we love God and keep His commandments. For this is the love of God that we keep His commandments. And His commandments are not burdensome. For whatever is born of God overcomes the world. And this is the victory that has overcome the world—our faith. Who is he who overcomes the world but he who believes that Jesus is the Son of God.—I John 5: 1-5

Now this is the confidence that we have in Him, that if we ask anything according to His will, He hears us, whatever we ask, we know that we have the petitions that we have asked of Him.
—I John 5: 14-15

And we know that the Son of God has come and has given us an understanding, that we may know Him who is true; and we are in Him who is true, in His Son Jesus Christ. This is the true God and eternal life.—I John 5: 20

Revelation

So then because you are lukewarm and neither hot nor cold, I will vomit you out of my mouth.—Revelation 3:16

After these things I looked, and behold, a great multitude which no one could number, of all nations, tribes, peoples, and tongues, standing before the throne and before the Lamb, clothed with white robes, with palm branches in their hands, and crying out with a loud voice, saying, "Salvation belongs to our God who sits on the throne, and to the Lamb!"—Revelation 7: 9-10

And they overcame him by the blood of the Lamb and by the word of their testimony.—Revelation 12: 11

But there shall by no means enter it anything that defiles, or causes an abomination or a lie, but only those who are written in the Lamb's Book of Life.—Revelation 21: 27

Calluses On My Knees

Life is full of troubles.
Pray for help.
Life is full of joys.
Pray a prayer of thanksgiving.

My neighbor on the right is dying of cancer.
Pray for help.
My neighbor on the left just delivered a healthy baby boy.
Pray a prayer of thanksgiving.

My car just broke down.
Pray for help.
I received a refund check in the mail today.
Pray a prayer of thanksgiving.

Dear Lord, help me to always turn all things over to you,
Whether great or small, happy or sad.
Please let me have calluses on my knees from praying to you.

Amen
Christine Talley

Subject Index